W0037680

Whitestein Series in Software Agent Technologies

Series Editors:
Marius Walliser
Stefan Brantschen
Monique Calisti
Thomas Hempfling

This series reports new developments in agent-based software technologies and agent-oriented software engineering methodologies, with particular emphasis on applications in various scientific and industrial areas. It includes research level monographs, polished notes arising from research and industrial projects, outstanding PhD theses, and proceedings of focused meetings and conferences. The series aims at promoting advanced research as well as at facilitating know-how transfer to industrial use.

About Whitestein Technologies

Whitestein Technologies AG was founded in 1999 with the mission to become a leading provider of advanced software agent technologies, products, solutions, and services for various applications and industries. Whitestein Technologies strongly believes that software agent technologies, in combination with other leading-edge technologies like web services and mobile wireless computing, will enable attractive opportunities for the design and the implementation of a new generation of distributed information systems and network infrastructures.

www.whitestein.com

Chris van Aart

Organizational Principles for Multi-Agent Architectures

Birkhäuser Verlag
Basel · Boston · Berlin

Author:

Chris van Aart
Acklin B.V.
Taxandriaweg 12b
NL-5142 PA Waalwijk
The Netherlands
e-mail: chris@acklin.nl

2000 Mathematical Subject Classification 68T35, 68U35, 94A99, 94C99

A CIP catalogue record for this book is available from the
Library of Congress, Washington D.C., USA

Bibliographic information published by Die Deutsche Bibliothek
Die Deutsche Bibliothek lists this publication in the Deutsche Nationalbibliografie;
detailed bibliographic data is available in the Internet at <http://dnb.ddb.de>.

ISBN 3-7643-7213-3 Birkhäuser Verlag, Basel – Boston – Berlin

This work is subject to copyright. All rights are reserved, whether the whole or part of the
material is concerned, specifically the rights of translation, reprinting, re-use of illustrations,
recitation, broadcasting, reproduction on microfilms or in other ways, and storage
in data banks. For any kind of use permission of the copyright owner must be obtained.

© 2005 Birkhäuser Verlag, P.O. Box 133, CH-4010 Basel, Switzerland
Part of Springer Science+Business Media
Cover design: Micha Lotrovsky, CH-4106 Therwil, Switzerland
Printed on acid-free paper produced from chlorine-free pulp. TCF ∞
Printed in Germany
ISBN 10: 3-7643-7213-3
ISBN 13: 978-3-7643-7213-2

9 8 7 6 5 4 3 2 1   www.birkhauser.ch

Acknowledgments

This book has been written in the period 1999-2004 under the supervision of Prof. Dr. Bob Wielinga and Prof. Dr. Guus Schreiber of the department of social informatics science, University of Amsterdam. Hereby I would like to thank Bob Wielinga and Guus Schreiber, especially for their enthusiastic and intensive supervision, support and guidance.

During the writing of this work, I have been working on the IBROW project (IST-1999-19005) with the I-team: Wenjin Lue, Monica Crubezy, Arthur Duineveld, Enrico Motta, Mark Musen, Borys Omelayenko, John Dominque, Maite Lopez, Frank van Harmelen, Annette ten Teije and Mario Gomez.

At the University of Amsterdam, several people helped me with technical, administrative, LATEX related, Linux related, graphical, prolog related and juggling related issues. Therefore, I would especially like to thank Richard Benjamins, Anjo Anjewierden, Wouter Jansweijer, Jan Wielemaker, Maarten van Someren, Machiel Jansen, Saskia van Loo, Fransje Enserink, Laurens Ekkel, Vannessa Evers and Dennis Beckers.

Next, I would like to thank my old Bolesian colleagues: Gert-Jan Beijer, Kris Van Marcke, Bob Swart, Niels Postma, Paul Siteur en Dave Henneman who helped with developping of the 5C model.

The Beangenerator described in chapter 6 is developed in close cooperation with Telecom Italia Lab. Hereby, I would like to thank Fabio Bellifemine and Giovanni Caire for their review work on the original paper and the development of the JADE environment. Furthermore, thanks to Valentina Tamma for her expertise on the field of the English language and culture, Italian delicacies, ontologies and of course (semantic) webservices.

My colleagues at Acklin helped me with support, distraction, motivation, compiling Linux kernels at high speed, mathematical issues and lessons of life. Therefore, I would like to thank: Jan Smulders, Patrick Storms, Leo Blommers, Geert Graat, Michiel van Hulst and Joëlle Smulders.

Finally, I would like to thank my friends and family, who did not really understand the material I have been worked on, but supported me in several other ways, in particular: Jan en Wilma van Aart, Peter en Agnes Behet, Leon en Loes van Aart, Willem en Bianca van Aart, Paul, Ina en Gertske Kuiper, Hubert Borghans, Dr. C. Meijer, Marloes Wolfs, Rogier Thissen, Marie Pauline van Voorst tot Voorst and Nik Baerten.

Contents

Chapter 1

Introduction

1.1 Background

In this work, we develop a framework for the design of multi-agent systems inspired by (human) organizational principles. Organizations are complex entities formed to overcome various limitations of individual agencies, such as cognitive, physical, temporal and institutional limitations. There is a parallel between the complexity of organizations and multi-agent systems. Therefore, we explore the use of concepts, methods and techniques from human organizational design as architectural principles for multi-agent systems. Three research lines are presented: *organizational modeling and coordination, interoperability* and *agent models*. Organizational modeling and coordination are concerned with how resources (i.e. agents) can be identified and related to each other. In order to have agents cooperate, several issues of interoperability have to be addressed. Agent models deal with the design of individual intelligent software agents, taking into account typical features of agent intelligence.

Every (human) activity raises two challenges: *division of labor* and *coordination* [Mintzberg, 1993]. Division of labor is the decomposition of work (or goals) into various distinct tasks. Coordination refers to managing relations between these tasks to carry out the work. The patterns of division of labor, responsibilities (people who do the work), clustering of responsibilities into units and coordination between units can be defined by *organizational structures* [Galbraith, 1973]. The design of an organization should cover how one or more actors are engaged in one or more tasks, where knowledge, capabilities and resources are distributed. Such a design can be seen as a set of networks and procedures that link actors, tasks, resources and skills. The theory of division of labor originates from Adam Smith, who argues that organizations are characterized as a way for assigning resources and responsibilities to working "units" [Smith, 1776]. Every unit is responsible for a task related to its role within an organization.

One of the first studies on organizational modeling has been later classified as mechanistic organizational modeling. Mechanistic organizations are designed as machines.

This approach is known as *classical management theory* for designing organizational structures [Fayol, 1949]. Designing individual positions as part of a machine is known as *scientific management* [Taylor, 1947]. The mechanistic approach is effective in stable environments, but another approach to design organizational structures is *organic organizations*, where organizations are designed as if they were organisms. Organic organizations can be seen as open systems where the organizational members (i.e. staff) must survive (e.g. by adapting) in changing environments and have life cycles. The organic organizations approach is effective in situations characterized by rapid changes in the environment and the staff. Morgan adds another approach: the organization as an information processing brain [Morgan, 1996]. By combining different elements (i.e. competences), functionality can emerge. Knowledge is distributed and by removing one element, the function of that element is taken over by another element, making the organization "self-organizing". A discussion of studies on organizational structures can be found in [Morgan, 1996].

Several considerations can be made when making decisions about organizational design. Galbraith divides these decisions into *strategical, organizational* and *staff related* [Galbraith, 1973]. Strategic considerations look at the distinctive competence or domain of an organization. The structure of an organization will be formed according to products or services to be offered, customer/clients to be served, technology to be utilized or location at which work is to be performed. Furthermore, the objectives and goals of the organization play a major role. Types of goals range from long to short-term and from economic to social. The organizing mode determines how to decompose the overall task into subtasks combined with coordination mechanisms to reintegrate the results of these subtasks in order to achieve the overall goal. Considerations related to staff concern selecting people (actors), designing tasks and arranging incentives or motivations (such as rewards) for people to do their job.

Many human organizations can be viewed as information processing systems because many of their activities are concerned with transforming information from one form into another. In addition, organizational activity (like receiving orders, reporting and administrating) is frequently information-driven [Bond and Gasser, 1988]. Links between human organizations and computational systems are described by [Fox, 1981, Malone and Crowston, 1994]. Fox describes an organizational structure for a distributed system as the collection of processes (agents), communication paths and a control regime that coordinates the whole [Fox, 1981]. Malone and Crowston discusses the influence of coordination theory in resource allocation, management of unreliable actors, task assignment and information flow management [Malone and Crowston, 1994]. Hewitt points out that *in organization lies power* [Hewitt, 1991]. An elaborate study on the use of notions, concepts, mechanisms and patterns from organizational design in Distributed Artificial Intelligence research can be found in [Carley and Gasser, 1999].

Coordination is an essential activity in multi-agent systems, in that it permits agents to cooperate in order to achieve common goals. Based on division of labor, agents will perform a number of (specialized) tasks. Agents organized in a multi-agent system are capable of performing more complex actions, when they collaborate. However, in order to achieve common and individual goals agents need to interact in a coordinated manner. This means that an agent should be aware not only of the actions it can perform and the state it is in at any moment of the execution, but also of the actions other agents can perform and their states. Corkill and Lander point out the necessity for coordination in large agent-based systems [Corkill and Lander, 1998]. They describe a set of principles to argue that coordination structures will become an important aspect of effective system performance. The importance of organizations can be determined by looking at the number of agents they include, the duration of agent activities and the repetitiveness of activities. Another principle states that when a system is composed of distributed processes, such as *agents*, there is a need for coordination structures governing the interactions between these processes.

"Intelligent Agents" is a research domain within Artificial Intelligence that has received a great deal of attention over the past decade [Bradshaw, 1997, Weiss, 1999, Luck et al., 2003]. The fascination with this subject may be explained by the fact that most of the traditional AI problems (such as knowledge representation, machine learning, planning, problem-solving and reflection) come together within this topic, see for example [Bond and Gasser, 1988]. A lot of intelligent agents on the Internet are usually not so clever as the term suggests. The reason for this is that a lot of classical AI problems are not solved by the introduction of agent technology [Wooldridge and Jennings, 1998].

Several perspectives, property sets and classifications for intelligent agents are described within the literature, see for overviews [Franklin and Graesser, 1996, Nwana, 1996, Bradshaw, 1997, Jennings, 2000]. An example of a property that is generally associated with an intelligent agent is that they have a degree of autonomy, meaning that an agent can follow its agenda independently of others in order to meet its objectives [Wooldridge, 2002]. For that reason, an intelligent agent should be able to *perceive* its environment, e.g. via sensors, and respond in a timely fashion to changes that occur in it. Types of environments include the physical world, a user, a collection of agents and the Internet. Furthermore, an intelligent agent should be able to take the initiative, i.e. be *pro-active*, instead of simply reacting in response to its environment. Finally, an intelligent agent should be able to *interact* with other agents and humans in order to offer their services and cooperate with other agents. To be able to interact with others, intelligent agents must have the capability to communicate in one or more agent communication languages. In order to have agents understand each other, several standardization efforts have been carried out [FIPA, 2002d]. However, standardization of an agent communication language does not mean standardization of communication: problems at a semantic and coordination level still need to be solved. Several agent models and frameworks have been proposed within the agent literature [Franklin and Graesser, 1996]. Most of the time, they pay particular attention to multi-agent aspects: i.e. to inter-agent/social organization and to inter-agent interaction. Some frameworks make no commitment to the way an individual agent is organized internally; others make a commitment by imposing a certain technical mechanism which implements only one or a few intelligent agent properties [Wooldridge and Jennings, 1998].

Domains where multi-agent systems play a role are large scale problem-solving systems, comprised of multiple individuals or services, engaged in more than one task, goal-directed (where goals can change), able to affect and be affected by their environment, having knowledge, culture, memories, history and capabilities distinct from any single agent, and having a legal standing [Bond and Gasser, 1988]. Many existing (web) services are distributed, heterogeneous and rigid, in the sense that they can not easily be configured. For example, different languages will be used for competence representations and ontology representation [Powers, 2003]. The libraries of services (i.e. Problem-Solving Methods) of a future Semantic Web will be as heterogeneous as the current collection of search engines and other services that exist on the Web [Berners-Lee et al., 2001]. To take heterogeneity and distribution into account, agent wrappers can be built around these services, so that these services can cooperate (e.g. exchange information).

Given the possible distributive and heterogeneous nature of multi-agent systems several design decisions have to be made. Bond and Gasser divide these decisions into two levels: individual agent level and community level. Decisions at the level of individual agents are: *What becomes an agent in a system? How does each agent model the world? How are agents structured internally? Are the agents identical or heterogeneous?* In addition *Do the agents share common modules or differ in others?* Decisions at the level of a community are: *What is the population of a system? What communication channels do agents use? What communication protocols do agents use? How are conversations among agents structured? How is the configuration of the agent-community?* and *How do the agents coordinate their action?* [Bond and Gasser, 1988]

Little has been reported on theories and methods related to complex multi-agent architectures design. Therefore, we explore the use of existing organizational patterns as architectures for multi-agent systems to address a selection of the above-described design issues. In order to have agents cooperate within artificial organizations, interoperability problems will be examined. Furthermore, we investigate how individual agents can be analyzed and designed.

1.2   Research Questions

The general problem addressed in this book is:

> How can human organizational principles be used for multi-agent architectures?

We explore the possibilities of designing multi-agent systems as artificial organizations and we investigate the problems that arise when we want agents to behave as members within an artificial organization.

This general problem is refined by the following three research questions:

1. How can decomposition principles (i.e. division of labor) and coordination be applied in multi-agent architecture design?

   Despite the differences between intelligent agents and humans, we assume that human organizational principles can be used in multi-agent architecture design. Concepts, mechanisms and patterns from the field of organizational design have already been used as the basis for distributed intelligent system design [Fox, 1981, Corkill and Lander, 1998, Carley and Gasser, 1999]. However, little work has been reported on the explicit use of the notion of *organizations* in distributed intelligent system design. Moreover, Jennings argues that there are (still) insufficient mechanisms available for representing an agent-based system's organizational structure [Jennings, 2000]. However, several organizational structures and mechanisms are described within the organizational design literature. Therefore, we are interested in the use of this organizational knowledge in multi-agent architecture design.

2. HOW CAN AGENTS MAKE USE OF COORDINATION MECHANISMS?

When agents collaborate, they need to use and share coordination strategies in order to regulate joint actions. To share coordination strategies, agents will have to be able to share knowledge related to coordination models. Furthermore, to regulate joint actions, agents need to interoperate with each other. Interoperability issues are concerned with allowing agents to communicate with each other, coordinating agent communication and adding semantics to agent communication.

3. HOW CAN THE CAPABILITIES AND FUNCTIONALITY OF AN INDIVIDUAL INTELLIGENT AGENT BE ANALYZED AND DESIGNED?

This question relates to the issues discussed by Bond and Gasser: *how does an agent model the world*, *are the agents identical or heterogeneous* and *how are the agents structured internally* [Bond and Gasser, 1988]. There is a need for an integrated model that combines typical agent intelligence properties, such as autonomy, interaction, pro-activeness and reactiveness. This model should be able to guide designers in making conceptual, functional and technical design decisions. Such a model can take the form of a reference model for agent analysis and design in which issues related to coordination and organization are included.

1.3 Approach

In order to answer the research questions, we follow three research lines: *organizational modeling and coordination*, *interoperability* and *agent models*. In each research line, we present conceptual frameworks that are evaluated with technical experiments using prototypes. The three frameworks are described at the knowledge level: i.e. independent of implementation and symbol representation details. Prototypes are implemented (at the symbol level), as proof of concepts evaluating the plausibility of the presented frameworks.

To answer the research questions, we perform the following tasks:

- CONDUCT A CONCEPTUAL ANALYSIS OF ORGANIZATIONAL CONCEPTS, ORGANIZATIONAL MODELS AND COORDINATION MECHANISMS.

To set the scope of this book, we investigate the building blocks of organizational design that form the basis of an agent organization framework. Within this framework, a set of organizational structures will be discussed. A case study on supply chain management is analyzed with this framework, which results in three organizational structure designs. Finally, we describe a prototype application resulting from the three organizational designs.

- PROVIDE A FRAMEWORK FOR AGENT INTEROPERATION.

  In order to have agents "smoothly" collaborate with each other, we address the problem of enabling interoperation. We explore an interoperability framework consisting of four interoperability levels: *technical, syntactical, semantic* and *coordination*. The issues in the *technical interoperability* and *syntactic interoperability*, which are solved by applying standard protocols, methods and technology, are briefly discussed. The *semantic interoperability* level deals with ontologies that are used in agent communication. We investigate how these ontologies can be constructed and used by agents. The *coordination interoperability* level deals with how agents can be coordinated. We explore the use of Problem-Solving Methods (PSMs) to characterize coordination strategies that can be used by agents. Work on a multi-agent architecture capable of (semi)automatic reuse of (web) services is discussed.

- PROVIDE A CONCEPTUAL FRAMEWORK FOR ANALYZING AND DESIGNING THE CAPABILITIES AND FUNCTIONALITY OF AN INTELLIGENT AGENT.

  We present a conceptual framework for analyzing and designing the capabilities and functionality of an intelligent agent. Using the notion of *separation of concerns*, we define five dimensions of agent intelligence where each dimension plays a role in the development of intelligent agents. We report on two agent-based systems that are analyzed, designed and implemented using the conceptual framework.

1.4 Outline

The book is organized according to the outline presented below:

Chapter 2 - Agent Organization Framework In this chapter, we introduce general principles of organizational design related to decomposition principles, organizational structures and coordination mechanisms. A selection of these principles are gathered in a framework for multi-agent system design. In order to explore the application of the framework, a collection of organizational design steps is presented that assists in a task-oriented decomposition of the overall task of a system into jobs, the reintegration of jobs using job allocation, coordination mechanisms and organizational structuring. A case study on distributed supply chain management shows the process from task decomposition via organizational design to three architectures of multi-agent system designs.

Chapter 3 - Coordination Strategies for Multi-Agent Systems Models for coordination strategies, introduced in Chapter 2, are translated into Problem-Solving Methods. The coordination strategies are based on existing coordination strategies taken from organizational design theory and give agents a means to coordinate joint actions. We report on a small experiment in which three coordination strategies were implemented as problem-solving methods in a multi-agent system.

Chapter 4 - Five Capabilities Model In order to study how agents can be made to operate within organizations, we discuss the the *5 Capabilities (5C) model*. The 5C model is a conceptual framework for analyzing and designing the capabilities and functionality of an intelligent agent. Using the notion of *separation of concerns*, the 5C model defines five dimensions of agent intelligence, where each dimension plays a role in the analysis and development of intelligent agents.

Chapter 5 - Interoperation within a Complex Multi-Agent Architecture The problem of interoperation within a distributed architecture composed of heterogeneous components is discussed in this chapter. The architecture is able to compose applications from existing (web) services that reside on the Web. The agents within the architecture collaborate using collaboration patterns and specialized ontologies, which are part of an interoperability framework. This framework consists of four layers: coordination (based on the mechanisms described in Chapter 2), semantical, syntactical and technical. The collaboration patterns are operationalizations of the coordination methods described in Chapter 3. A proof of concept is presented that explains the dynamics of parts of the architecture. The design and use of specialized ontologies is described in Chapter 6.

Chapter 6 - Message Content Ontologies The semantical layer of the interoperability framework, introduced in Chapter 5, is discussed in detail in this chapter. We address the problem of how agents handle ontology-based communication. A theoretical framework for ontology-based communication is introduced. A pragmatic approach is presented that enables the creation and use of ontologies to support ontology-based communication between agents.

Chapter 7 - Conclusions This chapter concludes the book by answering the research questions, discussing the presented work and suggesting future research.

Chapter 2

Agent Organization Framework

In this chapter we present a framework for multi-agent system design which is based both on human organizational notions and principles for distributed intelligent systems design. The framework elaborates on the idea that notions from the field of organizational design can be used as the basis for the design of distributed intelligent systems. Organizational notions such as task, control, job, operation, management, coordination and organization are framed into an agent organizational framework. A collection of organizational design activities is presented that assists in a task oriented decomposition of the overall task of a system into jobs and the reintegration of jobs using job allocation, coordination mechanisms and organizational structuring. A number of coordination mechanisms have been defined in the organizational design literature. For the scope of this book we concentrate on: Direct Supervision where one individual takes all decisions for the work of others, Mutual Adjustment that achieves coordination by a process of informal communication between agents, and Standardization of Work, Output and Skills.

Three organizational structures are discussed, that coordinate agents and their work: Machine Bureaucracy, Professional Bureaucracy and Adhocracy. The Machine Bureaucracy is task-driven, seeing the organization as a single-purpose structure, which only uses one strategy to execute the overall task. The Professional Bureaucracy is competence-driven, where a part of the organization will first examine a case, match it to predetermined situations and then allocate specialized agents to it. In the Adhocracy the organization is capable of reorganizing its own structure including dynamically changing the work flow, shifting responsibilities and adapting to changing environments. A case study on distributed supply chain management shows the process from task decomposition via organizational design to three multi-agent architectures based on Mintzberg's organizational structures. This chapter will be published in the International Journal of Human Computer Studies [van Aart, 2004].

2.1 Introduction

In this chapter, we discuss a framework for the design of distributed intelligent systems. The framework is based on human organizational notions and principles, aimed at managing relations between organizational agents[1] and the activities they perform, rather than at the design of individual agents. The framework elaborates on the idea that notions from the field of organizational design can be used as the basis for the

---

[1]In this book, we use "agent" to refer to intelligent software agents.

design of distributed intelligent systems. Already in the eighties, links between human
organizations and computational systems were suggested [Fox, 1981, Malone, 1987].
Since then, organizational approaches have become themes in research areas for supporting coordination and framing control relations. Hewitt has pointed out that *in organization lies power* [Hewitt, 1991]. Indeed, despite the differences[2] between software
agents and humans a number of notions, such as concepts, mechanisms and patterns
can be used as principles for distributed intelligent systems design [Fox, 1981]. Different agent-oriented modeling techniques and methods have been presented, see for an
overview [Wooldridge et al., 2000]. For example, GAIA specifies agent systems in terms
of interaction roles. Roles are defined with responsibilities, permissions and protocols into
a role model. An interaction model defines a protocol for each type of inter-role interaction [Wooldridge et al., 2000]. However, GAIA only implicitly uses the notion of organizations and should be enhanced with organizational structures [Zambonelli et al., 2000].
Research efforts on agents and organizations have been reported in the organizational
design literature, including research on electronic institutions [Esteva et al., 2001], computational and mathematical models of organizations [Carley and Gasser, 1999] and organizational views on multi-agent systems [Ferber, 1999].

In spite of the work on agent organizations, Jennings argues that there are not sufficient mechanisms available for representing an agent-based system's organizational structure [Jennings, 2000]. Fox sees an organizational structure for a distributed system as the
collection of processes (i.e. agents), communication paths and a control regime that coordinates the whole [Fox, 1981]. Therefore, research efforts in the agent field have dealt
with the problem of enabling interactions among agents allowing information and knowledge to be transferred from one agent to another, middleware components (mediator,
information brokers) and infrastructures. However, the approach of the research efforts
reported in the agent literature is on the system (implementation) perspective.

Distributed Artificial Intelligence (DAI) has looked at overcoming limitations of
individual agencies by tackling problems through running distributed computational processes. For this reason, research in (distributed) knowledge models, communication and
reasoning techniques have led to ways in which agents can participate in societies of
agents, i.e. agencies. We see an agency as a society of agents, in which each of them can
be specialized with knowledge, one or more skills and has a sort of mechanism that permits the interaction with others. Examples of agencies are collections of individuals, including humans, machines and computational processes such as web services and agents.
A specific agency is a multi-agent system, which is defined by O'Hare and Jennings as
*a loosely-coupled network of problems solvers (i.e. agents) that work together to solve
problems that are beyond their individual capabilities* [O'Hare and Jennings, 1996]. Every agent has one or more limitations, which can be categorized into *cognitive*, *physical*,
temporal and *institutional limitations*. Cognitive limitations model the fact that individuals are rationally bounded. It means that the data, information, and knowledge an individual can process and the detail of control an individual can handle is limited. As tasks

---

[2]For example, agents can be cloned but agents do not have the ability to learn as quickly as humans from
each other.

grow larger and more complex, techniques must be applied to limit the growth of information and the complexity of control. Individuals can be limited physically, because of their physiology or because of the resources available to them. Temporal limitations exist where the achievement of individual goals exceeds the lifetime of an individual, or the time during which resources are available for this goal. Finally, institutional limitations means that individuals are legally or politically limited.

Social systems, i.e. groups of humans and social connections, can be viewed as computational systems. Many human activities are concerned with transforming information and knowledge from one form to another. In addition, human activities (such as receiving orders, reporting and processing) are frequently information-driven [Galbraith, 1973]. An example is an agent-based system for digital cross-border information flow within a European network of insurance companies. In this case, agents that exchange the same information via the Internet replaced people who exchanged information by telephone [van Aart et al., 2002b]. However, when designing complex systems with multiple agents and multiple tasks, it is likely that social rules will lead to systems that are hard to design and maintain. If every agent is equipped with social rules prescribing the way it should behave in the system, these rules will have to be valid in every situation. The result can be a set of agents where the rule base for social rules is more complex than their competences. At the moment, if a task, domain or group of agent changes, every agent (and its social rule base) has to be adjusted.

The remainder of this chapter is organized as follows. In Section 2.2, we investigate the building blocks from organizational design that form the basis of our framework. Organizational structures are described in Section 2.3. Section 2.4 describes a collection of organizational design activities that operates within the framework. In Section 2.5 a case study on supply chain management is analyzed with the framework, which resulted in three organizational structure designs and a small prototype application. Finally, we discuss issues arising from this study and suggest future work.

2.2 Building Blocks of Agent Organizational models

This section discusses a number of concepts, organizational relation and coordination mechanisms from organizational design that will be used as building blocks in our agent organization framework. We will start by examining the work of Mintzberg. He has argued that: *Every organized human activity from baking a cookie to the placing of a man on the moon gives rise to two fundamental and opposing questions: how to divide activities into various tasks and how to coordinate these tasks to accomplish the activity?* [Mintzberg, 1993]. One of the answers Mintzberg gives to the first question is that activities should be broken down into a technical part and a management part. *Operators* will be responsible for performing the technical part of the work, such as producing output. *Managers* will be responsible for the control over Operators. With this approach, the performance of work is explicitly separated from the control over it.

One of the answers to the second question is to place Operators and Managers into a (hierarchical) structure, where Managers control Operators in order to achieve coordination. Another approach is to place Operators into a structure of commitments (also known as *locker room agreements*), wherein the Operators have reached an agreement on how to collaborate with each other. This means that the work and communication patterns of Operators are standardized. Mintzberg's breakdown of tasks into smaller activities can be seen as hierarchical task decomposition. This means that tasks are broken down into smaller subtasks. This breakdown repeats until the subtasks are small enough to be allocated to an Operator. A stop-criterion for decomposition is the amount and complexity of the knowledge needed for executing a subtask.

We assume that a task is known beforehand and that subtasks will not be conflicting. Other decomposition strategies include *Skill oriented* , *Process oriented* and *Knowledge oriented decomposition*. Skill oriented decomposition looks at the expertise of components (humans, machine or agents) already available. For example, in the design of a system that is able to search on the Web, one can utilize already existing search engines, such as Google. Process oriented decomposition tries to define the goal of a system in terms of transactions between steps. This can be useful in domains where the steps to be undertaken are deterministic and the transactions between the steps can be described as sequential. For example, in the process of assembling a car, there is an assembly line that represents the medium for sequential transactions between the assemble jobs. Knowledge oriented decomposition will look at the knowledge of components (humans, machine or agents) already available. For example, in order to facilitate a one-stop shop[3] for law assistance, a number of existing knowledge bases on the domain of law can be coupled, by wrapping agents around them. An example of this functionality is discussed in Section 6.5. In the remainder we will use task decomposition as mechanism for division of labor.

Another principle from organizational design is the contingency theory (see for an overview [Morgan, 1996]). It claims that: *There is no best way to organize*. This means that there is not one organizational structure that can handle every problem in every domain. The theory states that the appropriate form of an organizational design depends on the task and the environment. Tasks range from highly routine to highly innovative. For example, the task to assemble a car can be seen as a routine task. The design of a car can be seen as an innovative task. Environments can be characterized on a scale ranging from relatively stable to highly unpredictable.

The next section starts from the theory of Mintzberg by describing an ontology that can be used for Multi-Agent System analysis and design. Based on the contingency theory we discuss several organizational forms in Section 2.3.

2.2.1   Concepts

One individual (such as person, machine, agent or web service) can handle many tasks on its own. However, when one of these individuals encounters one or more limitations, a solution is to have the task be executed by a set of individuals. To define what has to be done (i.e. the decomposition of the overall task), by whom (set of Operators and task al-

---

[3]A system where one point mediates between user and available services.

location) and how (methods and knowledge), a selection of concepts from organizational literature has been placed in a context as illustrated in Figure 2.1.

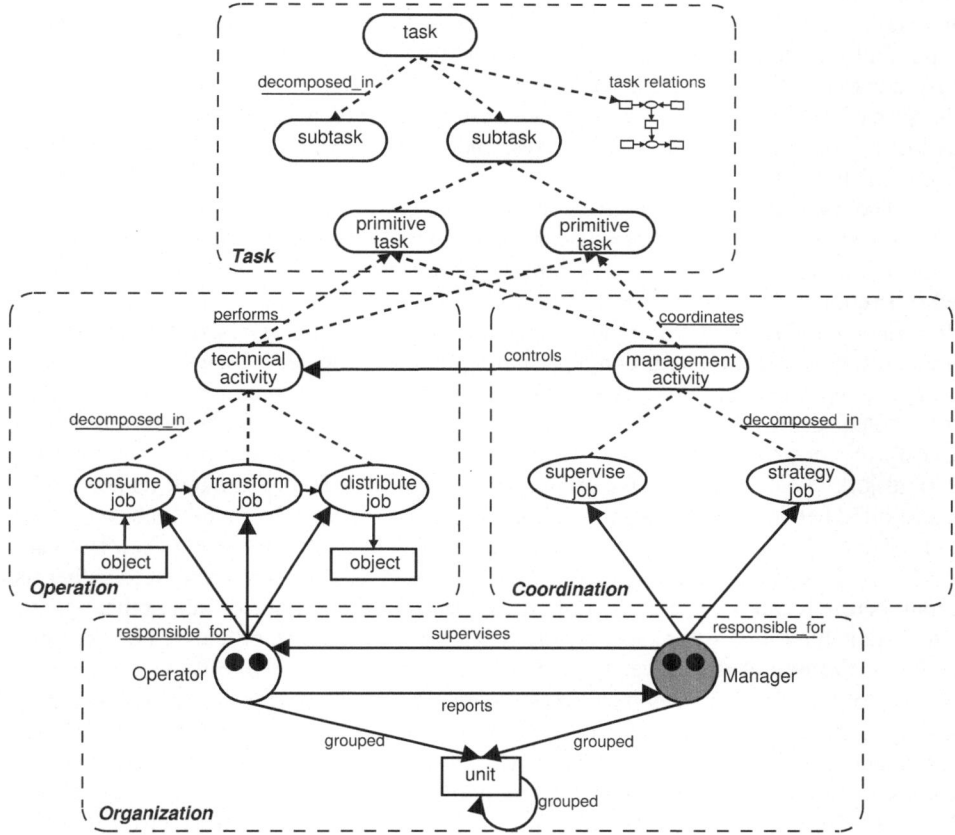

Figure 2.1

Framework context, showing the four perspectives of the framework, its concepts and main relations. The task perspective consists of *tasks* and task decomposition expressed in *task relations*. The operational perspective consists of *objects, technical activities* and *jobs*. The coordination perspective is concerned with the control of technical activities in the form of *management activities* and *jobs*. The organizational perspective is concerned with who does what (job allocation) and consists of *positions* (such as operator and manager) and *units*.

The **task perspective** consists of *tasks* and a task decomposition expressed in *task relations*. A *task* can be seen as the overall duty of an organization. Tasks can be defined as work in a domain, e.g. production of cars or finding scientific literature on the Web. In detail, a task definition specifies the subtasks that should achieve that goal of the task, input and output specifications and a control structure. A control structure specifies a methods to handle the dependencies between subtasks. This corresponds to Mintzberg's division of work into tasks. *Task relations* describe dependencies of these subtasks, such as the sequence of execution. This corresponds to Mintzberg's coordination of tasks to accomplish the work.

The **operational perspective** consists of objects, technical activities and jobs. An *object* is something that can be consumed, produced (created, cloned), transformed (altered, combined) or used by tasks. Examples of objects are data, information and knowledge. In some cases, objects can be stored in a warehouse or a repository (e.g. a database). *Technical activities* deal with objects typically leading to a piece of work where objects are consumed (used, altered, combined) and produced (created, cloned). The pieces of work are represented by *jobs*. A technical activity consists of three jobs: (1) Consume job, which secures the inputs (that is objects) for production (2) Transform job, which transforms (or produces) the input to outputs via a transformation process and (3) Distribute job, which distributes the outputs (that is objects). Sometimes objects need to be transported between producing and consuming jobs. For example, there can be a unit for item discovery and a unit for item classification. The jobs Consume and Distribute are explicitly defined to assist the process of coordination. Every agent has first to gather its input, before it can operate on it. Then it can be distributed to one or more other agents. The idea behind this is that these two jobs can be either passive or active. For example, if the job Consume is passive, agent A will wait until agent B will offer its consumable objects to Agent A. This can be seen as re-active behavior of agent A. If the job is pro-active, agent A will take initiative to gather its input by contacting agent B that distributes the object agent A needs. This can be seen as pro-active behavior. So called broker agents can assist in these processes, for coupling demand (Consume) and offer (Distribute). Interaction protocols can be applied, such as the Contract Net protocol which is based on announcements (call for proposals), bids (proposals) and awarded contracts (acceptance) [Davis and Smith, 1983]. In traditional software engineering the flow of objects are handled within the internals of a system or an inference mechanism. For example, one does not have to design the flow of objects in the programming environment Prolog, the internal inference mechanism will take care of this.

The **coordination perspective** is concerned with the control of technical activities in the form of management activities. Management activities deal with coordinating technical activities, transport of objects and decision-making. For example, when assembling a car there is a decision to make when to start, in what sequence the car should be assembled and how objects (i.e. parts) flow between the assembly jobs. Management activities consist of two jobs: Strategy job, which is in charge of ensuring that the organization serves its mission in an effective way, for example by configuring technical activities. The Supervise job supervises technical activities, by for example controlling the flow of objects between jobs. In more complex organizations where there is a hierarchy of management activities, the management activity should staff this authority hierarchy. This is what Mintzberg calls the middle line, i.e. the collection of Managers between the lower hierarchy and the top Managers [Mintzberg, 1993].

The **organizational perspective** is concerned with who does what (job allocation) and therefore consists of positions and units. A *position* is the characteristic and expected (social) behavior of an organizational individual. Organizational individuals populate an organization and are grouped into larger individual groups, such as units or departments. The behavior of an organizational individual can be described in terms of responsibility for carrying out a set of jobs (including objects to be consumed and produced), required expertise, skills or competences. Examples of positions are archivist, Operator, mediator, planner, coordinator, decision-maker, observer, executive, communicator and Manager. A position can fulfill multiple activities or a set of positions can fulfill one activity. Positions range from specialized by performing only one job to general (omnipotent) performing multiple or all jobs. To make things not too complex, we distinguish between two types of positions, OPERATORS and MANAGERS. An OPERATOR is responsible for a limited set of technical activities. A MANAGER is responsible for management activities. The difference between a MANAGER and an OPERATOR can be seen as the separation of control knowledge and object flow between agents in distributed intelligent systems. A *unit* is a group of positions that can be seen as a distinct entity within an organization [Mintzberg, 1993]. Similar concepts are agency, department, cluster, team and (sub) society. Six bases for grouping are commonly considered: grouping by knowledge and skill, by work process and function, by time, by output, by client and by location. At the end, the assignment of Operators and Managers, their grouping into units, and the grouping of units into other units can form an organization.

2.2.2 Organizational Relations

Between the concepts defined in the section above relations and dependencies exist. These relations are defined by Mintzberg and are discussed below for relations that connect two or more positions. The relations are also summarized in Table 2.1.

The *Producer/consumer relation* exists in the execution of activities, one Operator with one or more other technical activities produces objects that are to be used by technical activities that are allocated to other Operators. Sometimes transportations (i.e. transactions within the flow of objects) have to be performed to move objects between Operators. The *Consumer/producer relation*, is present where one or more Operators need objects that are to be produced by one or more other Operators. The distinction between producer/consumer relations and consumer/producer relations is that if OPERATOR A has a producer/consumer dependency with OPERATOR B, OPERATOR B has a consumer/producer relation with OPERATOR A. The *Common limited object relation* exists between multiple Operators when they need to access an object produced by one Operator. In this case, the technical activities of the Operators are mutually exclusive in the sense that they cannot be performed at the same time. For example, an Operator that needs a long time for transforming, such as complex calculations, can lock an object.

The *Report relation* means that an Operator has to report to a Manager. Type of

	OPERATOR with TECHNICAL ACTIVITIES	MANAGER with MANAGEMENT ACTIVITIES
OPERATOR with TECHNICAL ACTIVITIES	producer consumer consumer producer common limited object	report conflict
MANAGER with MANAGEMENT ACTIVITIES	command and instruct direct supervision delegate	delegate

Table 2.1
Relations between OPERATORS and MANAGERS with technical activities and management activities.

reports can be the beginning and the ending of an activity including the state of the produced object. The *Conflict relation* means that an Operator has to report to a Manager in case of a conflict between either another Operator, another Manager or a conflict with an object.

The *Command and instruct relation* means that a Manager will instruct an Operator in what manner to execute its technical activities and the moment of execution. An instruction consists of three sub-instructions: (1) what objects to consume from what Operator(s), (2) how to transform these objects, and (3) to what Operator(s) to distribute the transformed objects to. With the *Direct supervision relation*, a Manager will inform an Operator what next job to perform after finishing a job of a technical activity. For example, when an Operator performed a transform job, the Operator has to ask the Manager what to do with this new object. The Manager can respond with "distribute the object to Operator B". In short, the Manager makes all decisions on the perspective of the jobs of a technical activity.

The *Delegation relation* means that a Manager will delegate its responsibility to either another Manager or an Operator. In case of complex activities, a hierarchy of Managers can be defined that are capable of controlling on different perspectives of execution. For example, the management activities higher in a hierarchy use another perspective of detail than the management activities that control the operation. In a car factory, the higher Managers will look at the number of produced cars and the demand of customers. At the lower perspective of the organization, the Managers will control the process of manufacturing.

2.2.3   Coordination Mechanisms

Malone defines coordination as the operation of complex systems made up of components [Malone and Crowston, 1994]. It is the act of managing interdependencies between positions and activities performed to achieve goals. Mintzberg has defined the following mechanisms that can be applied to coordinate dependencies between positions and activities.

The first coordination mechanism, *Direct Supervision* achieves coordination by having one individual take responsibility, which is taking all decisions for the work of others, issuing instructions to them and monitoring their actions. This mechanism can be seen as a pattern for one central reasoning service (i.e. the MANAGER) with several information providing processes (i.e. OPERATORS). This form of coordination is suited when there is a clear distinction between decision-making and operation. In Section 3.3.1 (p.50), we discuss this coordination mechanism in detail.

The second mechanism, *Standardization of Work* achieves coordination by specifying, i.e. programming, the content of the technical activity. The content of the activity is specified in every step, from getting the input objects (Consume), what to do with it (Transform) and to whom to distribute it (Distribute). For example, when installing a gear into a car a piece of this specification will look like "take the two-inch-round-head Philips screw and insert it into hole H1, attach this to part P2 with the lock washer L2 and hexagonal nut N1, at the same time holding....". In distributed intelligent systems design this means a hard coded procedural program that dictates the behavior of an agent, without any room for negotiation with other agents. In case of a conflict (for instance exception), it will be reported to the supervisor (Manager). *Standardization of output objects* achieves coordination by only specifying the result (i.e. produced objects) of the activities. For example, taxi drivers are not told how to drive or what route to take; they are merely informed where to deliver their fares. This can be applied when only the configuration of the outgoing objects of activities matters. For example, web servers produce web pages in the HTML format. For the reader of those pages, it does not matter *how* these pages are produced, as long as they are in the HTML format. For distributed intelligent system design, this means the specification of interfaces (e.g. output objects) of agents and exchange mechanisms, like languages and ontologies. *Standardization of skills* achieves coordination by only specifying what competences are needed for the activity. For example, when two surgeons meet in an operating room to perform surgery, they need hardly communication, by virtue of training, they know exactly what to expect of each other [Gosselin, 1978]. When designing distributed intelligent systems, the knowledge required for specific activities has to be specified and agents need to be equipped with knowledge about the competences of other agents. By means of protocols, they can collaborate. In Section 3.3.2 (p.55), we discuss "Standardization of Work" in detail.

Finally, *Mutual Adjustment* achieves coordination by a process of informal communication between positions. This means that positions are capable of solving coordination issues by themselves. For distributed intelligent system design, this means that agents have social abilities in the sense that they are capable of interacting and reasoning about each others interfaces, knowledge and competences and activities to achieve, without hardly any standardization or protocols. In Section 3.3.3 (p.59) we discuss this 'Mutual Adjustment" in detail.

The choice of a coordination strategy depends on a number of factors, such as the type of environment, the type of activity and the style of organizing. For example, "standardization of technical activities" is an option when the multi-agent system needs to operate in a stable environment where activities will not change and there is a need for tight control over the Operators. The agents will not have to be equipped with organizational knowledge nor the ability of negotiation. "Mutual Adjustment" is an alternative, in case of a dynamic environment where it is unknown what activities need to be performed. Furthermore, the type and number of agents are not known on forehand meaning that agents themselves have to get in contact and discuss the allocation of activities and responsibilities. Accordingly, the agents have to be capable of modeling the environment (such as constructing a world model). Furthermore, the agents have to figure out what overall goals (if any) to achieve.

2.3   Organizational Structures

Organizations are complex artifacts that are made by design or that have emerged over time. A design of an organization should show flow of objects between positions and the interrelationships between these positions. An *organigram*[4] is an often used means to represent organizational designs [Mintzberg, 1993]. An organigram shows a picture of the division of labor, what positions exists, how these are grouped into units (or clusters) and how formal authority flows.

We propose to use organigrams as a mechanism for representing a distributed system's organizational structure in answer to the issue of the availability of insufficient mechanisms for representing a system's organizational structure as mentioned by Jennings [Jennings, 2000]. The grouping of these agents can be shown by units. Furthermore, the flows of authority show the responsibility of Managers in terms of the Operators they control. Imagine a hypothetical distributed system for classification of items on the Web, such as documents and images. This system includes specialized agents for crawling, document classification and image classification. The organigram in Figure 2.2 shows the collection of organizational properties for this system. Firstly, what positions exists in the system and what agents occupy these positions. For example, the agents Crawler1 and Crawler2 occupy the position of WebCrawler. The agents Classifier1 and Classifier2 occupy the position of DOCUMENT CLASSIFICATION AGENT Secondly, how these agents are grouped into units, e.g. the units **Operation**, **WebCrawling** and **Classification**. Thirdly, how control and coordination flows among them, e.g. the unit **Operation** controls the units **WebCrawling** and **Classification**.

With the discussed organizational properties in mind, we will look at three organizational structures as described by Mintzberg [Mintzberg, 1993]. The next sections describe these organizational structures in detail.

2.3.1   Machine Bureaucracy

The Machine Bureaucracy[5] is an organization where tasks are decomposed into highly routine technical activities. The relations between technical activities are sequential, therefore relations can be coordinated using formalized rules and regulations, based on

---

[4]Also known as organizational chart.

[5]The term *bureaucracy* was introduced by Max Weber as a technical term to describe a type of organization where behavior is predetermined or predictable, which can be seen as "standardization" as discussed before. The management and human resource management literature, has labeled the term "Bureaucracy" as a 'dirty word'. In this book we refer to the technical use of "Bureaucracy".

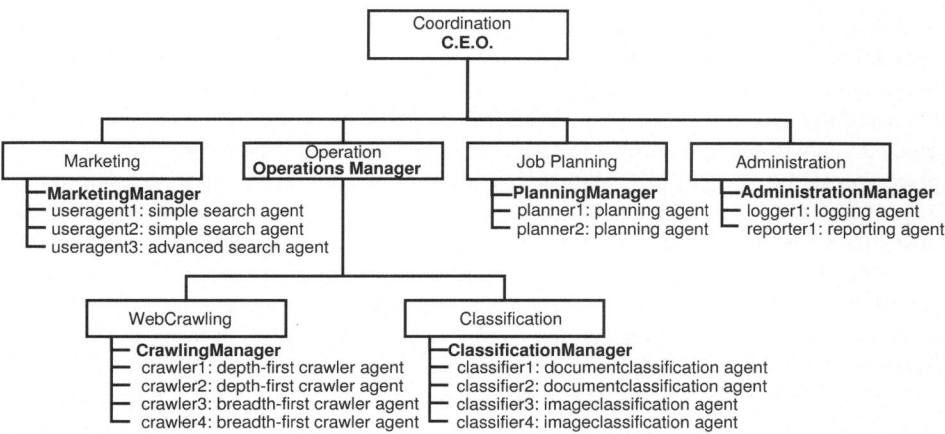

Figure 2.2
Organigram of a multi-agent system for classification of items on the Web. Boxes represent units, lines represent authority structures, **bold font** words represent manager positions and regular font words represent agents.

the coordination mechanism of standardization of technical activities. The positions are grouped on the basis of work processes into functional units. For example, one unit for pre-processing, one unit for transforming and one unit for packing.

There is a centralized authority, which means that all decision-making is done centrally and follows a chain of command from the top of the hierarchy to the Operators below. Given the functional units and the centralized decision-making, the form of the hierarchy of the organization is steep. The type of agents are very controllable, they do not have many decision-making capabilities and operate in subordination. Furthermore, there is a sharp distinction between technical positions and management positions. An example of a Machine Bureaucracy is a steel factory [Mintzberg, 1993]. The environment is stable and the nature of the tasks is routine and sequential, e.g. produce x products of type t. Furthermore, the jobs are rather simple and repetitive.

2.3.2 Professional Bureaucracy

The Professional Bureaucracy is an organization were technical activities are performed by highly skilled Operators. The nature of the jobs is highly complex, meaning that a lot of knowledge is required for them. Therefore, the control is decentralized and depends on internal professional standards. The positions are grouped based on skills into specialized units. For example, one for cardiology, one for neurology and one for surgery. The form of the organization is flat. The prime coordination mechanism is standardization of skills. The nature of the tasks is cyclic and the environment is predictable.

To understand how a Professional Bureaucracy operates, one has to think of a set of technical activities that can be applied to predetermined situations. The skill of an Operator is defined as the technical activities it can achieve. The idea is that Operators are categorized, based on their skills. When a problem has to be solved, the problem will be compared to one of the predetermined situations. From there, one or more Operators are selected that will solve the problem. Mintzberg has associated the term *pigeonholing* with this process [Mintzberg, 1993]. With this, Mintzberg means that Operators are placed into "pigeon holes" labeled with one ore more predetermined situations. Given a problem, the most suited Operator will be "grasped" from a "pigeon hole" on the basis of its label.

The process of pigeonholing is the responsibility of the strategy job. Given the activities to be performed, one can decompose these into technical activities and allocate these to specialized Operators. Pigeonholing can be seen as an assessment task for Managers. Based on the case it will decide which Operator will be assigned to it.

The difference between a Machine Bureaucracy and a Professional Bureaucracy is the pigeonholing process. The Machine Bureaucracy is a single-purpose structure, where Operators execute standard sequences of jobs. The Professional Bureaucracy will first examine a case and then select an Operator for it. In machine bureaucratic organizations, such as a car factory, Operators always perform the same job. For example, there is an Operator that classifies documents and an Operator that classifies images. In professional bureaucratic organizations, such as a hospital, the case of a patient will first be classified into for example, a heart defect. Secondly, it will be coupled to an Operator with the appropriate skills, i.e. a cardiologist.

Another difference between a Machine Bureaucracy and a Professional Bureaucracy is how technical activities are allocated to Operators. In a Machine Bureaucracy, there is a clear distinction between the positions that are occupied with technical activities and the positions that are occupied with management activities. Operators only perform technical activities and Managers are occupied with management activities. This means that Managers interfere with the consume, transform and produce jobs of Operators. This can be seen as management on a functional level. A Professional Bureaucracy uses the pigeonholing process for technical activities allocation.

2.3.3 Adhocracy

The two organization forms discussed above are not capable of *innovation*, i.e. breaking away from established organizational patterns. We see innovation as the ability of one or more agents to define new technical activities for new situations. New situations are found in dynamic and unpredictable environments. Therefore, the structure of the organization should have great flexibility. For that reason, the organizational structure of an Adhocracy has no hierarchical form. With the use of Mutual Adjustment the Operators are capable of performing innovative tasks, i.e. solving problems in a sophisticated and on an ad hoc way. Decision-making is done decentralized by multiple Managers. The prime coordination mechanism is Mutual Adjustment, which means that execution of the task relies on agent negotiation. An example of an Adhocracy is an Internet start-up with a limited number of employees, where the type of products and services frequently changes to find and serve customers.

The difference between an Adhocracy and the two bureaucracies is that within an Adhocracy there is no standard set of jobs and no classification of predetermined situations. For every case, Operators within an Adhocracy have to find creative solutions to unique problems. This has to be done using forms of negotiation on the basis of argumentation. When an Adhocracy grows older, it could reconfigure itself to a Machine Bureaucracy or a Professional Bureaucracy.

The organizational structures *Machine Bureaucracy, Professional Bureaucracy* and *Adhocracy* and their properties are summarized in Table 2.2.

Organizational Structures

	Machine Bureaucracy	*Professional Bureaucracy*	*Adhocracy*
environment	stable	predictable	dynamic
task nature	routine	skilled	innovative
activity allocation	static	pigeon holing	innovative
form	steep	flat	none
coordination mechanism	Standardization of Technical Activities	Standardization of Skills	Mutual Adjustment
decision making	central	decentral	decentral
type of agents	controllable	cooperational	autonomous

Table 2.2
Organizational structures and their properties.

2.4 Agent Organizational Design Activities

Based on Figure 2.1, we see an organizational *structure* in terms of flows between agents. These flows can be the movement of objects between Operators, commands from Managers to Operators and reports from Operators to Managers. This view, the discussed organization principles and organizational design are accompanied by three organizational design activities: *Task Analysis*, *Operator Collaboration Design* and *Organizational Design*.

2.4.1 Task Analysis

Task Analysis is concerned with the breakdown of work into subtasks. When a subtask is small enough to be performed by one agent, we see that as a primitive task. A primitive task is specialized into a technical activity. Accompanied with this breakdown is the identification of task dependencies. In this step, the primitive tasks are allocated to technical activities. For this step, UML activity diagrams can be used to show the technical activities, the transform jobs of technical activities, task relations and the flow of objects. Individual tasks can be described in terms of needed skills, task relations, input and output objects.

We use Bond and Gasser's conceptual distances as *rules for decomposition* [Bond and Gasser, 1988]. Firstly, *computation cost*, that is the costs for using information, knowledge or drawing on a specialized skill (measured in time, space, or other resources). For example, it is cheaper to produce cars in Asia or it is cheaper to use the services of Google instead of building a new search engine. Secondly, *spatial distance*, which can be expressed in a measure of distribution of processes, information or knowledge. Both computational and human information processing depend upon sensing data, information and knowledge. These processes occur at spatially distributed locations and on different and therefore distributed devices. There is a (possibly large) cost involved in moving these input data to a single central point in the system for processing. For example, in the car factory there will be assembly lines. It is impossible to see what is going on at the beginning and at the end of the assembly line at the same time. Another example are web services which can be implemented differently and running on different servers. Thirdly, *temporal distance*, means that data, information or knowledge may not be available at a given time, because they have not yet been produced or derived. For example, it can take time to transport information from one point to another. Finally, *semantic distance*, knowledge can be clustered into specialized tasks. There is then a distance between these specialized tasks. For example, in a car factory, one position will reason about the number of produced cars and one position will reason about the demand of customers. Another position will reason about the process of manufacturing, for instance sequence of assembly, work schedules and conflict handling.

2.4.2 Operator Collaboration Design

After determining a set of technical activities, these are to be allocated to Operators. An Operator can be specified in terms of responsibility, (expected) behavior, used interaction strategies, and relationships with other Operators and Managers.

We assume that Operators are rationally bounded, meaning that data, information, and knowledge an Operator can process and the detail of control it can handle is limited. Therefore, techniques must be applied to limit the increase of information and the complexity of control. For that reason, one or more of the coordination mechanisms are to be chosen, given the nature of the task and the nature of the environment. For example, when using direct supervision, positions must allow Managers to steer their object flows. AUML sequence diagrams (cf. [Odell et al., 2000]) can be used to express interactions between agents. AUML is an extension of UML for expressing concepts and mechanisms, such as agents, interactions and protocols. An AUML sequence diagram can show patterns of interaction between the agents, i.e. Operators. These interactions dictate what control between the Operators has to be managed.

2.4.3 Organizational Design

The step Organizational Design is concerned with the definitive organizational design. Given the collaboration model, Manager tasks have to be specified. This can be illustrated in a control flow diagram showing the flow of control between the management activities and the Operators. Furthermore, it shows the sequential flow of objects. Two examples of control flow diagrams can be found in Figure 2.6 (p.30) and Figure 2.8 (p.32).

An *organizational structure* can be used for the agent organizational design, given the type of environment and the type of task. The characteristics of the organization can be expressed as in Figure 2.2 showing the organizational positions, their grouping and the flows of authority.

2.5 Agent-Based Supply Chain Management

Supply Chain Management (SCM) is a process where different types of distributions can be found, both spatial and semantic. Existing retailers are now offering their products and services online via web shops[6]. When a customer orders a set of products, the retailer has to figure out how to deliver these products. Furthermore, the retailer should give an indication of the price and the moment of delivery. In this case, a chain of stores uses couriers to assemble orders and deliver the products to customers. Chains of stores can include different kind of stores having heterogeneous assortments. The couriers have to travel via multiple stores and multiple customers in an optimal route to satisfy customer orders. The idea is not to let the couriers plan a route, but to introduce a central planning process, represented by a *planner*. This planner will have information about what stores are present, what assortment the stores carry and what couriers exist. Besides that information, it will have knowledge on one or more planning strategies operationalized by planning algorithms. The planner will instruct couriers what to do, in terms of a route. The problem is that the planner does not know whether a product is in the stock of a store and what the costs are to retrieve the products from the stores. Furthermore, in spite of the instructions of the planner, it does not know what the trip of an individual courier is, because the courier can get stuck in traffic-jams or get in trouble with its vehicle. The planner has to build a chain from stores to customers via couriers using real time information. The system has to make use of legacy systems, because the stores have already computational systems (back offices) that handle parts of their business by monitoring sales and stocks. Finally, customers, stores, and couriers are physically distributed.

Huget has described a comparable agent-based approach to supply chain management [Huget, 2002]. His approach focuses only on interaction protocols.

2.5.1 Task Analysis

We make use of the spatial distribution rule, because customers, stores, and couriers are physical distributed. Furthermore, the system has to make use of legacy systems. The result of the breakdown of tasks into technical activities is illustrated in Figure 2.3. There are four technical activities: ORDERING, PLANNING, PRODUCING and TRANS-PORTING, which are identified in the activity diagram as swimlanes. The flow of information and decisions begins when a customer places an order, via the job place order. This job produces the object order that is consumed by PLANNING.

---

[6]Acklin B.V. provided input for this case (for more information see www.acklin.nl).

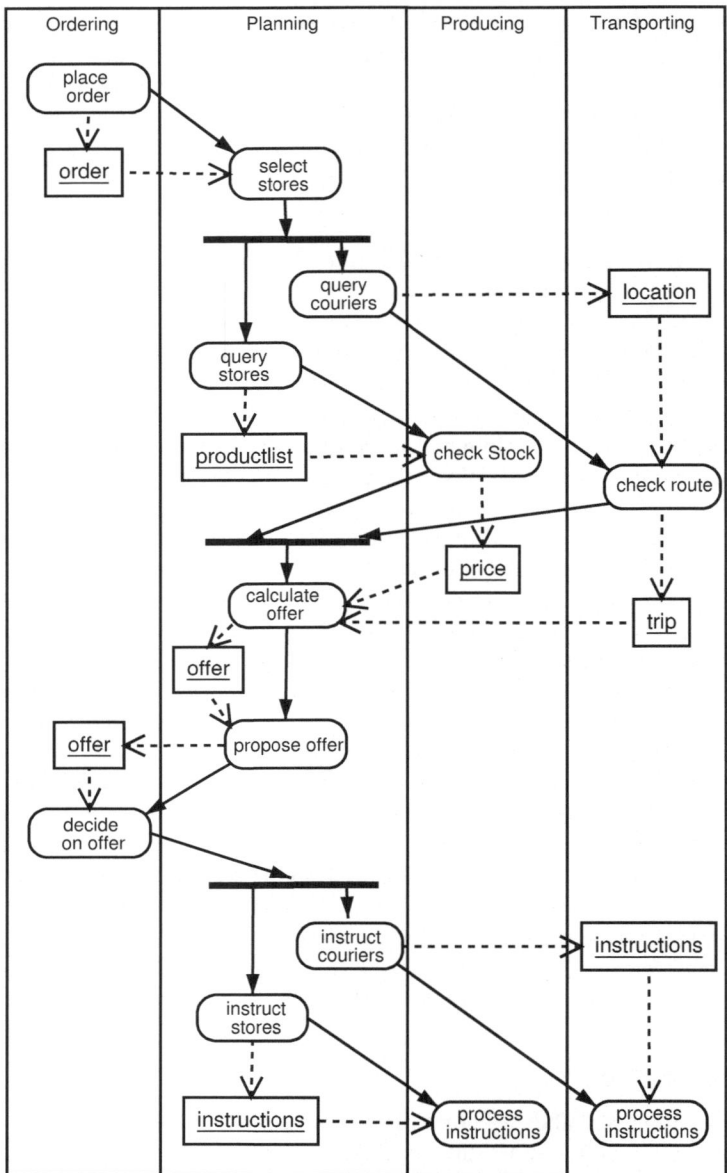

Figure 2.3
Task analysis for the Agent-based Supply Chain Management case in a UML activity
diagram. The swim lanes represent what technical activities are to be done. The rounded
boxes show the transform jobs of technical activities, the square boxes show the objects
(see also Table 2.3), the straight arrowed lines show the task relations and dotted arrowed
lines show the direction of the object flow.

The job **select stores** select a number of stores and consult the jobs **query stores** and **query couriers**. The job **query stores** takes as input the object <u>order</u> and consults a number of stores (i.e. the task PRODUCING). Based on the location of the user and location of the selected stores, the job **query couriers** consults a number of couriers (i.e. the task TRANSPORTING).

The job **check stock** (part of PRODUCING) consumes the object <u>productlist</u>, calculates a price and distributes the object <u>price</u> to the job **calculate offer** (part of PLAN-NING). Parallel to the job **check stock**, the job **check route** (part of TRANSPORT-ING) is consulted. This job calculates for a particular courier, a trip from its current position, via the selected store to the customer and back. The result of the calculation is the object <u>trip</u> which is distributed to the job **calculate offer** (part of PLANNING).

After receiving the objects <u>price</u> and <u>trip</u>, the job **calculate offer** produces an <u>offer</u>, which is distributed by the **propose offer** to the customer. The customer decides on the offer via the **decide on offer**. When the customer accepts the <u>offer</u>, PLANNING will instruct stores and couriers using the jobs **instruct stores** and **instruct couriers** and the objects <u>instructions</u>.

The dependencies between the technical activities are seen as producer/consumer relations (see Table 2.1), because of the obvious information-driven character of the work flow. The dependencies between the tasks are described in Table 2.3.

	ORDERING	PLANNING	PRODUCING	TRANSPORTING
ORDERING	-	p/c for <u>order</u> c/p for <u>offer</u>	-	-
PLANNING	c/p for <u>order</u> p/c for <u>offer</u>	-	c/p for <u>productlist</u> p/c for price	c/p for <u>location</u> p/c for <u>trip</u>
PRODUCING	-	p/c for <u>productlist</u> c/p for <u>price</u>	-	-
TRANSPORTING	-	p/c for <u>location</u> c/p for <u>trip</u>	-	-

Table 2.3
Dependencies between the input and output objects of the technical activities as a result of the task analysis of the Agent-based Supply Chain Management case. **p/c** stands for producer/consumer dependency and **c/p** stands for consumer/producer dependency. These relations are reflected in the task analysis in the form of a UML activity diagram in Fig. 2.3.

2.5.2 Operator Collaboration Design

Based on the identified technical activities, the skills of the Operators are determined. Given the obvious spatial (i.e. customers, stores and courier are geographical distributed) and semantic distribution (i.e. customer reason about products, stores about stocks, couriers about trips and the planner about supply chains), we choose to allocate tasks to Operators in a fixed manner. This means that allocation decisions are made at design time. Another approach is making allocation decisions at run time, meaning that agents have to decide what agents perform what tasks. Several techniques are reported including market mechanisms, planning and voting [Bond and Gasser, 1988].

The following technical activity allocations (expressed by the symbol "↦") to Operators have been made:

ORDERING ↦ CUSTOMER Every customer will be offered a `customer agent`, which will take care of the communication with the other agents of the system. This can be in the form of a user agent as a desktop application or as a web service.

PLANNING ↦ PLANNER There will be a `planner agent` that is wrapped around existing planning algorithms.

PRODUCING ↦ STORE Every store will be equipped with a `store agent` that is wrapped around the existing store information system (i.e. back office system).

TRANSPORTING ↦ COURIER Every courier will be assigned a `courier agent`, able of tracking the whereabouts of the courier and able to present plans from the `planner agent` to the courier.

The sequence diagram in Figure 2.4 shows the pattern of interactions between the initial group of agents. Agent Interaction Protocols (AIPs) describe communication patterns as an allowed sequence of messages between agents and the constraints on the content of those messages [Odell et al., 2000]. The content of the messages is defined with a *message content ontology* as discussed in Section 2.5.5. The definition and use of Message Content Ontologies are discussed in Section 6.3.

As shown in Figure 2.4, existing AIPs are placed in sequence to enable the technical activities as described above. The used AIPs are part of the Contract Net protocol (cf. [FIPA, 2002e]) for enabling standardization of output of work.

2.5.3 Organizational Design

We design the definitive configuration of relations between Operators for controlling the process. This will be done by integrating Managers that are occupied with management activities. Both Figure 2.3 and Figure 2.4 show that PLANNER has a broad responsibility, it has to gather objects from CUSTOMERS, STORES and COURIERS. Furthermore, it has to calculate offers within a given time limit. When the number of CUSTOMERS, STORES and COURIERS grows, PLANNER will form a potential bottleneck for the efficiency of the overall system.

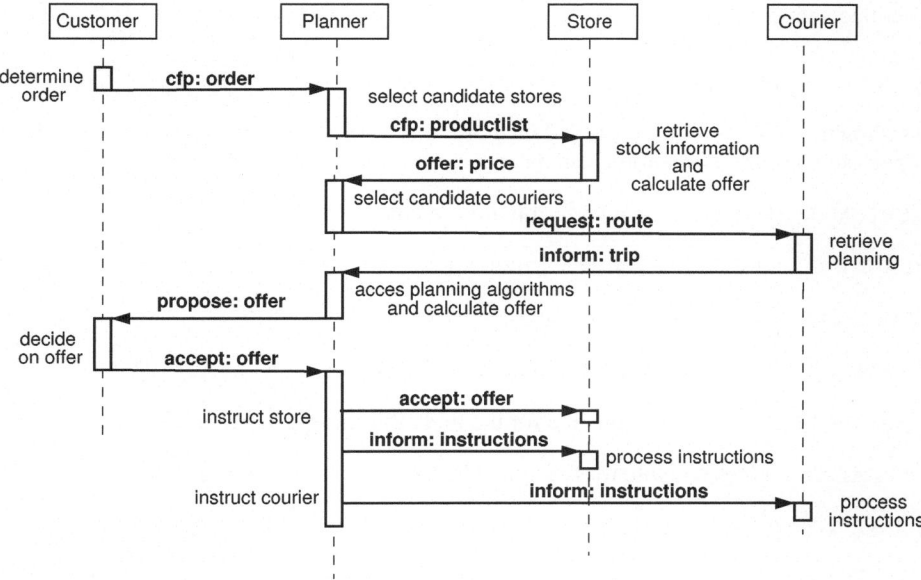

Figure 2.4
Operations design expressed in an AUML sequence diagram showing patterns of interaction between the operators. Lifelines of positions are represented by the dotted lines. The arrowed lines show interactions between the operators, which are instances of interaction protocols. The term "cfp" stands for "Call For Proposal".

Given Table 2.2 and the claim that there is not one best way to organize, we will look at three possible organization patterns that will cope with the information and control complexity of the PLANNING activity. The choice of the three organizations is based on different interpretations of the environment. If we see the environment as stable we can apply the Machine Bureaucracy, see Section 2.5.3.1. We do not expect that there will be any changes in terms of the number or types of stores, products and couriers. When we see the environment as instable although predictable, we apply the Professional Bureaucracy (cf. Section 2.5.3.2) We expect that the number of stores, products and couriers is dynamic meaning that stores, products and couriers can enter or leave the system at any time. However, we do not expect that the process will change. We apply the Adhocracy (cf. Section 2.5.3.3), when the environment is unpredictable because the process may change due to, for example, new forms of customer services where the customer can choose how to collects its goods.

2.5.3.1   Machine Bureaucracy

As shown in Figure 2.5, several Management activities are introduced that use direct supervision as a coordination mechanism:

CUSTOMER RELATIONS is responsible for the Operators CUSTOMER.

PLANNING is responsible for the Operators PLANNER.

STOCK is responsible for the Operators STORE.

TRANSPORT is responsible for the Operators COURIER.

CHAINING SERVICE is responsible for the units **Planning** and **Stock**.

OPERATIONS is responsible for the units **Chaining Service** and **Transport**.

C.E.O. is responsible for the units **Customer Relations** and **Operation**.

The agents are grouped into functional units, which are put in a steep hierarchy. For example the line of authority from `coordinator agent` to the `planner agents` flows from the units **Operations**, **Chaining Services** to **Planning**.

The control flow as illustrated in Figure 2.6 shows the sequence of interactions within the Machine Bureaucracy. The process starts with a CFP[7] with an <u>order</u> sent from CUSTOMER to CUSTOMERMANAGEMENT in message labeled with "1". OPERATIONSMANAGEMENT receives the <u>order</u> via GENERALMANAGEMENT via the messages 2 and 3. From there, OPERATIONSMANAGEMENT will query for available couriers via TRANSPORTMANAGEMENT via messages 4,5,6 and 7. TRANSPORTMANAGEMENT will select for every job what agents to query. As shown, every Operator has to report to the unit's Manager. Given the object <u>trips</u> the position CHAININGMANAGEMENT will query STORES for <u>prices</u> given a <u>productlist</u> via the messages 9,10,11 and 12. Then PLANNER

---

[7]CFP stands for Call For Proposal.

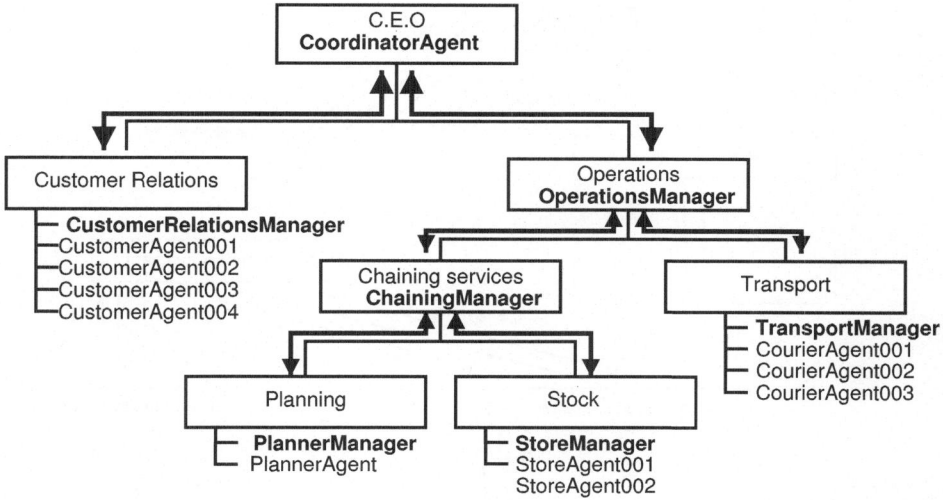

Figure 2.5
Organigram of the supply chain management organization as a Machine Bureaucracy, where boxes represent units, lines represent authority structures, bold font words represent management positions and regular font words represent operational positions. The black arrowed lines represent control and the grey arrowed lines represent Standardization of Output.

will be instructed to construct a <u>chain</u> via the messages 13 and 14. The <u>chain</u> will be reported to CUSTOMER via the messages 15,16,17,18,19 and 20. Then CUSTOMER can choose to refuse or accept the offer. In case of acceptance, STORES will be instructed via the messages 23,24,25 and 26. COURIERS will be instructed via the messages 23, 27 and 28.

The technical activities are seen as highly routine operating jobs, therefore the type of agents has to be very controllable and will not need to do much decision-making. Furthermore, the nature of the flow of objects is seen as sequential. There is a sharp distinction between technical positions and management positions. For example, the management positions COORDINATORAGENT, OPERATIONSMANAGER and CHAININGMANAGER only control other units being in charge of making the decisions for this units. For example, the planner does not have to know *how* the store and courier agents return their real time information. Figure 2.5 illustrates the resulting agents, grouping and the authority structure of the agent organization with the COORDINATOR AGENT as the C.E.O. of the system.

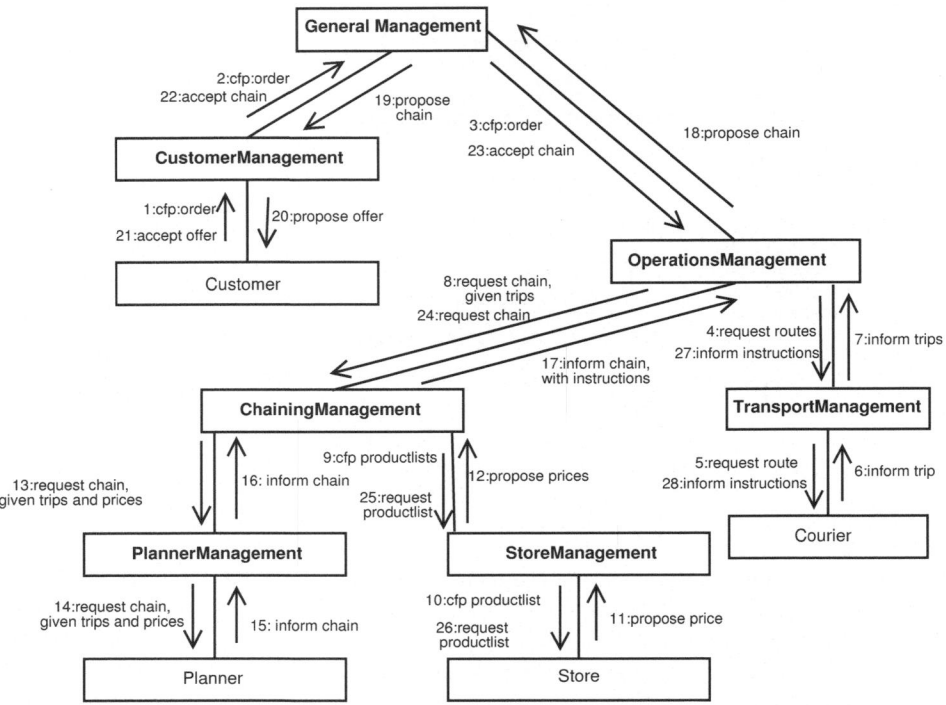

Figure 2.6
Flow of control within the Machine Bureaucracy, showing the sequence of messages, their intention and content.

2.5.3.2 Professional Bureaucracy

When applying the Professional Bureaucracy as organizational structure, we see the nature of the environment as dynamic but predictable. The nature is dynamic in the terms of the come and go of existing and new stores, products and couriers. The nature is predictable, when we assume that these processes will not change. For that reason, the system has to be able to handle a dynamic number of agents. For this, management activities are equipped with skills for determining the number and type of available agents. For example, when the PLANNER is to query available STORES, the system has to determine which STORES are available.

Figure 2.7 shows the organigram of the Professional Bureaucracy. The form of the organization can be seen as flat, because the positions are grouped on basis of skills into specialized units. The units reflect the distribution of already existing competences, i.e. the backoffice systems of the involved parties. The unit **ChainingServices** is designed around the existing planning algorithms, the unit **Stock** is designed around the computa-

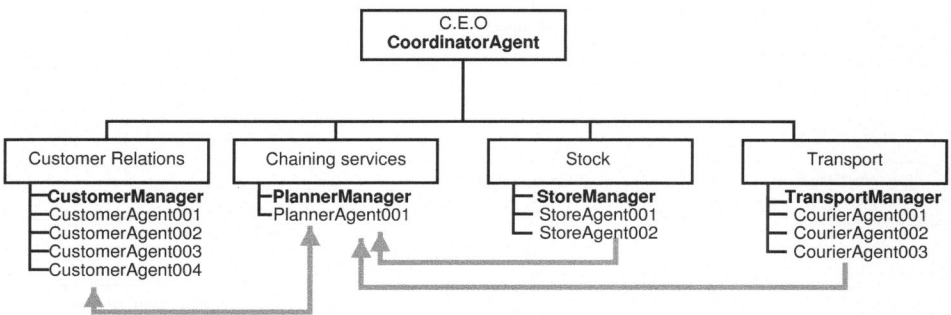

Figure 2.7
Organigram of the supply chain management organization as a Professional Bureaucracy, where boxes represent units, lines represent authority structures, bold font words represent management positions and regular font words represent operational positions. The black lines represent control and the grey arrowed lines represent Standardization of Output.

tional systems of the stores and the unit **Transport** is designed around the computational systems of the couriers. To coordinate the flows between the units, we have chosen "standardization of skills" as prime coordination mechanism.

The control flow as illustrated in Figure 2.8 shows the sequence of communication. It starts with a CFP containing an <u>order</u> sent from CUSTOMER to PLANNERMANAGEMENT in message 1. PLANNERMANAGEMENT will select a PLANNER using the "pigeonholing" principle, which is a selection from a set of available planners, and sends the <u>order</u> in message 2. The planner will query STORES and COURIERS via STOREMANAGER and TRANSPORTMANAGER. The STOREMANAGER will select a store and TRANSPORTMANAGER will select a courier both using the pigeonhole principle. The query process is illustrated in the messages 3,4,5,6,7 and 8. After acceptance of a proposed chain via the messages 9 and 10 the planner will instruct the STORE and COURIER via the messages 11 and 12.

An alternative approach using the Professional Bureaucracy as organizational pattern is when every store has its own transport service. The PLANNER will only have to contact STORES to ask for price offers. These price offers will include the costs related to transport. of the products. The STORES will determine what COURIERS to contract. In this scenario, a part of responsibility of the PLANNER is given to STORES. The advantage is that every STORE can apply its own strategy to compile its offer. Furthermore, STORES will have more control over how goods are transported from stores to customers.

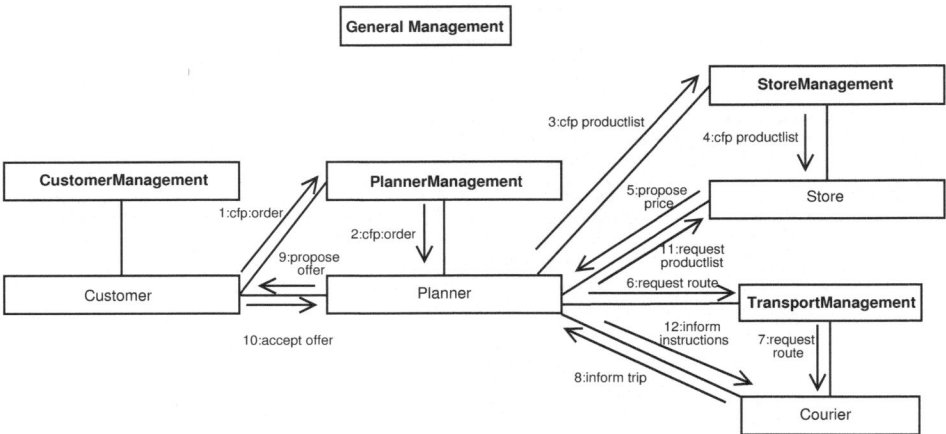

Figure 2.8
Flow of control within the Professional Bureaucracy, showing the sequence of messages,
their intention and content.

2.5.3.3 Adhocracy

The agents within an Adhocracy use Mutual Adjustment as a coordination mechanism
to determine what has to be done and by whom. For this every agent has to be able
to communicate with other agents. Therefore, there is no clear organizational structure.
Furthermore, decision-making is performed decentrally by individual agents.

The knowledge required for solving the problem is distributed over the individual agents. For example, the `customeragent` has knowledge about available `courieragents` and `courieragents` have knowledge about available
`storeagents`.

The method used to coordinate the agent-based supply chain system is having every
agent distributing its output to all available agents. The idea is that if an agent receives an
object that it can consume, the agents will do so, transform the object and distribute the
object to all other available agents.

We did not draw a control flow diagram for the Adhocracy because we cannot design the flow of communication a priori. Still we can illustrate a possible communication path. Suppose `CustomerAgent002` has as goal to get an order delivered for a customer. For that, `CustomerAgent002` will first try to find
an agent that is cable of handling an <u>order</u>. In this scenario, we assume that
`CustomerAgent002` already knows that `CourierAgent001` is able of handling <u>orders</u>. As shown in Figure 2.9,`CustomerAgent002` send a CFP (message
1) to `CourierAgent001`. To determine a price, `CourierAgent001` contacts
`StoreAgent001` and `StoreAgent002` with messages 2 and 3 to queries for prices.
The storeagents propose a price in messages 4 and 5. Next, `CourierAgent001` pro-

poses to `CustomerAgent002` in message 6 to take care of the <u>order</u> given <u>price</u>. `CustomerAgent002` agrees under the condition that it will be delivered within two hours (message 7). `CourierAgent001` agrees with this condition and rises the <u>price</u> (message 8). `CustomerAgent002` gives `CourierAgent001` the order to deliver <u>order</u> by agreeing (message 9) on the offer. Finally, `CourierAgent001` notifies `StoreAgent002` that it accepts the price.

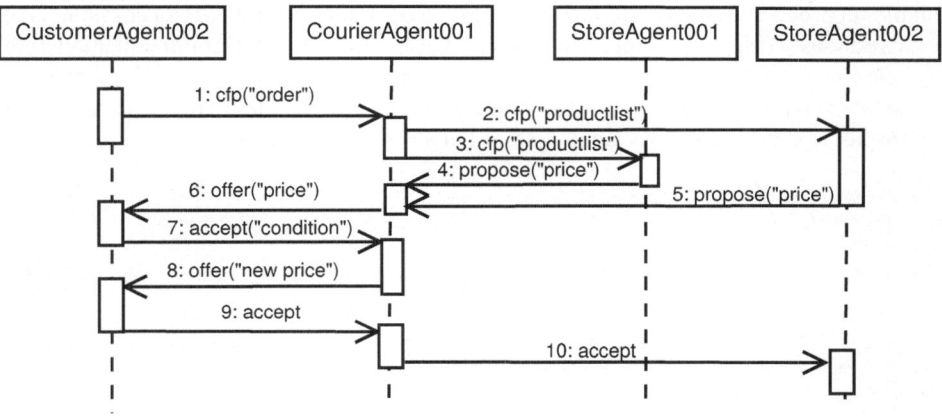

Figure 2.9
A flow of control within of a possible scenario of the Adhocracy, showing the sequence of messages, their intention and content.

2.5.4 Implementation

We implemented three small multi-agent systems based on the Machine Bureaucracy, Professional Bureaucracy and Adhocracy designs as discussed above. In these systems, we see positions as intelligent software agents that are relatively independent and have responsive and pro-active behaviors. The behavior of an agent can be seen from the outside as information-processing and interacting in structured communication networks. This behavior is implemented as:

- Select a message from the *mailbox*. In order to determine the priority of the message, the agents use processing rules. These priority methods are based on queuing techniques such as FIFO or based on the organizational position of the sender

- Process message, that is to carry out the jobs that are triggered by *the content of a received message*. For example, calculating, reasoning or searching.

- Generate new instances of jobs *based on the agenda* of *the agent*.

- Send communication to other agents via *mailboxes*. The agents can send messages
  to Operators and Manager containing commands or reports. Sending a message
  from one agent to another technically means that the sending agent adds a record
  via an agent platform to the mailbox database of the receiving agent.

The agents are implemented as JAVA-thread objects on top of the JADE toolkit that
satisfies the behavior as described above. This means that every agent is a separate computational process with its own internal control and a mailbox. Agents can communicate
asynchronously using each other's mailboxes. This method is called communication with
asynchronous mailbox semantics [Schmidt et al., 2000]. The mailboxes are implemented
as databases with records representing incoming messages. Besides that, all variables that
represent the state of an agent are also stored in a model state database.

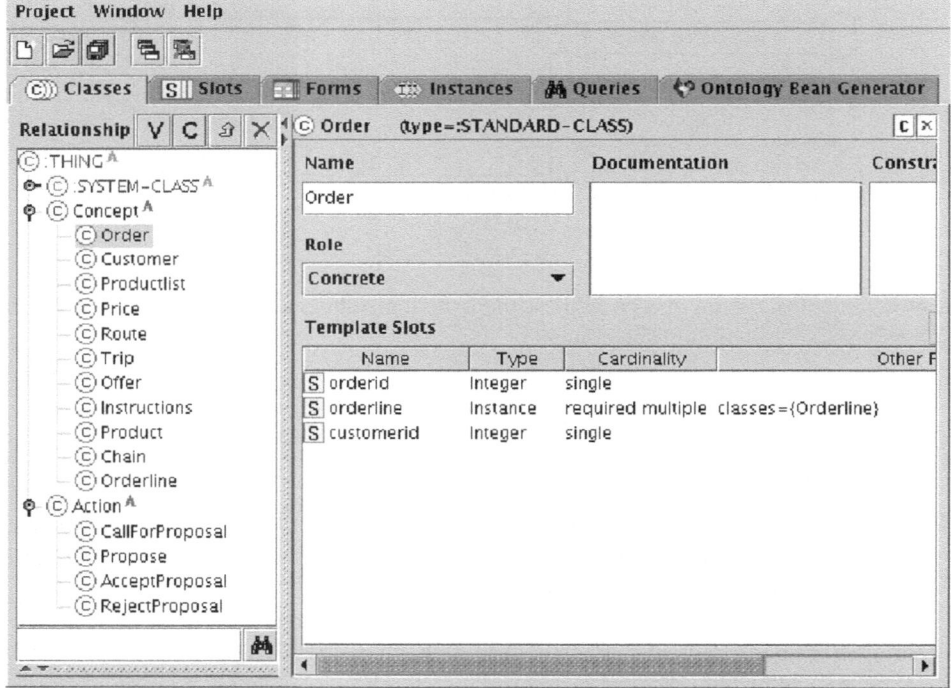

Figure 2.10
Message Content Ontology design showing Concepts and Actions. We refer to Section 6.3 (p.142) for a definition of message content ontologies and to Section 6.4 (p.158)
for the use of message content ontologies.

To process the content of a message, such as in Figure 2.11, the agent has to have knowledge about how to handle messages. Concepts such as *Order*, *Price* and *Offer* are standardized in a message content ontology (message content ontologies are defined in Section 6.3 and their use is explained in Section 6.4). The ontology used in this application is shown in Figure 2.10. The concepts *AgentActions*, such as *CallForProposal*, *Propose* and *AcceptProposal* are used to give intentions to messages. Every AgentAction is connected to one or more *processing rules*. For example, a processing rule for the agent `PlannerAgent` can start the job Planning after receiving a message of the type REQUEST. The job planning will produce a set of outgoing messages and change the internal state of the agent, including new message templates. For example, when sending a REQUEST message to agent A, a processing rule will be instantiated that will listen to messages received from agent B. After triggering, the appropriate actions will be undertaken.

```
(CFP
 :sender (agent-identifier :name Customer)
 :receiver (set ( agent-identifier :name CustomerManager))
 :encoding   String
 :language <?xml version ="1.0"?>
 :ontology   www.acklin.nl/Supermarket/SupplyChainOntology.xsd
 :content
   <order id="1569244107" customerid="6315178">
      <orderline product="product001" quantity="1" />
      <orderline product="product004" quantity="2" />
      <orderline product="product015" quantity="1" />
   </order>
  :protocol   FIPA CONTRACT-NET
  :conversation-id  Req1008770622742
  :reply-with Req1008770622742
)
```

Figure 2.11
Example ACL Message, which represents a Call For Proposal (CFP) message part of the FIPA Contract-Net protocol, sent from `CustomerAgent` to `CustomerManager` containing a request for proposal of an order.

The experiments were run on three separate test machines. One machine for serving a customer with one customer agent, i.e. `customer`. The second machine acted as agent platform server together with one planner agent, i.e. `planner`. The third machine was equipped with three store agents, i.e. `store001`, `store002` and `store003`, and three courier agent, i.e. `courier001`, `courier002` and `courier003`. The machines were connected with each other in a LAN.

| Organizational | Parameter | |
structure	Production Costs	Coordination Costs
Machine Bureaucracy	0.9 s	39
Professional Bureaucracy	0.5 s	17
Adhocracy	0.6 s	30

Table 2.4
Comparison between organizational structures. The "Productions Costs" are expressed in seconds (i.e. the duration of the operation). The "Coordination Costs" are expressed by the number of messages sent within the operation.

2.5.5   Results

The results of the experiments with the three designs can be inspected graphically using the Agent Organization Console, see Figure 2.12 (p.39), Figure 2.13 (p.40) and Figure 2.14 (p.41). This tool draws special purpose "pseudo interaction diagrams" on the basis of communication logs of the involved agents. This means that every agents writes its communication to a central database, see also Section 5.5.4 (p.126). The ellipses show agents and the arrowed lines show flow of messages between agents. The labels represent type of message and an object as configuration. For example in Figure 2.12, the label "1: cfp(order)" corresponds with the ACLMessage in Fig. 2.11.

We compared the three runs based on two types of costs for organizational structures (cf. [Malone, 1987]). Firstly, *production costs*, the costs of production and the costs of delay in processing. In our experiments, we interpreted this rule as the difference between the end of the process and the beginning of the process. Secondly, the costs of maintaining communication paths and the costs of exchanging messages along the paths, i.e. the *coordination costs*. We interpreted this rule as counting the number of messages sent.

Table 2.4 shows the comparison between the organizational structures. The number of message sent for one customer order with the Professional Bureaucracy (17 messages) is less then in the Machine Bureaucracy (39 messages). The reason for this is that the agents within the Professional Bureaucracy have more knowledge about the process. It makes the agents more independent and flexible. For example, if we want to add another technical activity to the system to enrich the process, we only have to adjust a limited set of agents. In the Machine Bureaucracy a large part of the machinery has to be adjusted.

For a designer or maintainer of the Professional Bureaucracy system, processes and flow of objects are less controllable and predictable than in the Machine Bureaucracy system. If something goes wrong, it is harder to track the source of a problem. Furthermore, it is also difficult to determine the state of the system at a given time. Possible stores, i.e. the ones that will pay for the system, will want to have a feeling of control over the system. A possible extension of the system is a logger or reporting agent.

The number of messages (i.e. 30) sent in the Adhocracy are justified by the fact that in the start of the process `customer` and `planner001` send a CFP to every known agent in order to locate agents that can fulfill some service. Another way to locate an agent is to contact a broker. This structure can be useful when the number and type of agents are not known on forehand. However, one can never be sure whether the system will reach its intended goal. For a designer or maintainer of the system, processes and flow of objects are very uncontrollable and unpredictable. The agents have to be equipped with a large knowledge base containing knowledge about communication languages, negotiation strategies and interaction protocols. When the type of objects, agents and tasks are not known at design time, the agents should also be equipped with learning abilities.

Although the time measurements are influenced by available network bandwidth and running of other experiments on the test machines, the Professional Bureaucracy turned out to be the fastest organization. This can be explained by the fact that there is no management overhead as in the Machine Bureaucracy. Both the agents within the Adhocracy and the Professional Bureaucracy have knowledge about others agents.

2.6 Discussion

The goal of this chapter is to get insights in the application of human organizational principles in distributed intelligent system design. We discussed a collection of organizational concepts, organizational models and coordination mechanisms. As argued by Jennings, organizational relationships need to be explicitly represented [Jennings, 2000]. Therefore, "Organigrams" have been used as a mechanism for representing a system's organizational structure. This resulted in an agent organization framework with four perspectives: task, operation, coordination and organization. Furthermore, a collection of organizational design steps was presented containing three steps: process analysis, operation design and organizational design. The steps assist in the decomposition of the overall task of a system into jobs and the reintegration of the jobs into the overall task using job allocation, organizational structuring and coordination mechanisms.

The case study presented in this chapter, showed that the repetitive nature of the tasks allowed the relations between agents to be identified only once. A reason for this is that supply chain management can be seen as information-driven, due to its repetitive nature. In the prototypes, we implemented Direct Supervision, Standardization of Output and Mutual Adjustment. Furthermore, the Agent Organization Console showed that the progress of the organization can be monitored by tracing the flow of objects within messages.

If we see supply chain management as competence-driven, i.e. the process relies on the problem-solving skills that agents have, other organizational structures and coordination mechanisms can be applied. With the pigeonholing process, the competences of the agents can be categorized and mapped on a categorization of predetermined situations. The pigeonholing process is the main difference between Professional Bureaucracy and Machine Bureaucracy. A Machine Bureaucracy is task-driven, i.e. the organization is a single-purpose structure, which executes only one standard sequence of jobs. Whereas the Professional Bureaucracy is competence-driven, i.e. a part of the organization will first examine a case, match it to predetermined situations and then allocate an Operator with a standard set of jobs to it. Using one or more of the coordination mechanisms presented in Section 2.2.3 the agents can choose a strategy, which can lead to more interesting solutions to complex problems. For example, if standardization of output, in terms of standardized ontologies and languages, fails for some reason, it could be resolved by giving one ore more agents the ability of failure detection and failure resolution.

The difference between an Adhocracy and the two Bureaucracies is that within an Adhocracy, agents have to find creative solutions to unique problems using forms of negotiation such as argumentation. In an Adhocracy, the agents should be capable of reorganizing their own organization including dynamically changing the flow of objects, shifting responsibilities and adapting to changing environments. For this reason, the agents should have a notion of the environment, abilities to determine the overall tasks, and have knowledge to reason about the actions they can perform.

The work presented in this chapter showed that notions from organizational design such as task, job, position, direct supervision and standardization can be used in the design of distributed intelligent systems. A more formal approach subject issue for future research. Furthermore, coordination can be handled by various methods, leading to different organizational structures. Finally, organigrams can support the visualization of organizational structures, by showing the agent staff, the grouping of the agents and the authority structure that connects the units and individual agents. However, organigrams only represent a static perspective on an organization and only suggest a coordination strategy. Together with diagrams in UML and AUML, it could form the basis of a graphical distributed intelligent systems modeling language.

Future research includes extensions to the existing framework, which should be of assistance in the organizational design decision process to bring coherence between the goals or purposes for which the organization exists, the patterns of division of labor, patterns of coordination, and the agents that performs the jobs. The extensions should help designers to address more precisely an organization's overall task and environment. One of the extensions will address technology to be utilized, for example, technology as described by FIPA (agent standardization), the grid (peer-to-peer computing) and the semantic web (service discovery and composition). When using FIPA standards, our method should be compliant with models and technology that draw on interaction protocols and agent services, such as white, yellow and blue pages.

Many web services (which can be seen as agent-based service) are available. However, the notion of negotiation has only recently begun to be an issue of research in the semantic web community. Moreover, web services tend to follow the classic client/server model, where web services behave as servers and will only answer to a client directly. In an agent setting, an agent service can be configured to give its answer to another agent service, which leads to a chain of services.

In the end, the framework should assist in the formalization of the overall behavior of a distributed intelligent system in terms of organizational structure and organization behavior. Predictable and controllable behavior of agents will lead to reduction in the variability of systems. Furthermore, agents in an organizational setting should have means (e.g. methods, procedures and knowledge) to handle uncertainty and unpredictable events

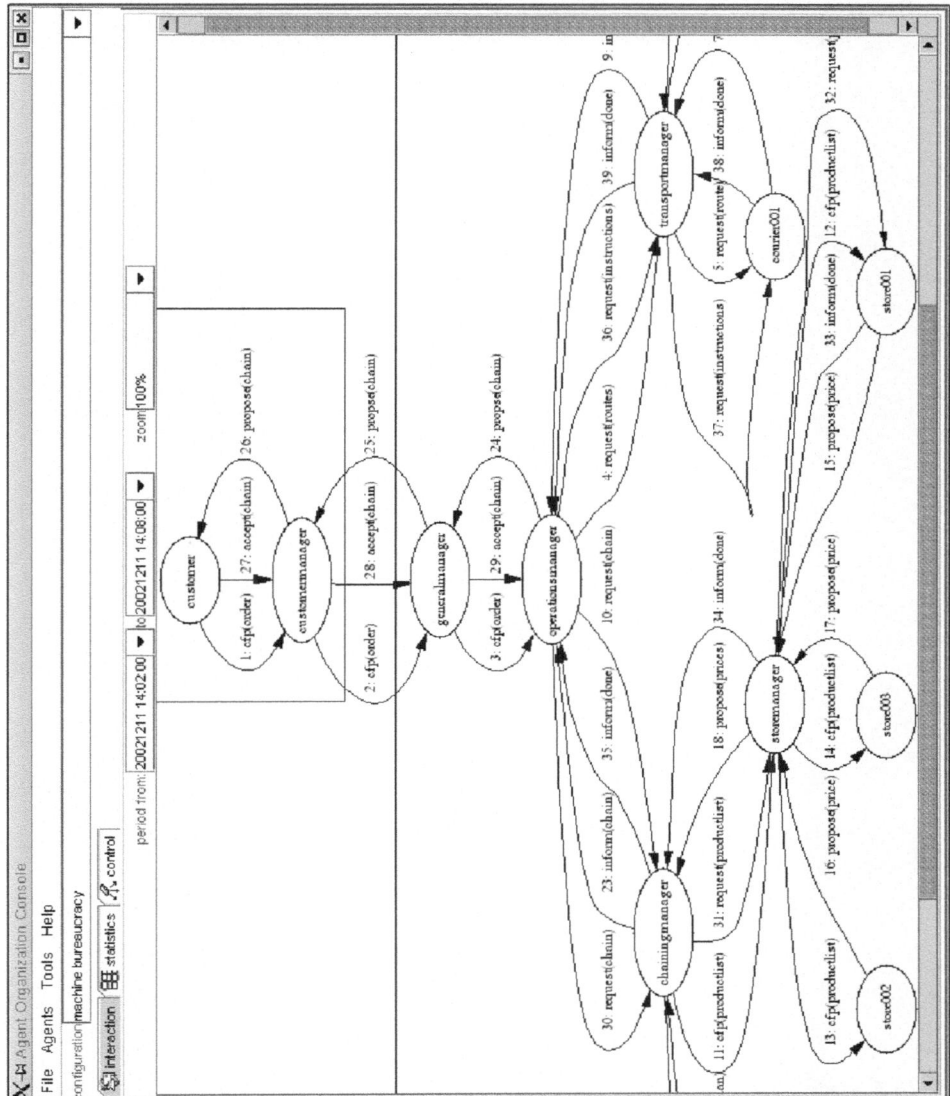

Figure 2.12
Screenshot of the Agent Organization Console that shows a part of a special purpose Pseudo Interaction Diagram for the supply chain scenario with the Machine Bureaucracy design. The ellipses represent agents and the arrowed lines represent flow of messages between agents. The labels represent the type of message and an object as configuration. For example, the label "1: cfp(order)" corresponds with the ACLMessage in Fig. 2.11 (p.35).

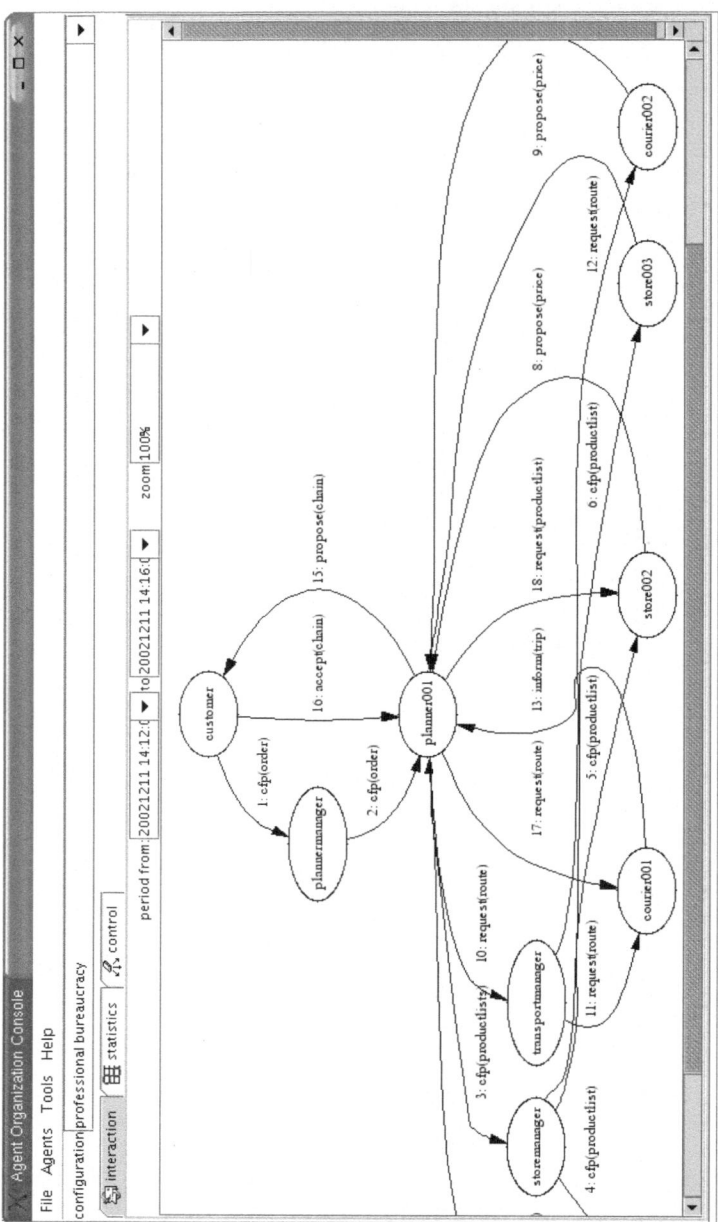

Figure 2.13
Part of special purpose Pseudo Interaction Diagram for the supply chain scenario with the
Professional Bureaucracy design.

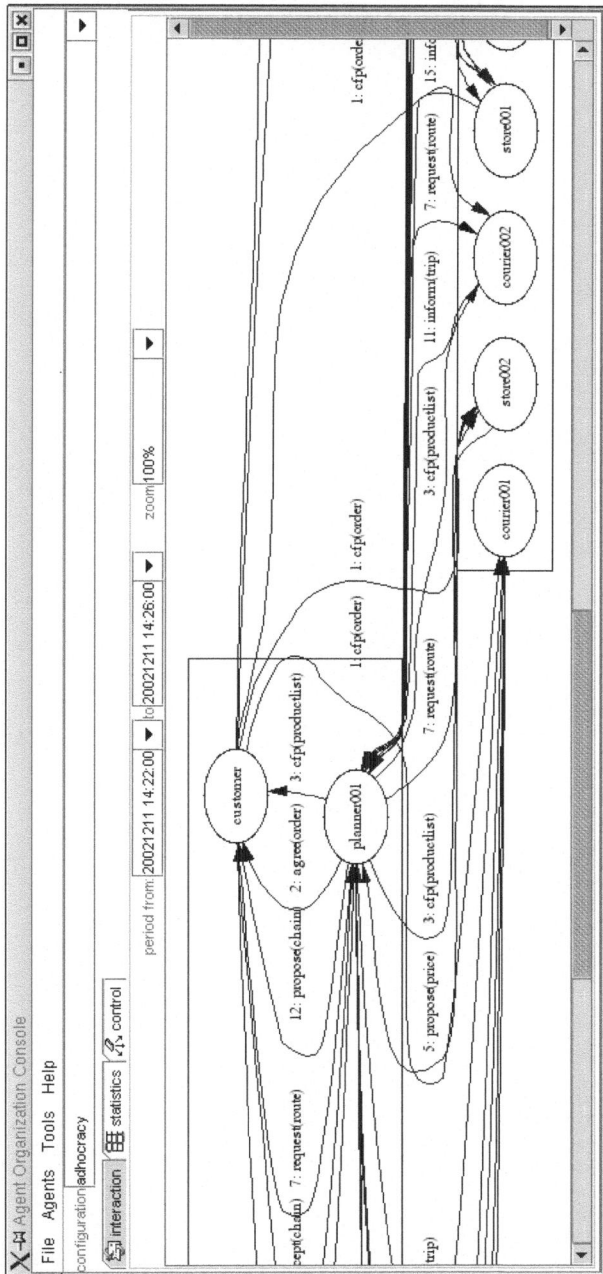

Figure 2.14
Part of special purpose Pseudo Interaction Diagram for the supply chain scenario with the
Adhocracy design.

Chapter 3

Coordination Strategies for Multi-Agent Systems

In this chapter, we elaborate on the coordination perspectives of the organizational framework, introduced in Section 2.2.1 (p.12). The operational perspective is concerned with modeling technical activities performed by Operators. The coordination perspective is concerned with modeling coordination over these technical activities. In order to assist Managers in reasoning about coordination, strategies are represented in the form of problem-solving methods. Agents that need coordination, can agree to commit to one or more coordination strategies. Underlying the problem-solving methods is a coordination ontology that models the concepts and relationships describing the coordination domain. The coordination strategies are based on existing strategies, which were introduced in Section 2.2.3 (p.16). We report on a small experiment in which three coordination strategies were implemented as problem-solving methods in a multi-agent system.

The outcome of the experiment gives us observations concerning the appropriate use of coordination strategies. These observations are based on efficiency (the costs of communication and process time) and comparison between the strategies.

3.1 Introduction

In the organizational framework, introduced in Section 2.2.1 (p.12), we have defined four perspectives: task, operational, coordination and organizational. In this chapter, we focus on the coordination perspective, which is concerned with the control of the (technical) activities and the regulation of object flows from the operational perspective. In order to elaborate on coordination, we discuss a "common sense" definition for coordination: *Coordination is the act of working together harmoniously* [Malone and Crowston, 1993]. If we extend this definition to include agents, an interpretation of this definition can be, that *the act of working* implies that *agents* perform *activities*. Activities need *input* to produce *objects*. The activities are performed in order to achieve a *task*, i.e. a specification of the work to be done. *Together* refers to the fact that there are *interdependencies* between activities. An example of interdependency is the consumer/producer relation, see Section 2.2.2 (p.15). *Harmoniously* implies that relations between different activities have to be managed.

There are two common approaches to coordination in multi-agent systems, implicit and explicit. In *implicit coordination*, agents share common models of coordination and there is no explicit communication related to coordination activities. Every agent maintains internal models (e.g. goals, state and strategy) of all other agents. However there are various reasons why this is not feasible. One might think of all administrative activities agents need to perform in order to acquire information (e.g. state and locations) about other agents. These activities could lead to overloading the network in which the agents operate. Furthermore, these activities could be more demanding than the goals the agents are supposed to achieve.

In explicit coordination, there is an explicit "Manager" and "Operator" role, where Managers and Operators agents explicitly communicate information related to coordination. For example, there could be agents that control other agents by sending them instructions. These controlling agents (i.e. Managers) make use of a coordination strategy. A coordination strategy can be seen as a pattern of decision-making and communication among a set of agents that perform activities to coordinate task execution [Malone and Crowston, 1994]. The idea is that the controlling agents choose a coordination strategy and then coordinate other agents.

Several coordination strategies are available in the literature. Mintzberg has described coordination strategies that can be found in Machine and Professional Bureaucracies and Adhocracies [Mintzberg, 1993], see also Section 2.3. These strategies are: *Direct Supervision* where one individual takes all decisions for the work of others, *Mutual Adjustment* that achieves coordination by a process of informal communication between agents, and *Standardization of Activity*, *Output* and *Skills*. The problem is that these coordination strategies are described informally. Therefore, in their original form, they cannot be used in multi-agents system.

There are several ways to model coordination methods and strategies. For an overview of coordination modeling approaches, we refer to [Ossowski, 1999]. In this book, several semi-formal and formal approaches are described, including coordination as the basis for optimization problems, computational games and social laws. However, most of these approaches are implicit coordination methods. Furthermore, these methods cannot be easily shared and reused by other agents. The reason for this is that most research on coordination in DAI has not taken into account that agents within a multi-agent system are inherently heterogeneous [Wooldridge and Jennings, 1998]. This means that the same engineers do not necessarily build all the agents participating in a multi-agent system. Therefore, the behaviors of these agents differ and are not built for the same purpose.

The focus of this work is how to model explicit coordination strategies in such a way that they can be shared and used by agents. These coordination strategies are of interest to agent engineers, because they can be used to *control* agents within a multi-agent system. If coordination patterns are stored in libraries, agent engineers can model agent behaviors according to these coordination patterns. In addition, Managers can be equipped with knowledge to select a coordination strategy and to reason about it. Furthermore, a group of agents could negotiate about which coordination strategy to apply.

As suggested in Section 2.4, there are three basic organization design steps: Task Analysis, Operator Collaboration Design and Organizational Design. Task analysis is concerned with the breakdown of work into subtasks that can be defined as (technical) activities. These activities can be performed by Operators. In order to let the Operators collaborate, coordination patterns can be applied that steer interactions between Operators and control the flow of objects between Operators. Finally, organizational design is concerned with the design of the organizational structure including the definition of management tasks.

In Section 3.2, we discuss the representation of coordination in a reusable and sharable format. Three coordination strategies are modeled and presented in Section 3.3. A possible alternative to design agents according to our approach is outlined in Section 3.4. In Section 3.5 we report on small experiments in which three coordination strategies were implemented as problem-solving methods in a multi-agent system.

3.2   Coordination as Problem-Solving

One way to represent coordination is in the form of Problem-Solving Methods (PSMs). Problem-solving methods describe the reasoning process of a knowledge based system, that can be thought of as an agent, in an implementation-and-domain independent manner [Benjamins and Fensel, 1998]. We use PSMs to characterize inference steps that need to be carried out in order to achieve coordination, and a control structure, that specifies the order of these inference steps. The operationalizations of coordination strategies are represented as PSMs, so that they can be shared and reused amongst different agents (cf. [Schreiber et al., 1999]).

To provide semantics to the PSMs we make use of a number of ontologies. Ontologies represent a shared and agreed upon abstraction of the domain of interest, represented in an explicit and machine-readable way [Studer et al., 1998]. In open environments, agents are able to join the interactions with no prior knowledge of other agents' internal states or of the strategies used to achieve coordination. By modeling coordination information in an ontology, we make this information explicit and sharable. One of the requirements for an agent joining the interactions is to commit to the shared information in the ontology. This information can be stored in a task-method ontology, which can be used for exchanging method independent concepts and relations for a particular set of tasks (goals) [Benjamins et al., 1998]. For example, a task ontology for diagnosis contains terms such as *hypotheses*, *symptoms* and *observations*.

We first model the coordination as a knowledge intensive task. Next, we model a task-method ontology, based on an interpretation of coordination.

3.2.1   Coordination Task

In our approach, *coordination* is seen as a knowledge intensive task, that we call the *coordination task* (Figure 3.1). The coordination task is concerned with how agents perform joint actions. The idea is that knowledge required by agents for coordination is independent of the actual operation. To make the separation between operation and coordination, we use the notion of *Manager* and *Operator*, as introduced in Section 2.2. The Manager is responsible for organizing agent relations, such as those described in Section 2.2.2, through a chosen coordination strategy. The Operator is only concerned with performing the actions that are instructed by the Manager. Furthermore, we make use of the notion of a Requester Agent. The *Requester* is an agent that delivers the *task* and input *objects*[1]. The results of the execution will be given to the Requester.

---

task coordination **is-a** management-task;
   goal : "manage interdependencies between the activities between operators
     in order to satisfy system's goal";
   roles :
     input : operators, system-task;
     output : instructions;
end task coordination;

Figure 3.1
Task specification for coordination in terms of goal and input and output roles. The syntax used is the *CommonKADS Knowledge-Model Language* as defined in [Schreiber et al., 1999].

The communication lines between agents, objects and agents involved are illustrated in Figure 3.2, in order to illustrate the context of coordination. This figure can be read as follows: the coordination process starts when the Requester agent sends a *task* to the Manager. The Manager translates the *task* into a set of *instructions* by selecting **sub-tasks**[2] from *task*. These instructions define collaborations that manage interdependencies between activities. The instructions are represented by `activities` or `procedures` that specify what agent (Manager or Operator) provides input-objects, what activities to perform and to what agent to the input-objects should be distributed.

Instructions will first be delegated to the Operators. Secondly, the Operators start the execution by asking input from the Requester. Then, the Operators perform the activities, instructed by the Manager. After execution, one of the Operators reports to the Manager. Finally, the Manager reports the results to the Requester.

Several methods (i.e. coordination strategies in the form of PSMs) can be applied to execute the coordination task. Before modeling these PSMs, we discuss a task-method ontology that provides semantics to the concepts and relations used in the task specification.

---

[1] An object can contain a primitive data-entity or a collection of other objects.
[2] Here we use sub-task to denote a piece of work that an Operator can perform, i.e. a primitive task. Primitive Task is defined in Section 2.2.1 (p.12).

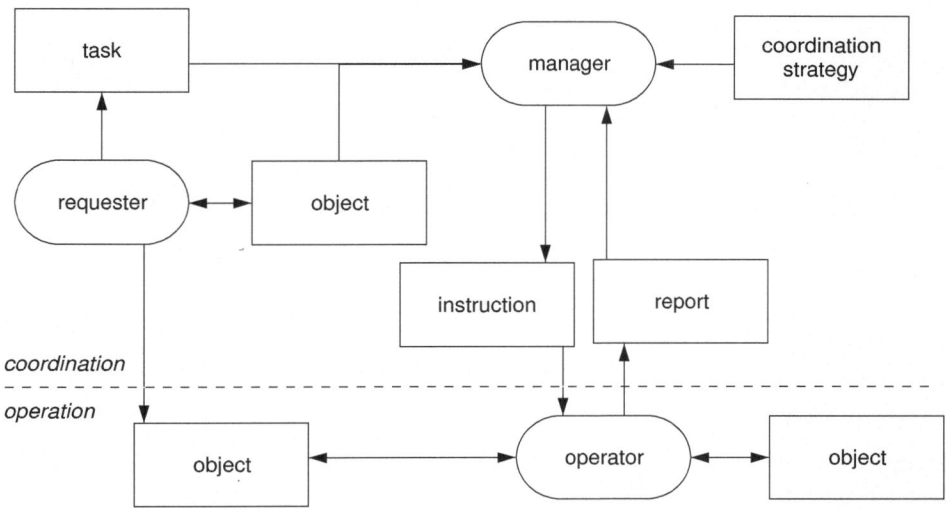

Figure 3.2

Context of Coordination in a pseudo collaboration diagram. Ellipses represent agents and the rectangles represent concepts. The arrowed lines represent communication lines. The Requester is an agent that sends a task to the Manager. The Manager will decompose the task and selects a coordination strategy to instruct available Operators. The Operators receive input objects from the Requester. The Operators exchange objects amongst each other. The Operators report to the Manager, which reports to the Requester.

3.2.2 Task-Method Ontology

In order to provide semantics to the coordination task, a task-method ontology has been constructed. A graphical model of parts of the ontology is shown in Figure 3.3. The ontology described here is semi-formal and is intended as a first version that has to be extended and formalized.

The three central concepts in the coordination task-method ontology are **task**, **operator** and **instruction**. The task represents the overall task of the system that has to be coordinated. Here, we semi-formally describe the task as a sequence of activities that have to be performed by a set of Operators. In Chapter 5, we elaborate on the specification of tasks and how they can be put together.

Activities need **input-object** to produce **output-objects**. The concept **Operator** represents the set of available Operators. It describes the physical address of the Operator (e.g. agent @ some machine), the services it can perform (e.g. get information from Google) and the history of the agent (e.g. this agent has just performed an activity and has successfully given an answer back). The set of services is called the Operator's competence. Operators will send **reports** containing results (i.e. **output objects**) of performed

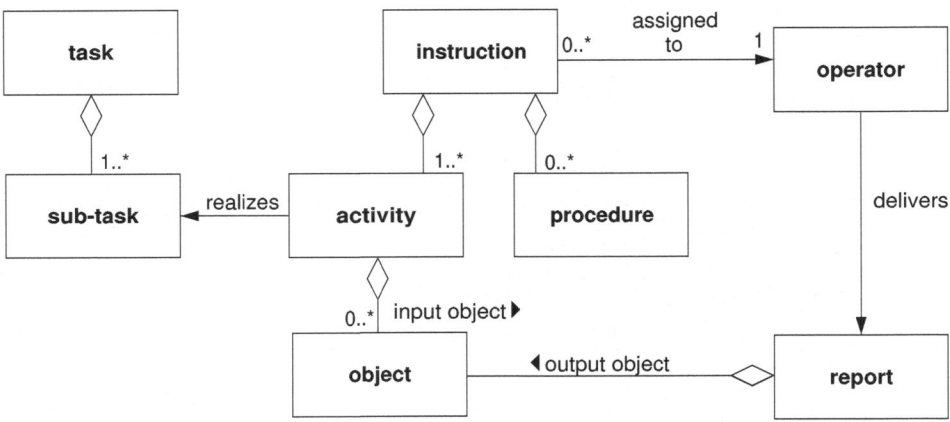

Figure 3.3
Domain Schema showing parts of the task-method ontology which represents the conceptualizations of our interpretation of the coordination task. The graphical notation used,
is defined in [Schreiber et al., 1999]. The three central concepts in the coordination task-
method ontology are task, operator and instruction. Activities need input-object to produce output-objects. Operators sends reports containing results (i.e. output objects) of
performed activities. There are two parts of instruction: activity, which is a request for
performing directly a technical activity including input-objects, and procedure, which is
a specification of an activity in combination with collaborations.

activities.

    Instructions can be assigned by the Manager to an Operator. An instruction tells an
agent what to do. In our ontology we have specified two parts of Instruction, i.e. **activity**
and **procedure**. An *activity* is a request for performing directly a technical activity on
input-objects. The results of an activity, i.e. output-objects, will be reported to the agent
that requested the activity. For example, if the Manager sends an instruction to Operator
A, Operator A will perform directly the activity specified in the instruction and report
back to the Manager.

    A *procedure* is a specification of an activity in combination with collaborations. A
collaborations tells the agent from whom to get the input for its activity and to whom
distribute its output to. For example, agent B is instructed to get a list of URLs (as input)
from agent A before it has to perform activity 2. Procedures can be used to first configure
the behavior of an agent, before the actual execution of a system.

    Using the above described concepts, we can describe the "common sense"
definition for coordination, i.e. *the act of working together harmoniously*
(cf. [Malone and Crowston, 1993]) as follows. The *act of working* can be seen as
Operators perform **activities**. The **activities** are performed in order to achieve a **task**.
Together refers to the fact that there are interdependencies between **activities**. These
interdependencies are the flow of **input-objects** and **output-objects** between Operators.

The **Operators** receive **instructions** so that the Operators can work harmoniously.

The above-described ontology can form the basis of the knowledge base of agents. The knowledge base of an Operator should be able to answer questions like: "What activities should I perform?" and "To whom do I have to report the outcome of activities?". Questions the knowledge base of the Manager should answer include:"How did I divide the overall task into activities?" and "To what Operators did I delegate activities?".

3.3 Coordination Strategy Methods

In this section we model three coordination strategies as PSMs, in order to show the variety of possible coordination methods. The strategies we selected from Mintzberg are *coordination by Direct Supervision*, *Standardization of Work* and *Mutual Adjustment* [Mintzberg, 1993]. We omit the strategies *Standardization of Skills* and *Standardization of Output*, because they can be seen as variations on *Standardization of Work*. As discussed in Section 2.2.1, these coordination strategies can be used to coordinate agent organizations. The strategy *Coordination by Direct Supervision* achieves coordination by having one individual directly controlling others. In *Standardization of Work*, control is delegated to others. *Mutual Adjustment* achieves coordination by a process of informal communication between agents. The strategies are illustrated in Figure 3.4. These strategies are selected, because they fit within the three organizational structure models from Mintzberg, as described in Section 2.3.

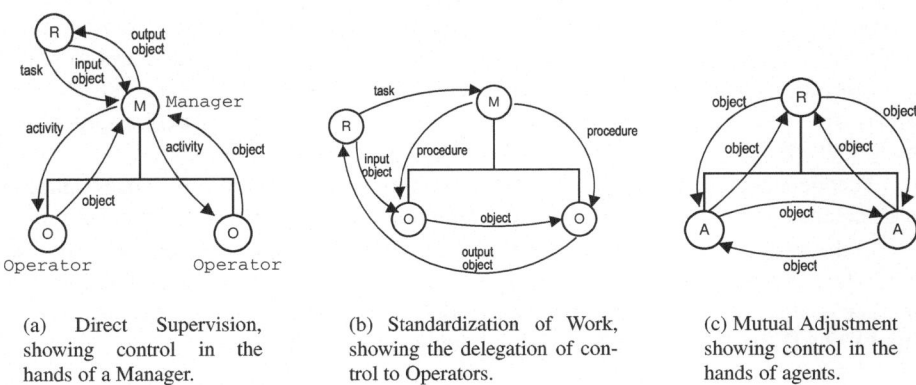

(a) Direct Supervision, showing control in the hands of a Manager.

(b) Standardization of Work, showing the delegation of control to Operators.

(c) Mutual Adjustment showing control in the hands of agents.

Figure 3.4
Three Coordination mechanisms. The circles represent roles of agents. The letter M stands for Manager and O for Operator. Authority structures are represented by the black lines that connect positions. The arrowed curved black lines represent message flows. In Fig. 3.4(c) there are no Manager and Operator roles, the R stands for requesting agent and the A stands for agent.

We discuss possible interpretations of these coordination strategies in the form of Manager and Operator PSMs and sequence diagrams. A *Manager PSM* defines the co-ordination behavior of an agent with the Manager role. An *Operator PSM* defines the coordination behavior of an agent with the Operator role. These PSMs are semi-formally specified by roles, inferences, functions and a description of the internal control. The Manager PSMs are methods based on the task described in Figure 3.1. The sequence diagrams show the sequence of interactions between the agents involved.

To illustrate the working of the PSMs by examples, we make use of a toy system. The task of this system is "classify resources on the Web into genres given queries". The objects involved are query, i.e. a representation of a search question, resource, i.e. a digital document or image and genre, i.e. a representation of a group of documents that share the same characteristics, e.g. scientific article, thesis or presentation. The environment is qualified as dynamic, since the Web constantly changes. As illustrated in Figure 3.5, the task is broken down into three technical activities and four objects. The activity SEARCH takes the object query as input and will produce the object candidate. A query can be a Boolean formula containing keywords.

For example, `glucose AND deprivation` can be used to search for material related to a pathological decrease of blood flow to the brain[3]. The candidates will be obtained consulting a search engine and are in the form of links (URLs) to resources. For example, `www.brainresearch.edu/introduction.pdf`. The activity OBTAIN takes the object candidate as input from SEARCH and produces resource. Resources are obtained following the URLs from candidates and downloading to a local repository. An example of a resource is a document expressed in PDF. The activity CLASSIFY takes the object resource as input from the activity OBTAIN and produces the object genre. Genres are determined by matching features from the resources found on the Web to features of the genre classes. The match criteria and attributes to match are retrieved from a classification knowledge base. For example, `if resource contains {abstract, introduction, conclusions, references} then genre-class=scientific_article`.

The dependencies between the three activities are consumer-producer relation, which means that there is an obvious sequential relation between the different activities.

In the system, four agents are involved, i.e. Manager, Searcher, Obtainer and Classifier. Manager plays the role of Manager agent and performs the coordination task. Searcher is able to perform the activity SEARCH, Obtainer is able to perform the activity OBTAIN and the CLASSIFY is performed by Classifier.

3.3.1 Coordination by Direct Supervision

The first strategy, *Coordination by Direct Supervision*, is based on the idea that there is one *supervisor* that will *direct* all the other Operators involved. [Mintzberg, 1993, p. 4] has defined Direct Supervision as:

---

[3] See www.wnc.lu.se/bkexpbr.html.

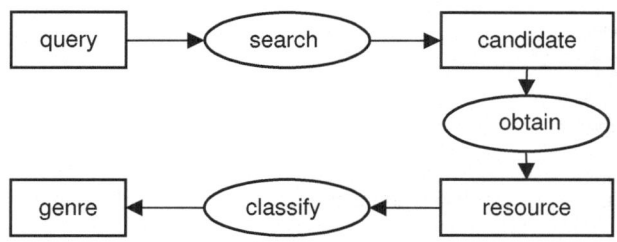

Figure 3.5
Example of a process for resource classification on the Web, showing three ellipses as technical activities (SEARCH, OBTAIN and CLASSIFY) and four squared boxes as objects (query, candidate, resource and genre). The arrowed lines show the sequence of execution.

> Direct Supervision achieves coordination by having one person take responsibility for the work of others, issues instructions to them and monitoring their actions. In effect, one brains coordinates several hands (...)

When we apply this strategy to agents, we can interpret it as follows. There is one dominant agent with all coordination knowledge, i.e. the Manager, which is in fact the *brain*. The Operators, i.e. the several more or less brainless hands, will be controlled by the Manager. The Manager regulates the process and keeps track of the state of the solution.

3.3.1.1 Manager PSM Specification

The strategy chosen in the PSM for Direct Supervision is having the Manager control the Operators in every job. The Manager will instruct the Operators using activities. The Operators respond with reports that contain the result of the performed activities, i.e. the output role if successfully. If not successful, the Operators will send a report with an error message.

The specification of the method is shown in Figure 3.6. The current-object role is initially filled by an input-object delivered by the Requester. The value of the current-object is used to specify the input-role for the activity to be performed next. The value of the current-object is updated using the value of the output-object of a report.

This process is designed as a **while** loop that selects sub-tasks from the task. An activity is specified based on the select sub-task and the current-object, which represents the input-object for this activity. Given the available Operators, an Operator is selected and assigned to the activity.

The Operator receives a message containing the activity description and an input-object. When the Operator has successfully performed its activity, it sends a report containing an output-object. The Manager updates the current-object with the output-object from the report sent by the Operators.

```
psm direct-supervision;
   can-realize : coordination;
   decomposition :
      inferences : specify, assign, select;
      functions : update;
   roles :
      input : operators, task, input-object, report;
      intermediate : sub-task, activity, current-object;
      output : instruction, output-object;
   control-structure :
      current-object := input-object;
      while has-solution select(system-task → sub-task) do
         specify(current-object + sub-task → activity);
         select(activity → operator);
         assign(activity + operator → instruction);
         if (report.status==success) update(report → current-object);
         else if has-solution select(activity → operator) do
               assign(activity + operator → instruction);
               else break;
               end-if
            end-if
         end while
end psm direct-supervision;
```

Figure 3.6
Method specification for Direct Supervision in terms or roles, inferences, functions and a control structure. The syntax used is the *CommonKADS Knowledge-Model Language* as defined in [Schreiber et al., 1999]. We added the function **break** as exit point of the **while** loop.

The corresponding inference structure for this strategy is shown in Figure 3.7. Four inferences and a transfer function are used in this method:

Select sub-task   The first step in the inference selects a sub-task to perform next from the specification of the task. In the example, the sequence of selected sub-tasks is search, obtain and classify.

Specify activity   The next step in the sequence specifies an activity based on the selected sub-task and the current-object. The current-object is either the initial input-object (e.g. query) or an intermediate object received from a report (e.g. candidate). The idea is that when Operators have performed their activity, they report to the Manager. The function update, updates the current-role.

Select Operator   An Operator will be selected to carry out the activity from the set of available Operators. Several methods exist to select an Operator. A possible method is to make a selection utilizing the required competence specified in the activity. If more than one Operators are available, other selection methods can be applied, such as ranking on availability, costs, trustworthiness or location.

Assign instructions   The last step is coupling the specified activity to the selected Operator. The instructions are sent in a message to the selected Operator.

Update Current-object   When the Manager sends instructions to the Operators, the Operators report (directly) back to the Manager. A report contains the output-objects generated by the reporting Operator. The function update, updates the current-object. The current-objects are used as input-object in the next activity assignment.

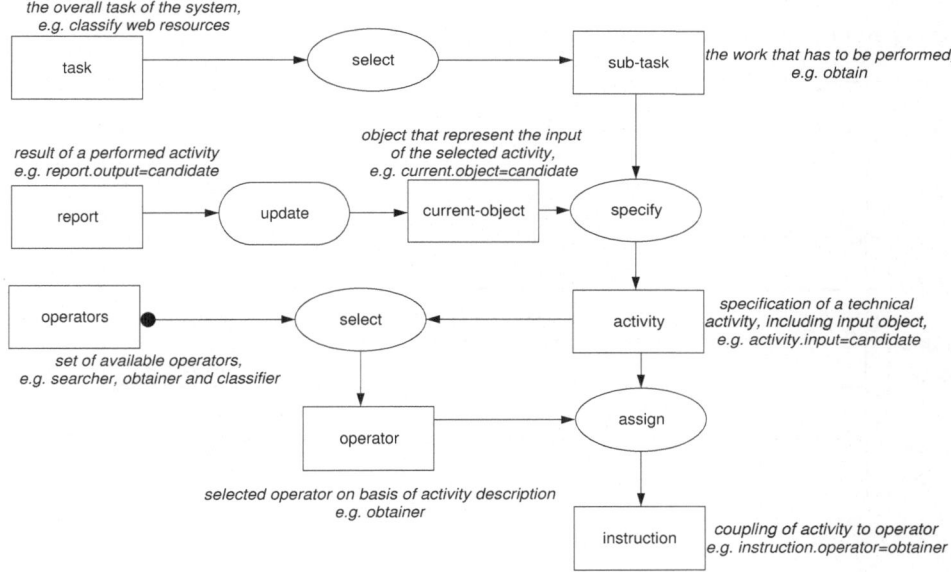

Figure 3.7
Inference structure (using the notation defined in [Schreiber et al., 1999]) of the Manager PSM for Direct Supervision. Boxes represent roles, ellipsis represent inferences and rounded boxes represent functions. Pointed arrows represent the control flow.

3.3.1.2   Operator PSM Specification

We briefly sketch the expected behavior of the Operator for this strategy. The function *perform activity* which are fed by the **instructions** (i.e. the activity description and input-objects) received from the Manager. The result of this function is a **report**, which is the result of a performed activity including output-objects. The results are to be sent to the Manager.

3.3.1.3 Sequence Diagram

An agent sequence diagram (according to AUML introduced by [Odell et al., 2000]) can graphically show a sequence of messages between agents. The expected sequence of messages to be sent in the Direct Supervision strategy is given in Figure 3.8. For now, we describe the content of a message informally. In Section 6.4, we discuss a method to fill the content of messages using message content ontologies.

The sequence diagram shows a centralized model, where the relations between the Manager and the Operators can be seen as Master-Slave, or Client-Server. This strategy is suitable when most of the agents are not capable of reasoning or cannot hold states. Furthermore, agent engineers can select this strategy, when they can have access to agents, but cannot influence the behavior of these agents. The Operators will not "know" that they form part of a specific multi-agent system.

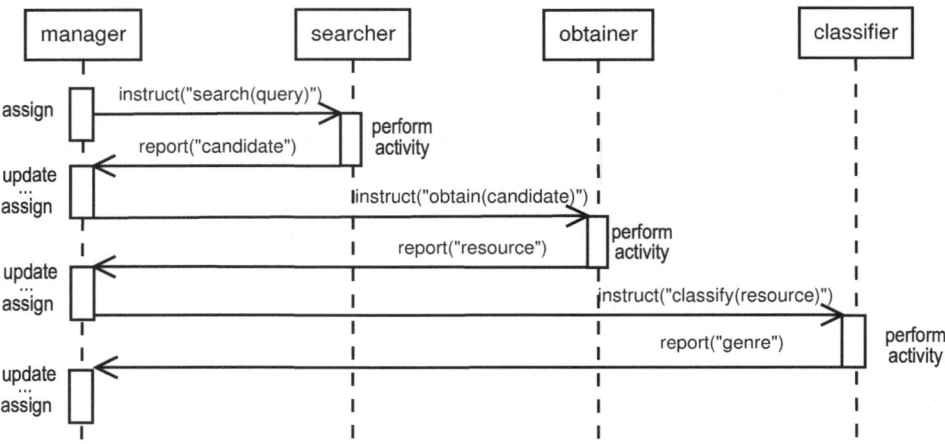

Figure 3.8
Sequence diagram showing collaboration patterns between the Manager and the three Operators using Direct Supervision as coordination mechanism.

3.3.1.4 Application

The coordination strategy "Direct Supervision" differs from classic functional decomposition, because in classic functional decomposition all control is in the hands of one control component. The agents in an agent system that apply "Direct Supervision", have independent behaviors. This means that the instructed Operators, still decide individually how to internally process the instructions.

All coordination knowledge is centered in one agent, i.e. the Manager. This can be attractive from a maintenance point of view, because the Manager is also the single point of failure. This means that if the Manager fails, the complete system will fail. If noticed, only the Manager needs to be restarted, replaced or modified. Moreover, if an Operator fails, the Managers resolves this by finding another Operator. The advantages and disadvantages of "Direct Supervision" are discussed in Table 3.5 (p.71).

When applying "Direct Supervision", one must assure that the Operators and Managers are able to interoperate with each other. This means that they use the same means to communicate and know how to process the content of messages (this is discussed in detail in Section 5.5.2.3). If multi tasks are to be executed at the same time (i.e. in parallel), the Manager and Operators need to keep track of multi tasks. This can be handled by annotating the exchanged messages, by an identifier, which refers to the identity of a task.

In case of a failing Operator, the Manager can use a time-out mechanism[4] to detect failures and respond accordingly by instructing a replace Operator or let's the complete process fail.

A Java implementation of Direct Supervision is given in Figure 5.13 (p.125).

3.3.2 Coordination by Standardization of Work

The coordination strategy, *Standardizing of Work* decentralizes the control over the workers involved. Standardization of Work has been defined by [Mintzberg, 1993, p.5] as:

> Coordination is achieved on the drawing board, so to speak, before work is undertaken. (. . .) Work process are standardized when the contents of the work are specified or programmed. (. . .) For example "Take the two-inch round-head Philips screw and insert into hole BX, attaching this to part XB with the lock washer and hexagonal nut, at the same time holding (. . .)

One interpretation of this strategy is to have a Manager that instructs Operators with procedures (i.e. work specification) before the actual operation. A procedure specifies how Operators should perform their work, such as how to acquire the input-objects, what to do with them, and to whom to distribute them.

The management of interdependencies, such as producer/consumer, consumer/producer and common limited object, will be delegated to the Operators. The main role of the Manager is to specify the work before the actual operation. From there on, the Operators are capable of coordinating themselves. The Operators store in their memories the procedures they have received. Using these procedures, they know how to act, when receiving an object from another agent.

3.3.2.1 Manager PSM Specification

In contrast to Direct Supervision, this method does not take into account the flow of objects. The idea is that control over the flow of objects is delegated to the Operators. Therefore the overall strategy has two phases: instruction and actual execution. In the

---

[4]The Manager waits for a certain period of time on an answer of an Operator. If the Operators does not respond within this time, the Manager assumes that the Operators has failed.

instruction phase, the Manager plays the dominant role by configuring the Operators involved. In the next phase, the Manager only starts the execution. The execution itself is controlled by the Operators in a decentralized model.

The method specified here only defines the role of the Manager in the instruction phase, see Figure 3.9. The **while** loop selects activities from the task. The next step is to determine the interdependencies of this activity with other activities. These interdependencies include consumer/producer and shared resources. Given the selected task and interdependencies, a procedure can be specified. The procedure contains a description of what activity to perform and how the flow of objects is regulated for this activity. The final step is the assignment of the procedure to an Operator.

```
psm standardization-of-work;
    can-realize : coordination;
    decomposition :
        inferences : select, abstract, specify, assign;
    roles :
        input : operators, system-task;
        intermediate : sub-task, procedure;
        output : instruction;
    control-structure :
        while has-solution select(system-task → sub-task) do
            abstract(sub-task → interdependency);
            specify(interdependency + activity → procedure);
            select(procedure + operators → operator);
            assign(procedure + operator → instruction);
        end while
psm standardization-of-work;
```

Figure 3.9
Method specification for Standardization of Work. The syntax used is the *CommonKADS Knowledge-Model Language.*

The corresponding inference structure of the strategy is shown in Figure 3.10. The inferences involved are:

Select activity   The first step in the inference is to select the activity to perform next from the specification of the system task.

Abstract interdependencies   The next step is to determine the relationships between the selected activity with other activities. In the example the activity CLASSIFY needs as input the output from the activity OBTAIN. The idea is that the Manager delegates the control over interdependencies to the Operators involved. Therefore, the Manager first has to find out what interdependencies exist.

Specify procedure   A procedure is generated with the selected activity and the associated interdependencies as input. For example, the procedure for the activity CLAS-

SIFY contains information on the source input (i.e. another Operator) and output directions. The source input is in the form of a `consume_from` relation. In this case the `consume_from` relation points to the Obtainer. The output directions are in the form of the `distribute_to` relation, which in this case refers to the Requester.

Select Operator   An Operator is selected from the set of available Operators, to carry out the activity. In this method the Manager selects an Operator out of the available Operators, based on the required competence for an activity. Within this strategy, the "pigeon-holing" strategy (cf. [Mintzberg, 1993], and Section 2.3.2 (p.19)) can be applied. The idea is that Operators are categorized, based on their competences, and that cases (i.e. activities) can be categorized into predetermined situations. Given a procedure, one or more Operators are selected.

Assign instructions   The last step in the inference structure is where the procedures are assigned to Operators.

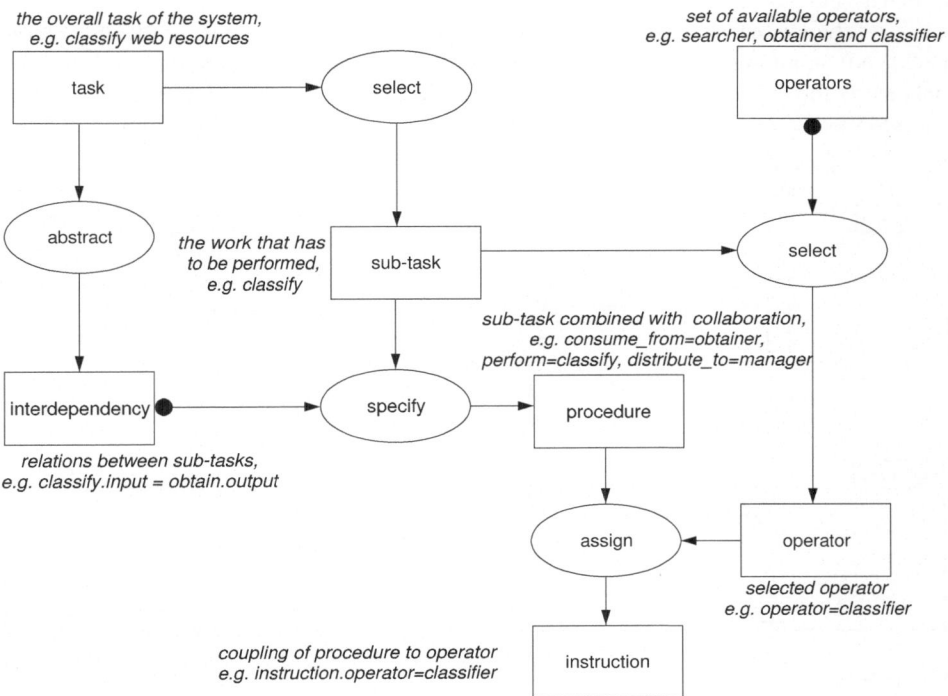

Figure 3.10
Inference structure (using the notation defined in [Schreiber et al., 1999]) of the Manager PSM for Standardization of Work.

3.3.2.2   Operator PSM Specification

The expected behavior of an Operator in this strategy is more complex then in the Direct Supervision strategy. Besides the **perform activity**, that transforms the input-object into an output-object, there are two additional inferences, **process instructions** and **produce output**. The inference **process instructions** is activated when the Operator receives an instruction from the Manager. The procedure within the instruction is stored in the memory (i.e. state) of the Operator and is consulted when the Operator receives an input-object. The inference **produce output** determines to which Operator the output-object is to be distributed.

3.3.2.3   Sequence Diagram

In Figure 3.11 the expected sequence of messages is given. The collaboration pattern shows the two phases of the strategy: the instruction phase and the actual execution. The two phases are represented by the UML packages *instruction* and *execution*, which are drawn as annotated boxes.

As shown, the Manager plays the dominant role of central planner in the instruction package by configuring the Operators involved. In the execution package, the Manager only starts the execution. The execution itself is controlled by the Operators in a decentralized model.

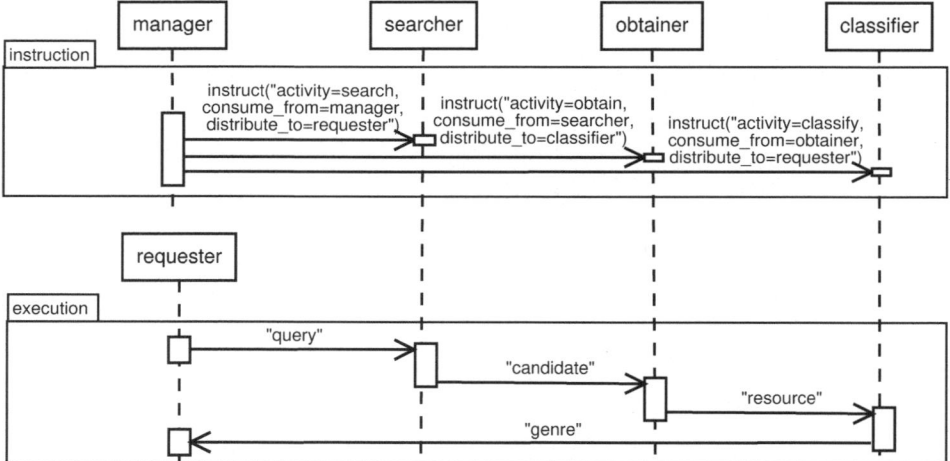

Figure 3.11
Sequence diagram showing collaboration patterns between the Manager, the three Operators and the Requester using Standardization of Work. In the instruction phase the Manager instructs the three operators. In the instruction phase the Requester interacts with the Operators. Furthermore, the Operators know how to accomplish the task.

3.3.2.4 Application

The strategy "Standardization of Work" requires that the Operators should be equipped with a memory, such as a database, where a configuration can be stored. It means that Operators should be able to "remember" their role in the multi-agent system. Furthermore, they should be able to interpret the procedures sent by the Manager.

The strategy is useful in situations where the multi-agent system has to perform a task multiple times, i.e. the task is of a repetitive nature. If the system's task only has to be performed once, the instruction phase can form a communication overload. As will be shown in the mini experiments (see Section 3.5), the breakpoint of overload is at two executions of the task. The advantages and disadvantages of "Standardization of Work" are discussed in Table 3.5 (p.71).

The role of the Manager is crucial in the instruction phase. When the strategy is in the execution phase, the role of the Manager is limited, which is an advantage in the overall performance of the system. The reason for this is that there is no redundant communication in the operation, in contrast with Direct Supervision.

An extension of this strategy can be that Operators are able to search for alternative Operators. This can be applied when an Operator itself is unable to follow the instructed procedure. For example, the Obtainer cannot process the object received from the Searcher, because it is in a format the Obtainer cannot read. To solve the problem, the Obtainer tries to find another agent that is able to process the object, e.g. Obtainer2,

Another situation is where an Operator cannot find the Operator to whom it is supposed to distribute its output. For example, Obtainer cannot locate Classifier, because the connection to Classifier is broken. Therefore, Obtainer will search another Classifier.

A Java implementation of Standardization of Work is given in Figure 5.11 (p.123).

3.3.3 Mutual Adjustment

Several articles are predicting agents that can freely travel on the Web and collaborate with any agent they encounter. For example, Hendler predicts that Web agents will be able to help users to find anything and regulate their needs on the Web [Hendler, 2001]. In order to do so agents should be able to interoperate with agents they never encountered before. In cases where agents are not equipped with the knowledge about how to deal with available coordination strategies (such as Direct Supervision or Standardization of Work) Mutual Adjustment can be applied as a coordination strategy. According to [Mintzberg, 1993, p.4]:

> Mutual Adjustment achieves the coordination of work by the simple process of informal communication. Under Mutual Adjustment, control of the work rests in the hands of the doers. (...) Because it is such a simple coordination strategy, it is naturally used in the very simplest of organizations (...). Paradoxically, it is also used in the most complicated ones (...)

There are several ways to interpret Mintzberg definition of Mutual Adjustment. Our interpretation is that in Mutual Adjustment there are no Manager and Operator roles involved. There are agents, which are aware of their own **competences**. A Requester will start "conversations" with all present agents.

One of the simplest ways to apply Mutual Adjustment is to have agents only to communicate objects to all known agents. This communication can be seen as a (network) broadcast, which can be envisioned as: "Hello All, I have object X, who can do something with it?". If an agent can do so, i.e. transform the received object into another object, this agent communicates the new object to all other agents.

Alternative method is to communicate both the object and the task. In order to limit the number of interactions, the agent could remember agents it was able to collaborate with. This can be seen as a list of preferred peers.

3.3.3.1   PSM specification

The specification of the method is given in Figure 3.12. When an agent (i.e. the Requester) has to carry out a task, it distributes the input-object to all available agents. When the input-object is received, the agents **match** the object to their competences and check whether they are capable of performing an activity with this object. If they do so, they define an internal activity, perform the internal activity and distribute the output-object to all other agents. From there on, the process repeats, until the Requester has received the output role it needs.

```
psm mutual-adjustment;
   can-realize : coordination;
   decomposition :
      inferences : match;
      functions : perform-activity;
   roles :
      input : input-object;
      intermediate : activity;
      output : output-object;
   control-structure :
      if has-solution match(input-object + competence → activity);
         perform-activity(activity + input-object) → object-object);
      end if
end psm mutual-adjustment;
```

Figure 3.12
Method specification for Mutual Adjustment. The syntax used is the *CommonKADS Knowledge-Model Language*.

The corresponding inference structure of the strategy is shown in Figure 3.13 showing one inference: **match competence**, and one function **perform activity**.

Match competence   This function is called every time an object is received from a broadcast. In this case the object is matched to the available services of the agent. When there is a solution an internal activity is generated that specifies an activity that can be performed using the received object.

Perform activity When the Match inference has found a match and has defined an internal activity, this function actually performs the activity. The output-object will be distributed (i.e. broadcasted) to all known agents.

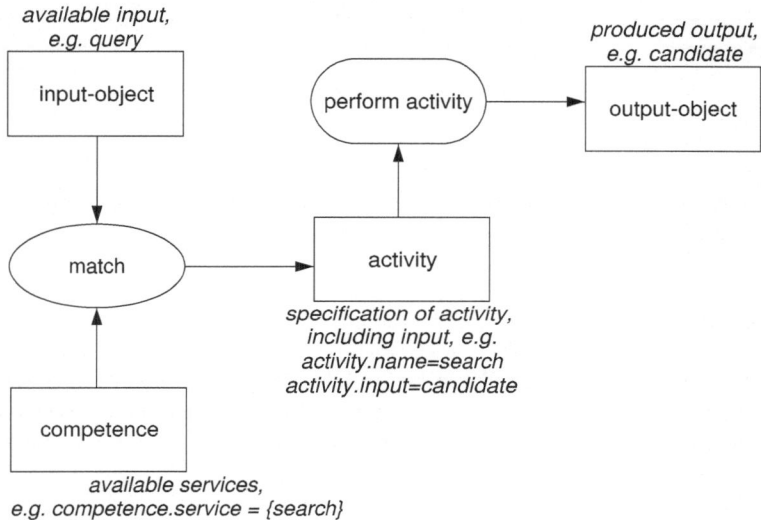

Figure 3.13
Inference structure (using the notation defined in [Schreiber et al., 1999]) for Mutual Adjustment.

3.3.3.2 Sequence Diagram

As shown in Figure 3.14 the interactions between the agents look like a broadcasting model. Although it looks like an overhead of exchanged messages, this strategy can be suitable when there is no control knowledge present. However it does not guarantee that the Requester will receive a solution to its problem. Furthermore, in this example, for every broadcast, exactly one agent can perform an activity given the broadcasted object. In other cases several agents could respond to a broadcast or no agent could respond. The main problem is that the state of the problem-solving is distributed so that no agent has control over it. This could lead to complete chaos or *emergent behavior*. Chaos can emerge when agents are continuously broadcasting problems and no single agent can solve it. Emergent Behavior could appear when agents that did not know of each other, would find each other and help each other in solving problems. Suppose multiple Operators start working on the same problem, several perspectives (or solutions) could emerge.

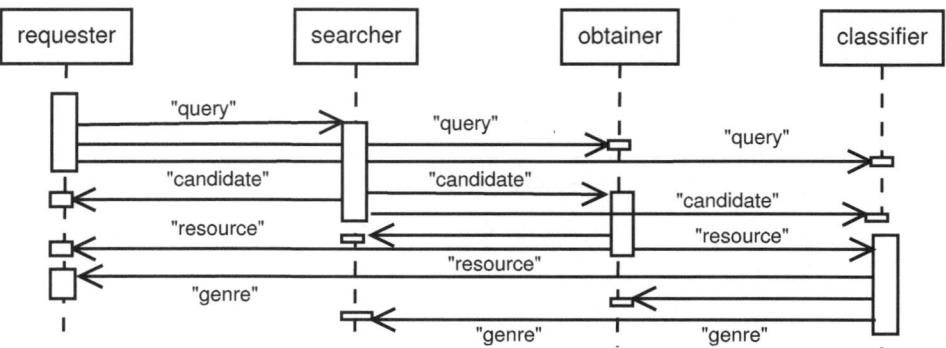

Figure 3.14
Sequence diagram showing collaboration patterns between the involved agents using Mutual Adjustment.

3.3.3.3 Application

The strategy "Mutual Adjustment" can be applied when the structure of a problem is unknown, unavailable or unreadable (i.e. the problem is expressed in an unknown format to the agent). It can also be applied when the agents are heterogeneous and cannot agree to use one of the other two strategies. For example, there is no Manager available, or the Operators do not want to be controlled by another agent.

As with "Direct Supervision" and "Mutual Adjustment", the agents need a common means to communicate with each other, such as message-based communication. Furthermore, to keep track of tasks, messages need to be equipped with identifiers to refer to task's identifications.

The advantage is that there is no central coordinator (Manager) and in an ideal case, the agents are capable of solving problems themselves. In other cases, where agents are not capable of solving problems broadcasted by other agents, this strategy cannot guarantee that the system is capable of executing every task. The advantages and disadvantages of "Mutual Adjustment" are discussed in Table 3.5.

3.4   Implication for External Agent Design

This section discusses how the PSMs can be integrated into the behavior of an agent. The behavior of an agent can be described using various techniques, such as activity diagrams, use case and state diagrams [Odell et al., 2000]. In this case, we will use state diagrams to describe the behavior of an Operator and of a Manager. The idea is that agent engineers can use these state diagram as a design pattern. In Section 5.5.2.1 (p.120), we discuss the application of the two behaviors described below.

3.4.1 Operator Agent Behavior

The behavior of an Operator consists of a composition of three life cycles: the *platform life cycle*, the *instruction life cycle* and the *execution life cycle*. A life cycle is a collection of *states* an agent can hold and *transactions* that allow traverse between states. This relation is of a cyclic nature, i.e. the states form a circle that can be traversed multiple times. The state diagram is illustrated in Figure 3.15.

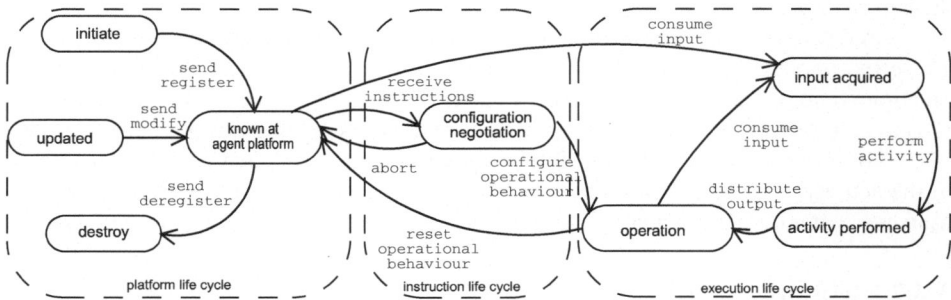

Figure 3.15
State diagram showing states (rounded boxes) and transitions (arrowed lines) of the three life cycles of the Operator's behavior.

The *platform life cycle* starts when an agent joins a multi-agent system. In order to do so, the agent has to register itself, in a pro-active manner, at an agent platform (cf. [FIPA, 2002c]). This registration is done at the AMS (the Agent Manager Service), which holds a register of the physical addresses (i.e. URLs) of agents. This can be seen as a white page service. For example, the Operator googlewrapper will register itself as googlewrapper@gaper.swi.psy.uva.nl.

Next, in order to be found by other agents, an agent has to register its services at the DF (Directory Facilitator). The DF, in fact a yellow page service, holds a directory of services of agents. A service can be "this agent can interact with the search engine Google. On the basis of a boolean query, a list of URLs and descriptions will be returned". In Section 5.2 we discuss an elaborate approach to describe and apply agent competences. The *platform life cycle* ends when an agent changes or wants to leave the multi-agent system. For that, it has to modify or de-register its services. The registration, modification and de-registration at the AMS and DF are described in the FIPA agent life cycle [FIPA, 2002c].

The state transitions, i.e. `register`, `modify` and `deregister`, are part of a pro-active behavior. This means that the Operator has to take initiative to make itself known at the agent platform.

The *instruction life cycle* starts when the Operator receives instructions from the Manager agent. The Operator will move to the `configuration negotiation` state. From this state, the Operator will try to configure its operational behavior. If successful, the Operator will be part of a (larger) application and will wait until it can enter the *operation life cycle*. If the configuration fails, the negotiation will be aborted and the

Operator will leave the instruction life cycle. Otherwise, the Manager will to report the Operator that the application execution is finished. In this case the Operator will reset the configuration of its operational behavior and leave the configuration life cycle.

The *execution life cycle* starts when the operational behavior is successfully configured. From there, the Operators wait to consume input. The Operator can consume input, from the *operation* state in case of "Direct Supervision" and "Standardization of Work" strategy. In case of the "Mutual Adjustment" strategy, the Operator can process input from the *known at platform* state.

An Operator can consume input both re-active as pro-active, see also Section 2.2.1. These two modes depend on the instructions from the Manager and the applied coordination strategy. In "Mutual Adjustment" and "Direct Supervision", the mode will be re-active. In "Standardization of Work" the mode depends on the Manager's instructions.

Given the acquired input, the Operator performs the instructed activity. The result of the activity, i.e. output-object, will be distributed according to the instructions of the Manager. After output distribution, the Operator will go back to the `operation` state.

3.4.2 Manager Agent Behavior

In "Direct Supervision", the Manager is involved in the configuration and execution phase. The Manager is only involved in the configuration phase when applying "Standardization of Work". In "Mutual Adjustment", the Manager plays no role in the two phases, however the Manager could facilitate negotiations between the requester and the Operators.

The behavior of the Manager consists of a composition of three life cycles, i.e. *platform life cycle*, *configuration life cycle* and *execution life cycle*. The platform life cycle is the same as the platform life cycle of the Manager, see Figure 3.16.

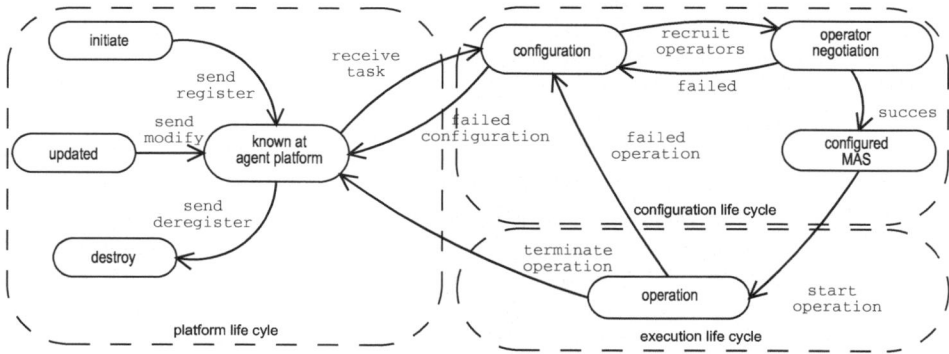

Figure 3.16
State diagram showing states (rounded boxes) and transitions (arrowed lines) of the three life cycles of the Manager's behavior.

The *configuration life cycle* starts when the Manager receives a task from the requester. The Manager will recruit Operators by consulting the agent platform's AMS and DF to search for relevant Operators. When a set of candidate Operators is found, the Manager will start negotiations with them. In case of success, the Manager will enter the *execution life cycle*.

Depending on the chosen coordination strategy, the behavior of the Manager is pro-active or re-active. When applying "Direct Supervision", the Manager will be actively involved in sending Operators instructions related to activity and the related input-role. In "standardization', the Manager can choose to play a role in execution. For example, the Manager can take care of the communication with the Requester.

3.5 Mini experiments

In this section we discuss results that are drawn from three mini experiments. For every described coordination method we implemented a prototype.

The experiments aimed to analyze alternative coordination structures applied to the web resource classification system as described in Section 3.3. The analysis is built up out of two parts: an efficiency analysis and a comparison between the three strategies. The qualitative analysis reports on the dynamics of the system. The quantitative analysis discusses the number of messages sent and the execution time. The aim of the quantitative analysis is to find out if there is a communication overhead and what influence this overhead will have on the system's performance.

The agents involved in the experiment are the ones that have been introduced in Section 3.3, i.e. Manager, Searcher, Obtainer and Classifier. We are interested in the performance of the three coordination strategies, not in the performance of the agents' competences. Another reason to disregard the use of web services, such as Google is that a lot of popular services only allow a limited number of request within a period of time. This means that after a number of requests, the service would deny a service request and therefore the experiment would fail. Therefore, we replaced the competences of the agents with *stubs*. Stubbing is a standard technique in software engineering in which only the external behavior of a process is built, to test this behavior in relation to other processes [Sommerville, 1995]. In this case, we simulated the behavior of a process by the expected time needed to perform the process. The implementations of the agents' competences are discussed in Table 3.1.

3.5.1 Direct Supervision

In order to describe the outcomes of the experiment using Direct Supervision, we discuss the dynamics of the Manager within the system. Using the activity log of the Manager, we constructed an inference trace. This trace is described in Table 3.2. The steps are described below.

In step 0, the roles *task* and *Operators* are initialized. Next in step 1, the inference *select* selects *search* as first activity, which is used in step 2 to specify *activity1*. The activity *activity1* instructs the Operator from whom to consume its input roles and to

Name	Activities	Implementation
Manager Agent	instruct(SystemTask, Operators) $\rightarrow$ instructions	Manager agent makes use of a coordination strategy.
Searcher	search(query) $\rightarrow$ item	Searcher makes use of external search services such as Google.
Obtainer	obtain(item) $\rightarrow$ resource	Obtainer make uses of standard Internet techniques, to download resources, i.e. HTTP protocol.
Classifier	classify(resource) $\rightarrow$ genre	Classifier makes use of an external classification library.

Table 3.1
Agents involved in the experiment and the implementation of their competences. The activities are notated as "transform job"("input") $\rightarrow$ "output", where "$\rightarrow$" means produces.

whom to distribute its output roles, after successfully carrying out its activities. In this case, the Operators have to consume and distribute their roles from and to the Manager. Next, the activity is assigned to the Operator Searcher in the form of instructions. When Searcher has completed its activity, it reports to the Manager in step 4. From there the Manager supervises Obtainer in the steps 4-8 and the Manager supervises Classifier in steps 9-12.

Step	Inference	Roles
0	init	System task = { search, obtain, classify } Operators = { searcher, obtainer, classier }
1	select sub-task	sub-task1 = search(query) $\rightarrow$ candidate
2	specify activity	activity1 = { consumeFrom(Manager), search(query), distributeTo(Manager) }
3	assign activity	instructions = { activity1, Operator(searcher) }
4	update current-object	current-object=candidate
5	select sub-task	sub-task2 = obtain(candidate) $\rightarrow$ resource
6	specify activity	activity2 = { consumeFrom(Manager), obtain(candidate), distributeTo(Manager) }
7	assign activity	instructions = { activity2, Operator(obtainer) }
8	update current-object	current-object=resource
9	select sub-task	sub-task3 = classify(resource) $\rightarrow$ genre
10	specify activity	activity3 = { consumeFrom(Manager), classify(resource), distributeTo(Manager) }
11	assign activity	instructions = { activity3, Operator(classifier) }
12	update current-object	current-object=genre

Table 3.2
Part of the interference trace of the Manager when applying Direct Supervision.

For every step in the task, the Manager has to send a direct order (i.e. send a message) to an Operator. The Operator reports (i.e. sending a message) directly to the Manager. Therefore there are two messages involved for every step. This regime does not change when the number of runs increases. The formula to determine the number of messages exchanged between Manager and Operators is given in Table 3.4.

3.5.2 Standardization of Work

Using standardization, the inference starts with an initialization of the roles *task* and *Operators* in step 0 (see Table 3.3). Next in step 1, the inference *select* selects *search* as the first activity which is used in step 2 to determine the collaborations. In this case, interdependencies for the activity *select* are getting the input role *query* and giving the output role to the activity *obtain*. Given these two interdependencies, the Manager specifies a procedure that contains one activity that tells the Operator to consume its input from the Manager, apply the activity *search* and distribute its output to Obtainer. Then the Manager assigns the procedure to the Operator Searcher. In steps 5-8 the Manager instructs the Operator Obtainer. The Operator Classifier is instructed through steps 9-12. The resulting collaboration patterns are illustrated in Figure 3.11. Details on the outcome of this experiment can be found in Figure 3.17.

Step	Inference	Roles
0	init	System task = { search, obtain, classify }
		Operators = { searcher, obtainer, classifier }
1	select sub-task	sub-task1 = search(query) $\rightarrow$ candidate
2	abstract interdependency	collaboration0 = { query, sub-task(search) }
		collaboration1 = { sub-task(search), sub-task(obtain) }
3	specify procedure	procedure1 = { consumeFrom(Manager), sub-task(search),
		distributeTo(obtainer)}
4	assign procedure	instructions = { procedure1, Operator(searcher) }
5	select sub-task	sub-task2 = obtain(candidate) $\rightarrow$ resource
6	abstract interdependency	collaboration2 = { sub-task(search), sub-task(obtain)}
		collaboration3 = { sub-task(obtain), sub-task(classify)}
7	specify procedure	procedure2 = { consumeFrom(searcher), sub-task(obtain),
		distributeTo(classifier) }
8	assign procedure	instructions = { procedure2, Operator(obtainer) }
9	select sub-task	sub-task3 = classify(resource) $\rightarrow$ genre
10	abstract interdependency	collaboration4 = { sub-task(obtain),
		sub-task(classify) }
		collaboration5={ sub-task(classify), genre }
11	specify procedure	procedure3 = { consumeFrom(obtainer), sub-task(classify),
		distributeTo(Manager)}
12	assign procedure	instructions = { procedure3, Operator(classifier) }

Table 3.3
Part of the interference trace of the Manager agent when applying Standardization of Work.

The formula to determine the number of messages exchanged between Manager and Operators is given in Table 3.4. The Manager instructs the Operators involved by sending one individual message to them, i.e. s messages, where s is the the number of steps (i.e subtasks) in the task. For every task, the Manager and Operators need $s + 1$ message: 1 message for Manager to the first Operator (i.e. the first step in the task), $s - 1$ messages for transactions between s Operators and 1 message for the last Operator (i.e. the last step in the task) to the Manager. The instruction has to be done once independently of the number of runs.

3.5.3   Mutual Adjustment

As illustrated in Figure 3.14 the agents send input roles to every known agent. The Requester sends the input role *query* to the agents Searcher, Obtainer and Classifier. The agent Searcher can match this input role to one of its activity in the agent's competence. Searcher performs the activity and sends its output-object to the agents Manager, Obtainer and Classifier. From there, Obtainer performs its activities and distributes the result to the other agents. Finally, Classifier performs its activity and after distribution, the Requester recognizes the output-object as solution to his problem.

The formula to determine the number of messages exchanged between Manager and Operators is given in Table 3.4. A "Mutual Adjustment" starts from the Requester sending $a - 1$ messages to all known agents, where a is the number of available agents. When an Operator processes a received message, it sends $a - 1$ messages to all known agents, including the Requester. This process repeats s times, until the Requester has received the solution to its request.

3.5.4   Evaluation

The experiments were run on two Linux machines (*gollem* and *gaper*) using four FIPA-compliant agent platforms[5]. Every machine was equipped with two agent platforms each inhabited by one agent. The agents Manager and Obtainer were located on *gaper*. The agents Searcher and Classifier were located on *gollem*.

The FIPA-HTTP message transport protocol was used for message transport [FIPA, 2002d]. This protocol was chosen, because this protocol expensive and could lead to a communication overhead of the agents.

3.5.4.1   Results

In order to measure the efficiency of the strategies, we examined the number of messages sent in order to determine the costs of communication and the process time. The Manager calculated the process time[6] needed to perform one execution run. Table 3.4 lists a quantified comparison of the three coordination strategies.

Both the communication weight as the process time show a linear relation[7] with the number of queries, see Figure 3.17. Due to a good network connection, the costs of communication *transport* can be discarded, in contrast to the costs of *processing* communication by the agents, which could lead to communication overhead. However, no (exponential) communication overhead has occurred. A possible reason for the fluctuating results of Standardization of Work (SW) and Mutual Adjustment (MA) is interfering network traffic, such as Internet traffic, backup mechanisms and other experiments.

---

[5]See http://gaper.swi.psy.uva.nl for more details on the *gaper* platform.

[6]The Manager agent used the system time to calculate the process time needed to perform tasks. The time provided to the Manager agent was dependent of the operating system, the agents were running on.

[7]The correlation coefficients of the three datasets are 0.998899 for "Direct Supervision", 0.639743 for "Standardization of Work" and 0.868646 for "Mutual Adjustment".

Strategy	Number of messages	Process Time
Direct Supervision	$m = 2qs$	$1786q + 141$
Standardization of Work	$m = s + (s+1)q$	$369q + 451$
Mutual Adjustment	$m = qs(a-1)$	$536q + 7832$

Table 3.4

Quantitative analysis of the three coordination strategies. The "number of messages" formulas are determined by counting the number of interactions in the collaboration diagrams in Sections 3.3.1.3 (p.54), 3.3.2.3 (p.58) and 3.3.3.2 (p.61). The "process time" formulas are determined by doing a regression analysis on the data gathered by the manager, as displayed in Fig. 3.17 The variable m represents the number of messages, s the number of steps in the task, q the number of queries (or runs) and a is the number of agents (i.e. number of Operators plus the requesting agent).

When looking at the process time, Standardization of Work appears to be the most efficient. The reason for this is that there is no superfluous communication. Moreover, the agents can process objects in parallel[8], thanks to a buffering mechanism. This means that the agents can add incoming messages onto a stack and process these one by one in the agent's own tempo. This is also the case in Mutual Adjustment. Direct Supervision cannot process objects in parallel, because in the given method, the Manager has to process all the objects one by one.

In Section 5.6, we discuss the application of "Standardization of Work" in a case study on classification of conference submissions. The operationalization of the "Direct Supervision" and "Standardization of Work" are discussed in the Sections 5.5.2.3 and 5.5.2.2.

3.5.4.2 Comparison

The results presented above give indicators of the performance of the system. One could also take into account the costs of equipping agents with reasoning power and the ability to self-configure. Other issues are summarized in Table 3.5.

The advantage of "Direct Supervision" is that the Operators are relatively small, because all control knowledge is maintained by the Manager. This can be preferable when the Operators cannot be changed, or when the Operators are not meant to be agents, such as P2P oriented (web)services. Furthermore, the control over the operation is centralized in the Manager. If an Operators fails to execute its activity, the Manager resolves the problem by locating a replacement Operator. From a maintenance point of view, this can be appealing.

A lot of design paradigms and methods are based on centralized control. Probably the first generation agent system, will be based on this strategy. However, centralizing control knowledge means building one "fat" agent that has to play the Manager role.

---

[8]Parallel processing in the sense that agents do not need to wait for each other. The agent still reasons in a sequential matter. The agent implementation does not take into account multi processors.

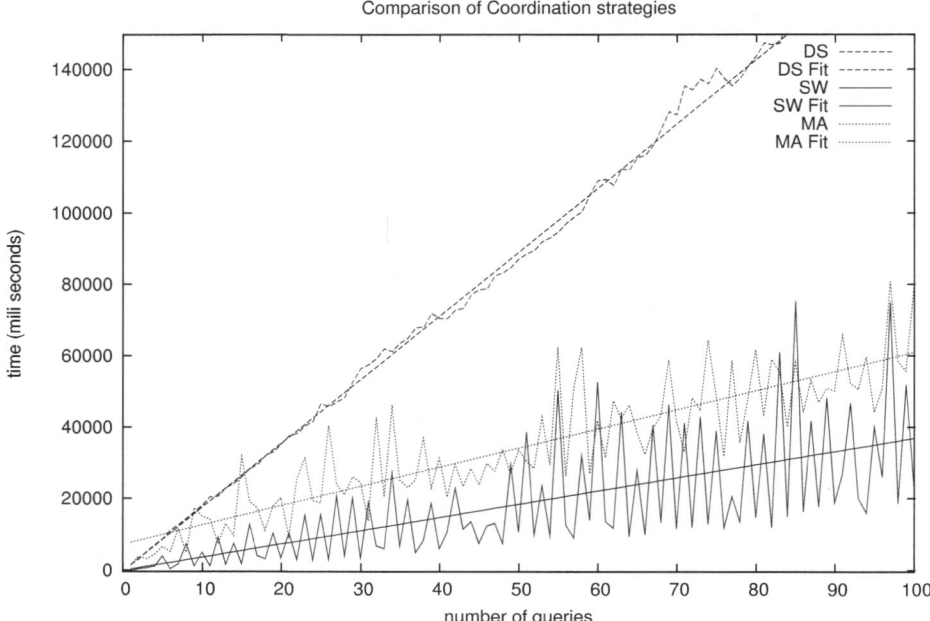

Figure 3.17

Results from three mini experiments comparing 1 to 100 queries against process time. The dashed line represents Direct Supervision(DS) combined with a line (DS fit) that represents the fit function for process time (see Table 3.4), the straight line represents Standardization of Work (SW) combined with its fit function (SW fit) and the dashed line with the "plus" symbol represents Mutual Adjustment (MA) combined its fit function (MA fit). The formulas for the fit functions for process time are given in Table 3.4.

When a lot of Operators are involved, the Manager could get too complex or too slow, i.e. the attention span can get overstressed. Moreover, if this agents fails, because it has to supervise too much Operators, the task cannot be performed. The point of having one big agent is also advised against in [Wooldridge and Jennings, 1995].

"Standardization of Work" has the advantage that it is efficient. This can be explained by the fact that the Manager delegates coordination to the Operators by exactly specifying their activities. There is a clear distinction between the instruction and execution knowledge. The Manager is occupied with instructions and Operators with execution, as devised in the division of work method described by Mintzberg [Mintzberg, 1993], see also Section 2.2.3. This means that the Manager does not interfere with execution, because the Manager has delegated the control to the agents. A reason for this can be that the execution of the Operators is too complex to supervise because many objects have to be transferred. Furthermore, the Manager can choose not to interfere in complex negotiations.

A disadvantage is that all the Operators involved need to be equipped with the ability to reason about procedures. Not in all situations, the designer has the means to alter existing agents or services. Furthermore, when something goes wrong, it is not clear how the Operators will resolve problems.

Strategy	Advantages	Disadvantages	Manager Knowledge
Direct Supervision	"Thin' Operators Control centralized	Single point of failure One "Fat" agent "Slow"	Task Coordination Available operators Input and output objects Fail-over mechanisms
Standardization of Work	Efficient Control in hands of operators	"Fat" operators Error handling	Task Instruction Available operators Standard situations
Mutual Adjustment	Emergent behavior Flexible Open	Chaos No solution guarantee Miscommunication	-

Table 3.5
Summary of advantages and disadvantages of the three coordination strategies, combined with the knowledge needed for the Manager.

From an agent perspective, "Mutual Adjustment" is the most interesting strategy, because it can lead to Emergent behavior. Unexpected dynamics can occur, thanks to different behaviors and expertise. The system can be flexible because there is no central control. Furthermore, the number of agents can be dynamic, meaning that agents can enter and leave the system during execution time.

A disadvantage is that this strategy cannot guarantee that tasks are solved. In an ideal situation, all existing agents could be contacted via communication. However, not for all problems agents or services exist. Furthermore, not all agents share the same conceptualization of problem, task, object and solution.

If every agent broadcasts objects (and tasks) to all known agents for every problem, a lot of this communication is purposeless and could lead to network overload. Furthermore, we did not(yet) take into account what happens when multiple agents can solve the problem. The Requester could compare multiple solutions and choose the one with the highest quality.

Another way to compare the strategies is to look at the amount and type of knowledge the Manager requires[9]. As described in Table 3.5 the Manager in "Direct Supervision" needs knowledge about the process in detail in order to directly instruct the Operators. Combined with this knowledge is a method to select the appropriate Operator from a repository of available Operators. Furthermore, it has to handle input, intermediate and output objects, which are exchanged between the Requester, Operators and the Manager. Besides that, it needs to apply one or more fail-over mechanisms, in case something goes wrong. The Manager in "Standardization of Work", only needs to know what Operators are available and the process. Furthermore, it needs to have a method to construct a

---

[9]With exception to "Mutual Adjustment", where there is no Manager.

Multi-Agent plan, including the allocation of an Operator from a repository of available Operators.

3.6 Discussion

We presented a knowledge-based approach to model coordination strategies in order to gain insights in the design of coordination structures in agents systems. We discussed the modeling of three known coordination strategies as problem-solving methods. The semantics for coordinating joint actions was made explicit and sharable by means of a task-method ontology.

From the three mini experiments we can see the differences between Direct Supervision, Standardization of Work and Mutual Adjustment. Direct Supervision shows a centralized model, i.e. all coordination knowledge (i.e. strategic and supervision) is concentrated in the Manager. The Manager takes care of managing the relations between activities and Operators. In Standardization of Work we can see a pattern of a decentralized model, where the Manager only plays the role of a strategic planner. Knowledge about coordination is distributed among the Operators. In Mutual Adjustment there is no division of roles into Operators and Managers. The pattern shows a broadcast communication model where every agent tries to communicate with all available agents. The patterns looks expensive, however the costs of building a Manager should be subtracted.

We have shown, to some extent, that a knowledge-based approach can represent our interpretation of concepts and relations of coordination. PSMs were applied to show how agents can be equipped with lines of reasoning for handling coordination. However, the inference structures for the different strategies are still of a provisional nature. More elaborate structures have to be defined. For example, ontologies and PSMs could be specialized on the grounds of the type of agents, environment, task or domain.

From an agent point of view, the Mutual Adjustment strategy is the most appealing. There is no central coordinator (Manager) and the agents are capable of solving problems for themselves. However, applying this strategy does not guarantee that the agents do so. For example, if an input is distributed (broadcasted) among agents and no agent is capable of performing an activity with it, the problem is not solved. In that case the agent that started the Mutual Adjustment could try to modify the input-object or choose another coordination strategy

Another approach could be that the agent that started the Mutual Adjustment would distribute an expected output. Instead of matching their competence based on input-objects, they could use the output-object as reference. When an agent has found a match, the agent needs an input-object. To acquire input-objects, the agent can ask other agents if they can provide these objects. However, from a traditional software engineering point of view, the engineer and possibly the end-user want to have control over the system.

We discussed several considerations for choosing the appropriate strategy to use. One of these considerations is related to the number of agents. For small systems, where there is a limited set of agents, Direct Supervision could be a good candidate, because the Operators do not need to be equipped with additional functions in order to reason on instructions as within Standardization of Work. The advantage and perhaps also the disadvantage of Direct Supervision is that control is centralized. When the number grows, both the attention span of an agent engineer and a Manager agent can be overstressed. In this case (i.e. larger distributed systems) the other two strategies are better candidates.

When a task is repetitive, Direct Supervision seems to be the best candidate. However, if the environment is dynamic, the instructions of the Manager could not be suitable anymore. When Operators do not want to agree on having a Manager or the task description is not present, Mutual Adjustment could be applied.

The costs of building a centralized or decentralized Manager should also be taken into account. In addition, one should also consider the costs of equipping Operators with reasoning power. From that perspective, the Manager of Direct Supervision is the most expensive Manager. The agents in Mutual Adjustment are the most expensive Operators.

When there are multiple ontologies involved, ontology translation can be allocated to one agent, i.e. the Manager, when applying Direct Supervision. In the other strategies the Operators need to be equipped with ontology translation knowledge.

In Section 5.4 (p.108), we discuss how a number of the coordination strategies ("Direct Supervision" in Section 5.5.2.3 (p.122) and "Standardization of Work" in Section 5.5.2.2 (p.122)) are embedded into an interoperability framework.

Chapter 4

Five Capabilities Model

In this chapter we present the *5 Capabilities (5C) model* which is a conceptual framework for analyzing and designing the capabilities of an intelligent agent. The 5C model defines five dimensions of agent intelligence - using the notion of *separation of concerns* - where each dimension plays a role in the development of intelligent software agents. These dimensions are communication, competence, self, planner and environment. The company Bolesian B.V. first proposed the 5C model during an EU-funded project, called MARTRANS [van Aart et al., 2000]. From there it was developed as a part of internal Bolesian development projects and prototypes were built in Java and Delphi. Later it is was refined and used as professional agent analysis and design framework by Acklin B.V. to develop commercial applications. This chapter is partly based on two articles: *Agent-based Logistic Service Provision* co-authored by Kris van Marcke, published at *the Fifth International Conference on the Practical Application of Intelligent Agents and Multi-Agent Technology (PAAM 2000)* and *International Insurance Traffic with Software Agents* co-authored by Kris van Marcke, published at *the 15th European Conference on Artificial Intelligence (ECAI 2002)*.

4.1 Introduction

The *Five Capabilities (5C) model* is a conceptual framework, based on a generalization of different types of agent capabilities, which can be found in the agent literature. The 5C model has been the design guide for the development of a series of intelligent agent application prototypes and commercial applications. The development of the applications showed that functional as well as technical constraints can be reflected along the five dimensions, using the notion of separation of concerns. Depending on the requirements of the application one can focus on each capability that needs attention, without getting lost in the complexity of the entire design. Applications that have been developed according to the 5C design guide include:

Supply in e-retail Special orders placed through the Internet to a retail-chain are delivered within hours to the nearest shop.

Intelligent Freight Planner IFP Requested by the European Commission (DG7): a distributed transport planning application was implemented to help organizing inter modal freight transportation processes [van Aart et al., 2000].

International claim handling with the KIR system A multi-agent application that
runs across different insurance companies to facilitate cross-border claim handling [van Aart et al., 2002b]. In Section 4.4 we discuss this application in detail.

The questions that lead to the development of the 5C model are the following: *How
do the relevant agent requirements come together?*, *What is the role for each of the agent
requirements to play in the final picture?*, *How can we understand the relevance and
importance of a single detailed contribution in the context of this complex collection?*
and *How to understand and be able to explain the real added value of agent technology?*
    To give answers to these questions we will define five dimensions of agent intel-
ligence - using the notion of *separation of concerns* - where each dimension can play
a role in the development of intelligent software agents. In the following section, these
dimensions are is explained in further detail.

4.2   The Five Dimensions

An agent in the 5C model is separated into five distinct dimensions: *communication*, *competence*, *self*, *planner* and *environment*. The dimensions are framed into models where
each model is responsible for one particular kind of capability an agent requires. One
of the inspirations of the 5C model is the metaphor of an individual agent as an information processing brain, where functionality emerges by combining different specialized
elements, i.e. models that cooperate [Morgan, 1996]. Another rationale behind the dimensions of the 5C model is a method to couple heterogenous expert systems (or knowledge
based systems) [van Aart et al., 2000]. In this method, we extend existing expert systems
with agent capabilities. Such a system, i.e. agent should be able perform a number of
tasks. Furthermore, the agent should be able to communicate with other agents and systems. In order to cope with complexity, we applied the separation of concern principle
and defined a *competence model* and a *communication model*. The competence model
is responsible for executing tasks and the communication model handles all interactions
between agents and other systems. The communication model has interpretation, conversation and ontology handling functions using knowledge of messages, languages and
protocols (see Section 4.2.2). Next to communication, information about others actors
is to be acquired and stored. Therefore we defined the *environment model*, which gives
the agent a view on the world it operates in (e.g. which other agents and systems it can
interact with, see Section 4.2.5).
    The process of task execution proceeds three steps: *tasks identification*, *task plan-
ning* and *actual task execution*. To determine what tasks have to be performed, we defined
the *self model*. This model gives the agent an idea of what the agent is doing (e.g. what are
its tasks, goals, jobs, states, capabilities) and should be able to facilitate self-monitoring,
self-maintenance and self-steering (see Section 4.2.3). The planning of the execution of
tasks is the concern of the *planner model* that enables an agent to autonomously decide
how to spend its time. The model can contain various planning strategies for meeting the

dimension	concept	capability	learning
communication	messages, language, protocol, message content ontology	interaction, converse, ontology handling	interpretation
competence	tasks, methods, domain knowledge	task execution memory	skills
self	identity, name, goals, state role, competences, location	introspection, reflection, life cycle management, instruct planner	self perception
planner	autonomy, agenda	task selection, execution control, monitoring, emergency handling	emergencies, task performance
environment	actors, perception, sensors and effectors	reaction, actor modeling	accumulate and explore environment

Table 4.1
The five dimensions of the 5C model with concepts, capabilities and learning abilities as rationale for the breakdown of an agent into the five dimensions. The relations between the models depend on individual designs. One example of an agent design according to the 5C model is described in Section 4.4. Considerations when to use or omit a model are given in Table 4.3 (p.96).

agent's goals (see Section 4.2.4). Finally, the *competence* model contains the methods and knowledge that enables an agent to execute the tasks it is designed for (see Section 4.2.1). How each of the dimensions will eventually be given shape, depends on the particular kind of agent or the particular application.

In the remainder of this chapter we discuss the dimensions in more detail. For every dimension we discuss the generalization of different types of agent capabilities categorized in *concept*, *capability* and *learning abilities*. An overview of the dimensions is given in Table. 4.1. We should note that the 5C model is intended to be a conceptual model, rather then a technical framework. Most of the issues we try to allocate into 5 dimensions - e.g. "reflection" or "actor modeling" are not resolvable in general terms. Technical implementations can be be partial and biased to the agent application in mind. One example of an agent design conform the 5C model is discussed in Section 4.4.

4.2.1   Competence Model

An agent is designed to perform - even to excel in - one or a small number of **tasks**. We see task offering as service offering. An agent can either perform the task or service itself if it is part of the agent. Otherwise, the agent can consult another non-agent system, such as a legacy system [Genesereth and Ketchpel, 1994]. In Sections 4.4.4 and 5.3.3 (p.105), we discuss how agents can access legacy systems.

The designer expects the agent to be *competent* and *rational* in this task performance [Newell, 1982]. Agent types are often named after the tasks they are designed for, such as "searcher", "analyst", "bidder", "buyer" and "seller". For example, for knowledge-based agents (i.e. agents that perform knowledge intensive tasks) the competence model can consist of **problem-solving methods**. For tasks of a different nature, it can rely on other techniques such as algorithmic models, databases or statistical models. The competence model finally encompasses the **domain knowledge** required for the correct execution of its problem-solving methods.

A *competence model* can embody the capabilities: **task execution** and **memory function**. Task execution is the ability to do the job (purpose) it was designed for. Tasks can have a reactive or a proactive nature. The memory capability represents the ability to exchange information between different task instantiations. It usually requires that information acquired during the execution of one task instantiation is preserved for an extended period of time. An example of the use of this capability is an internal blackboard, which is used by tasks to exchange information.

The sub-capabilities **information accumulation** and **forgetting** can further characterize the memory capability. Information accumulation refers to the ability to accumulate information during a particular task execution, but also to the ability to store and retrieve that information. Forgetting may have both pragmatic and functional purposes. When information is accumulated at a high rate, there may be an information or storage overload. To overcome this pragmatic constraint, information that looses relevance, may be forgotten. A second, more functional, aspect occurs when old information starts to mislead the problem solver because of changes in the environment.

Learning in the competence model reflects the agent's ability to become better in its task execution capability, i.e. **skilled** by virtue of experience. Maes puts a lot of emphasis on learning, e.g. learning by being trained [Maes, 1994]. She argues that learning is the most efficient way for an agent to become competent and trustworthy, above the two alternative strategies of having the end user program the agent at the one hand or having a knowledge engineer design the competence model at the other hand.

4.2.2   Communication Model

Besides being able to perform its task(s), an agent is expected to master the ability to **communicate** (social competence cf. [Gaspari and Motta, 1994, Wooldridge and Jennings, 1995]). Communication implies **interaction** and interaction implies **sending and receiving messages**. Messages are expressed in an **Agent Communication Language**, such as FIPA-SL0 [FIPA, 2002i]. **Protocols** prescribe the sequence of messages. The vocabulary used in messages is defined in **message content ontologies** [FIPA, 2001].

Next to message exchange, communication also includes **interpretation** of the message, **validation** that a message has been correctly interpreted and taking **corrective measures**. It is argued that communicating agents use languages comparable to a knowledge level of abstraction [Gaspari and Motta, 1994, Bradshaw, 1997]. This means that agents use communication primitives which support the use, request and supply of knowledge independently of implementation-related aspects.

The *communication model* is responsible for the following capabilities, **interaction, converse**[1] and **ontology handling**. Interaction refers to a situation where two (or

---

[1]By converse we mean "talking" with other agents.

more) agents get in contact to exchange information or requests. The message is the typical vehicle for interaction. It stands for the total package which is exchanged between agents in an interaction. *Converse* is seen as a small process, which may involve one or a small number of interactions, in order to accomplish a shared understanding of the intention of the originator of the conversation. Interaction can be further specified by the sub-capabilities **generate message**, **send message**, **receive message**, **parse and verify message syntactically** and **interpret and verify message semantically**.

Generating messages involves the creation of new messages upon demand in order to send messages to external actors (such as information sources, others agent and users). Sending messages is the ability to engage in an interaction as the taker of the initiative. Receiving messages is the ability to engage in an interaction for which the initiative was taken by another actor. Parsing or syntactic verification involves verifying whether the format of an incoming message is understandable. Interpretation or semantic verification involves verifying whether the content or meaning of an incoming message is understandable, and extracting that content from the message. The Speech Acts theory (cf. [Searle, 1969]) is an example of a theory to attribute intention to messages, which can be applied for example when negotiating with other agents on the basis of arguments. We discuss the Speech Act theory in detail in Section 6.3 (p.142).

When a conversation requires multiple interactions between agents, it becomes important to keep a conversation trace of the ongoing communication. Otherwise, the agent cannot distinguish an incoming message which is a continuation of an ongoing conversation from an incoming message which starts a new conversation. Ontology handling refers to the ability to work with shared conceptualizations, see Section 6.3 (p.142) for a detailed discussion on agents and ontologies.

Learning for the communication model, in its most natural form, would denote the ability of an agent to improve its ability of **interpretation** of messages. For example, when two agents use a partially different ontology, the communication may be initially very difficult; i.e. each communication requires several interactions to accomplish this common understanding. The model may gradually improve its communication abilities by incrementally learning the ontology which is used by the other agents, or by broadening one's own ontology.

4.2.3 Self Model

An agent has an **identity** including a description of its **name**, **goal**, **state**, **organizational role**, **own capabilities** and **computational location**. If an agent moves from one server to another, we would assume it to be still the same agent. This implies that the physical process that runs the agent cannot be a part of its identity.

The *self model* entails the following capabilities: **introspection**, **reflection**, **life cycle management** and **instruct planner**. With the capability introspection we refer to the ability to inspect or inform about the agent's global status: what is the list of the agent's current task instantiations, what is the status of those task instantiations, what are the agents goals, capabilities or objectives, what is the agent's current occupation, abilities, experience, memory, etc., see also [Maes, 1986]. With reflection we refer to the agent's ability to reason about and to act upon the agent's performance: e.g. "how well did I solve this task?" and " how can I do this better?", see also [Maes, 1998].

The life cycle management capability refers to the ability to follow life cycles as defined in 3.4.1 (p.63). For example, in Figure 3.15 (p.63), a life cycle containing a *platform life cycle*, the *instruction life cycle* and the *execution life cycle* is given. The self model knows in what state the agent is and to what states to traverse. With the capability instruct planner the self model translates internal goals to instructions to the planner model. An example of this capability is given in Figure 4.5, where the self model instructs the planner model to plan a goal.

The self model stands for the agent's perception of its own being and state (i.e. introspection). In its simplest form, the self model contains just a collection of ongoing tasks (monitoring). But for all but the most basic forms of autonomy and problem-solving more elaborate forms of reflection will become an issue. To give a very simple example, when an agent receives a request to perform a certain task within a limited time (say 20 seconds), the agent should be able to judge whether there is a fair chance to be able to perform the task within the given time. This judgment requires reflective reasoning about the current life cycle state, the agent's own competence (i.e. tasks from the competence model), the role the agent plays in an organization and goals of the agent. An agent can have long term and short term goals. Most of the goals can remain implicit, i.e. be hidden in the agent's design. However, in more complex cases agents will have to reason explicitly about their goals, trying to reach their goals in the most rational way. A good example is the Belief-Desire-Intention model [Rao and Georgeff, 1995].

The applied learning method for self perception could make use of the agent's history. It could reason about what strategy did fit best a certain problem, what tasks and methods were applied and whether the identity of the agent changed. Ideally, using reflection the agent should be able to change the self model's behavior in order to optimize its performance.

4.2.4   Planner Model

One of the most distinguishing features of an intelligent software agent is **autonomy** [Gaspari and Motta, 1994, Wooldridge, 2002]. Whereas an expert system is designed to perform a task in a rational way but anchored in a fixed environment that determines its behavior or process, the software agent's rationality is extended to a number of decisions including: whether to perform, when to perform, how often to perform and how long to perform the task. Furthermore, an agent has control over its own actions and internal state [Castelfranchi, 1995]. The liberty given to the agent to make decisions that go beyond deciding about how to do the given task, is called *autonomy*. When autonomy is well operationalized, it enables the use of an agent for tasks that require more responsibility, that span a large time frame, or that take place in a less controlled environment. The planning of the agent's tasks can be represented by an **agenda**.

Although autonomy relies heavily on all of the dimensions described in the 5C model, we consider the *planner model* to be the component that is most prominent responsible for autonomous decision-making. The planner model is the model that enables the agent to reason about the tasks (jobs) on his agenda; i.e. not the generic tasks for which the agent is designed, but the concrete task instantiations or jobs during the agent's lifetime. The planner model is hence intended in a broader sense than the traditional AI conception of planning, which is constructing a series of activities that can lead the agent towards a desired goal state, although such a traditional AI planning function may sometimes be a part of it. Capabilities of the planner model are: **task selection, execution control, time monitoring** and **emergency handling**. Task selection is concerned with the next task to be executed or continued. Execution control is concerned with starting and stopping the execution of task instantiations. It can be further refined as follows: **Task launching**: starting the execution of a task. **Task interruption**: putting an unfinished task on hold. Finally, **task reactivation**: restarting a task which was put on hold.

For non-instantaneous tasks, time monitoring is an important capability of the planner model. This capability involves keeping an eye on the clock and triggering clock-sensitive events. An example of a clock-sensitive event is a task that needs to be executed every hour. Another example of a potential clock sensitive event is a task that is waiting for the input from another agent. In uncontrolled environments it may be the case that the input never arrives, which should not go unnoticed. In such cases, waiting for an input is a clock-sensitive event.

Emergency handling has to do with dealing with all kind of abnormal circumstances with respect to the execution of tasks. Typical cases of emergency handling are: **Conflict handling**: i.e. handling priority conflicts; **Time-bound handling**: i.e. detecting and reacting to task executions that do not end within the expected time frame (e.g. any-time algorithms); and **Handling long waiting times:** i.e. detecting and reacting to tasks that are on hold for a long time waiting for particular external input that does not seem to arrive (e.g. life-lock).

Learning in the planning area can deal with getting better in **handling emergencies** or surviving in dynamic environments. When dealing with different agents in dynamic environment, a lot of things can go wrong, for example another agent does not behave as expected and sends the wrong data. For that reason, the agent should apply strategies to resolve these exceptions. Another learning strategy is to accumulate data about how well **tasks perform** with respect to execution times and success ratio. With this data, the planner model can inform the self model about the agent's performance.

4.2.5   Environment Model

Software agents are situated in one or more environments (cf. [Nwana, 1996]) where they can interact with other **actors**, such as agents, people, external systems and information sources. The agent in its simplest form has an environment model that maintains links to all external actors with which the agent interacts. This can be seen as a kind of world model. When mobile agents travel in a complex, non-predictable environment, they may not have an accurate model of the environment. The environment model then becomes a model of the agent's **perception** of its environment (beliefs), rather than a model of the environment itself. An environment model may finally implement direct interaction with the environment through **sensors and effectors**.

The environment model includes the capabilities: **reaction, perceive, actor modeling**. One of the properties characterizing an agent is *reactiveness*, i.e. the ability to selectively observe its environment (which may be the physical world, a user, a collection of agents, the Internet, etc) and react [Bradshaw, 1997]. The environment model has to be able to extract the values of essential parameters from sensor information (perception) and translate parameter settings into commands of action. Etzioni et.al. describe their softbot's interface to the Internet with a strong analogy to a real robot, where the softbot's effectors include ftp, telnet, mail, etc., and sensor include Internet facilities such as archie, gopher and netfind [Etzioni and Weld, 1994].

In its simplest form, the environment model maintains contacts, a set of links to external actors (i.e. external information sources, other agents, users) or places. In FIPA-speak, it also contains a register of agent-descriptions. Sometimes an actor may also include the category of external information sources such as databases, web-pages or other processes. One step beyond knowing the roles of external actors is keeping a perception of their nature. User modeling is a typical example frequently mentioned in agent literature, but the concept can be broadened into actor modeling which also includes modeling another agent. Many examples of Internet exploring agents work with a model of their user, in which they store the user's goals, interests and preferences [Maes, 1994].

The environment model may define for each external actor how the actor needs to be approached. This can be registered in the form of interaction protocol definitions and shared communication languages. When agents cohabit within a complex social undertaking, for example as part of a multi-agent system architecture based on complex dynamics principles, they may not refer to one another directly, but only by virtue of the role each one of them plays in the total organization. A contract is a set of mutually agreed obligations and related authorizations between two agents about services provided to each other, together with rules [Verharen, 1997]. The agent has to keep track of its contracts with other agents.

In a dynamic or open environment, the environment is often not, or not completely, defined beforehand. In such a situation, the agent must be able to build up its own perception of the environment. This may imply finding out which other agents are around, which information systems are around, what the role of other agents is, etc. A particular form of environment learning that is already applied in practice today, is user model learning. In addition, physical agents have to model their environment in a certain geometric representation of the real world. Also models of other agents can be learned. Two possible learning strategies can be distinguished; **accumulate environment** and **explore environment**. With accumulate environment, the agent is incrementally learning about the environment as the agent is interacting with the environment for other purposes. With explore environment, the agent is pro-actively interrogating the environment to find out more about it. Mobile agents in an e-commerce application, arriving at a marketplace to do their business may not have the time to incrementally accumulate all information about the environment. Therefore, mobile agents can use world models provided by already present (possibly static) agents.

4.3 The 5C Architecture

Each model in the 5C model can be seen as a process collaborating with the other processes through internal messaging mechanisms, which are standardized cooperation patterns forming the glue between the models. The implementation of each of the five models is open to the particular application.

A possible approach is the structure preserving design principle. In this approach the five dimensions of the 5C model are mapped onto five parallel Java thread objects in a Java architecture. At the implementation level, each thread has a to-do list. This corresponds to the objects with "asynchronous mailbox semantics" design pattern, meaning that every model is a separate computational process with its own control and has a mailbox (i.e. to-do box) that it uses to communicate with other processes [Schmidt et al., 2000]. The to-do boxes play an important role because they serve as a medium between the threads and they organize the interaction between the different threads. With this approach the computation that takes place within each threads is de-coupled. The to-do boxes are implemented as databases with records representing incoming messages. Besides that, every variable is also stored in a model state database. Forwarding a message from one model to another means that the sending model adds a record to the to-do box of the receiving model. This ensures that when the agent or a model (i.e. Java thread) goes down, the state can be restored. Every action of a model is logged in a log file, for both maintenance reasons and tracking and tracing of flows within the agent.

In order to illustrate the working of the threads, a workflow has been described in Figure 4.1. Note that the environment thread has not been illustrated because it does not play a role in this particular workflow. Imagine the following scenario: A request-message has been sent by this agent to agent B. As a result, Agent B has sent an response to the request-message. This message enters the to-do box of the communication thread[2]. The communication thread forwards the message to its parser. The parser, while checking its syntactical validity, also makes a quick check to see whether this agent is indeed the intended receiver. For this it uses the identity component of the self-thread. When the message is parsed into an internal message, the dispatcher puts the internal message in the to-do box of the self-thread.

The self-thread picks the message from the to-do box, and gives it to the conversation manager. The conversation manager detects whether the message is a response to an existing conversation or not. The schema above assumes that it belongs to an existing conversation. The conversation manager also checks with the capability manager to find out how to process the message. In this case the content of the message contains an answer to a previous request, therefore the message is put in the to-do box of the planner-thread.

The planner-thread picks up the internal message from its to-do box and forwards it to its request manager. Normally, because it is an existing conversation, it should be a reply to an existing request. The existing request belongs to a waiting job on the planner's agenda. The planner takes this job and reactivates it. (If the competence-thread is doing something else at that moment, the planner marks this job as "ready-to-be-reactivated".)

---

[2]Technically, this is realized by an agent platform.

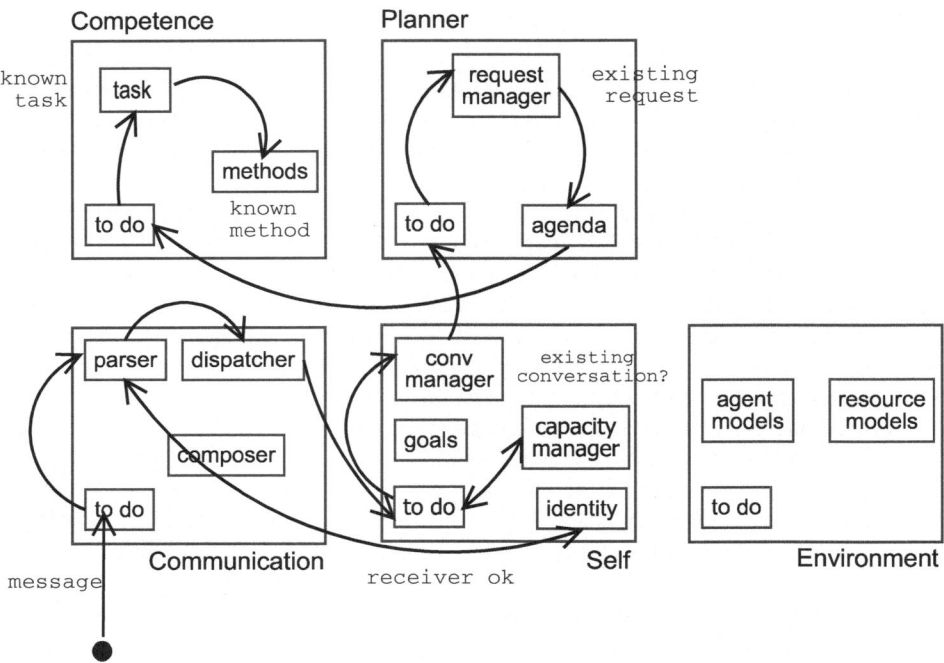

Figure 4.1
Workflow of the five Java threads showing how an incoming message (that contains a reply on a previous sent request message) is processed.

The reactivated job is put in the to-do box of the competence thread. The competence-thread picks the job from the to-do box, finds the task from which this job is an instantiation, and the associated method. Finally, this method is activated. The environment-thread has not been mentioned in this scenario, because there was already a conversation going on with a known agent. For the coding part of the agent, typical OO-inheritance was used.

4.4   International Insurance Traffic

In this section, we discuss a multi-agent system that has been develop using the 5C model. This system is operational since April 2001 and runs across different insurance companies to facilitate cross-border claim handling related to "Green cards" [van Aart et al., 2002b].

Green card traffic is the process where insurance companies exchange data for handling car accidents involving parties from different countries. Every country has a national green card institute responsible for handling international car accidents. The execution of green card traffic is handled by commercial insurance companies. 17 insurance companies in Europe form an international network of claim handling business called Euphoria. Claim handling works as follows: suppose a Dutch driver gets involved in a car accident in Germany. The accident is reported to a German insurance company, in this case, R+V in Wiesbaden (D). To settle the case, R+V will contact its Dutch partner, i.e. Interpolis in Tilburg (NL). R+V will open a new file containing information related to the incident and the involved partner. For this R+V has to contact Interpolis to verify whether the Dutch party is insured and covered. After exchanging details of the accident, the two bureaus will settle the case, determining who has to pay the costs.

The European Commission has recently enacted the so-called 4th guideline: *Fourth Motor Insurance Directive (Directive 2000/26/EC)* -operational from February 2003, that obliges all EU insurance companies to execute and settle insurance claim submissions within three months after the date of accident. If they do not, they receive a penalty as high as the total amount of the costs. Costs range from an average of 6,000 EURO for only material damage to 100,000 EURO for physical injury. The time needed and personnel costs involved are not included in these amounts. Interpolis is confronted with 3,500 cases involving international insurance takers each year. The average settlement time per case is approximate six months, involving four to six contacts at different times and dates between foreign insurance companies. The reasons for the settlement duration are due to the internal bureaucratic process of the insurance companies.

The problem is that all systems (back-offices) used by insurance companies are heterogeneous, in the sense that data is stored and used differently. Information between these companies is exchanged by hand, meaning that claim handlers within the network communicate largely by telephone, fax and mail. The first alternative suggested was to develop a central database in Brussels, where all companies upload their data, and where every company can retrieve data. One disadvantage of this approach is that every company has to make mappings from its back-office data to this central database including a synchronization mechanism. The largest objection however is that companies would have access to data of other companies, which can be used for other purposes. For example, one company could start to contact customers of other companies, offering their services. Therefore, the system should offer an arms length relationship between the involved parties: *"you can ask me questions, but you cannot have access to my information"*.

The second alternative was to give web-based access to every individual back-office. One problem here is that the definition of a single interface would lead to endless discussion on topics such as: in what language should it be? What functionality should it have? Furthermore, not all companies are able or willing to submit to a single technical implementation of the interface, and many companies are not ready to be on the Web. The major drawback is that the information still needs to be transferred manually between back-offices, because users have to copy information from a web-client into a back office client. The third alternative was to take an agent-based approach. Every company can connect to a network of information exchanging agents.

The KIR system[3] has been developed by Acklin using the agent metaphor, because it provides a natural and flexible way to reason about distributed heterogeneous components, processes and coordination [Bond and Gasser, 1988]. Business logic is encoded into the agents, on the one hand to assure the most fluent throughput of the process at stake; and on the other hand to respect the main business requirement, i.e. confidentiality. Furthermore, an agent-based system is far easier to extend in terms of functionality than a classical solution.

4.4.1 Approach

On the level of the business case we had to deal with the following functional constraints: (1) *No transparency in the market*, so it should not be possible that agents can query other agents' databases to retrieve data without a case, i.e. ensuring the arms length relationship; (2) The agents should have a high level of *robustness*, i.e. when the system or a part of the system goes down for some reason, it should go up without any problems, and go on with the tasks it was doing at the moment of the crash; and (3) The agents have to *operate within time windows* and should have *startup* and *shutdown procedures*. The back-office systems of Interpolis are operational from 6 a.m. to 11 p.m. from Monday till Saturday. All systems are started up and shut down via batch processes. The reason is that during the down period of the systems, maintenance can be performed, new systems can be installed and hardware can be replaced.

From a software engineering point of view we had to deal with the following technical/political constraints: (1) The agents should work with *existing infrastructure* of Interpolis and its 16 partners in Euphoria; and (2) The agents can have *no direct access to the back-offices*. The IT-department of Interpolis did not want to have an "exotic" piece of software, like agents "touch" its systems, because they do not have control over it.

To meet these concerns and constraints of the business case we applied the following approach. First, the process wherein companies have to cooperate to handle car accident settlements was analyzed. Second, the activities that the agents should perform are mapped on agent behavior and agent communicative acts framed in agent sequence diagrams. Third, an interface was designed to enable the agent to have (controlled) access to the required functionality, like finding, retrieving, creating and updating records in the database of the back-office. Finally, all pieces are put together in the KIR system which is presented in Section 4.4.5.

---

[3]KIR stands for KBC, Interpolis and R+V, respectively Belgium, Dutch and German insurance companies of the Euphoria network.

4.4.2 Green Card Traffic

The interaction between insurance companies starts after the report of damage caused by a car accident involving parties from different countries. The assignment of the handling bureau and paying bureau role in case of an accident involving drivers from different countries is done with the following rules. The company located in the country where an accident takes place, is the *handling bureau*. The company located in the country of the foreign driver, is the *paying bureau*. The handling bureau will start the settlement and sends a request for information (i.e. handling traffic) to the paying bureau. The paying bureau will respond to the handling (i.e. paying traffic).

Green card traffic starts when the manager of the "foreign claims department" of a handling bureau receives a report via one of the various channels including call centers, mail or fax. This report includes basic information (license plate, policy number and date of the accident), damage forms, police reports and witness declarations. The manager will delegate it to one of the claim handlers. The claim handler will open a new file in the claims database and starts identifying the involved parties. First the local party will be identified, using the green card number and license plate number. Next the foreign party has to be identified, checking whether this party is known and whether the information is consistent. For that, the claim handler of the handling bureau will contact its foreign partner, i.e. the paying bureau, sending green card number and license plate number of their insurance taker. If the party is not know, the claim handler will report this back to the manager who will end this process and starts another process that we will not discuss here. If the party is known, the handler will update the local file and will ask its partner whether the case is known. If the case is known to the partner it will send the date and its local claim number (database primary key) including all dedicated information to the handler. If the case is not known, the partner will create a new file and will also send the new local claim number to the handler. A part of this process is illustrated in Figure 4.2, drawn as a standard UML activity diagram.

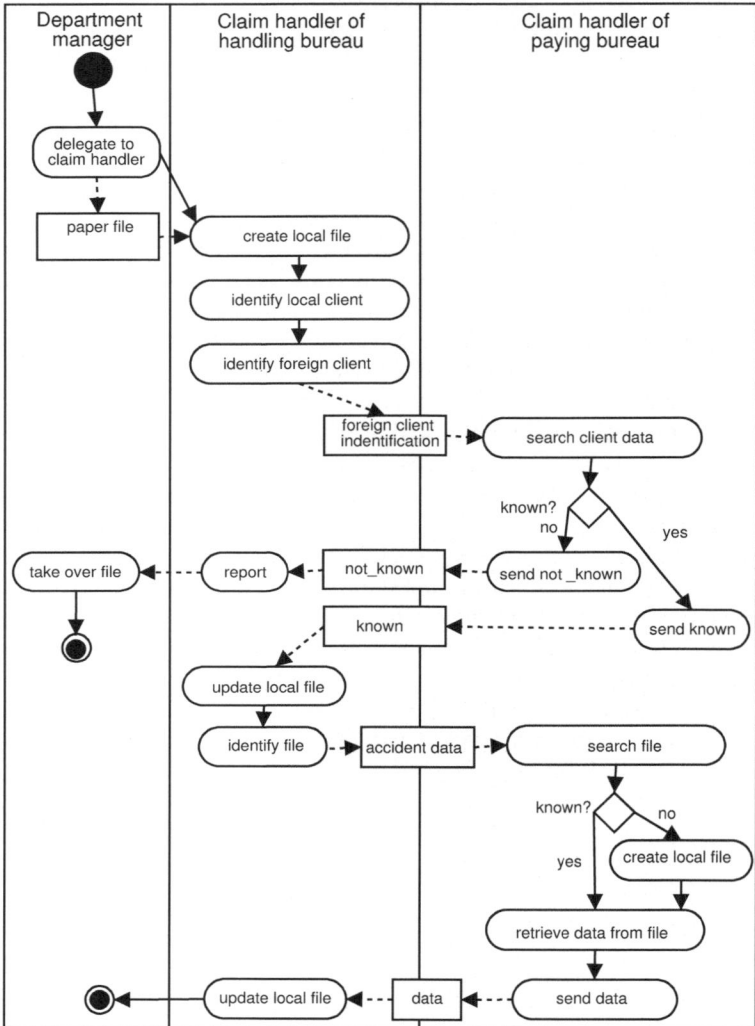

Figure 4.2
Green Card Traffic Process illustrated in a UML activity Diagram. The swim lanes represent the job allocation amongst actors. The rounded boxes show the jobs (activities), the square boxes show the resources, the straight lines show the direction of the sequence flow (control) and dotted lines show the direction of the resource flow (data flow).

4.4.3 Agent Collaboration

We mapped the green card traffic process on an agent sequence diagram in AUML introduced by [Odell et al., 2000]. The Green Card operations are illustrated in Figure 4.3 showing the handling and paying role and their pattern of interactions.

Two packages show the two main processes: (1) client identification using green card number and license plate and (2) case identification, using policy number and local claim number. A package shows the "agent interaction protocol" (AIP) used in this system for enabling the cooperation between the agents, where an AIP describes communication patterns as an allowed sequence of messages between agents and the constraints on the content of those messages. Here existing AIPs are placed in sequence to enable the process as described in Section 4.4.2. The AIPs used are all based on the FIPA REQUEST-protocol [FIPA, 2002h].

Communicative acts (CA) make up the process between a handling and paying bureau, and replace the interaction between humans by way of speech and handwriting into communication by agents as illustrated in Figure 4.3. The idea is that the manager of the department delegates the two identification tasks to the agent instead of a claim handler. The handling and paying bureau are here called *handler* and *payer*. It starts with a REQUEST-message for identification of the client. The identification contains a license plate and green card number. The payer validates the identification and can respond with: (1) a FAILURE-message containing *not_known*, which means that the client is not known. In many cases this is caused by typical errors such as data entry errors in the license plate or policy number as fed by the paper reports; or (2) an INFORM-message containing a policy number, meaning that the payer has identified the local insurance taker. Then a REQUEST-message for identification of the claim is sent. With this the handler asks for all known data from the file of the payer. The payer can respond with: an INFORM-message containing a policy number, which means that the payer has either created a new file with the data and locally know data, or has already created a file for this case. The latter can happen when the insured party has already registered this accident, before the handler asks for it. In both cases the payer will send a claim number, which is the key to the file of the accident.

4.4.4 Interface To The Back-Office System

There are a number of ways to give access to legacy systems. The main concern of the insurance companies is the security of their data and the stability of their back-offices. For that we built a transducer in the sense of [Genesereth and Ketchpel, 1994]. In Section 5.3.3 (p.105), we discuss the use of a transducer in interoperability problems in detail. This transducer maps instructions from the agent to the back-office and results from the back-office to the agent. This approach has the advantage that the agent does not need to have knowledge of the back-office, it only requires knowledge of the transducer. A more important advantage is that when the agent has to get access to other back-offices, only the back-office side of the transducer has to be altered. The transducer at Interpolis has access to a separate database where instructions and reports are written and read by the

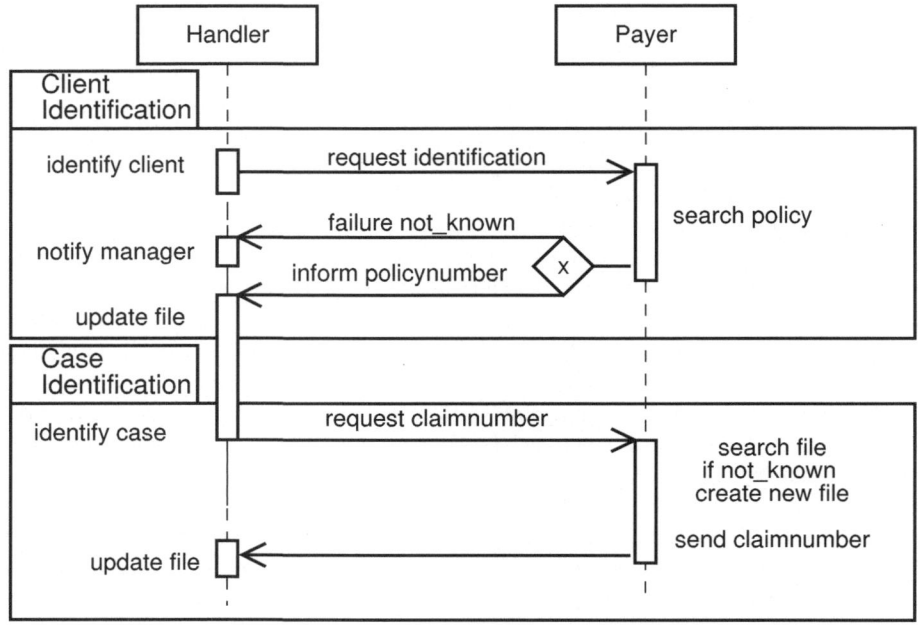

Figure 4.3
Green Card Traffic operation design in an AUML sequence diagram showing patterns of interaction within the operation. The dotted arrowed lines represent lifelines of positions. The arrowed lines show interactions and the packages show the applied agent interaction protocols.

agent. In this way the agent only has indirect access to the back-office, which in the case of Interpolis is built in "Powerbuilder" using a "Sybase" database.

The transducer between the agent and the back-office enables the agent to execute a number of actions: (1) `validate identification` using green card number and license plate number, (2) `search file` by policy number, (3) `create file` using policy and license plate number, (4) `retrieve data from file` using policy number, and (5) `update file` using policy number and received data.

4.4.5   The Kir System

The integration of the agents and the transducer results in the following architecture as illustrated in Figure 4.4. As shown every insurance company has installed one agent with a specialized transducer that is able to route handling traffic and paying traffic. This architecture provides not only a communication medium for the designer and builder at Interpolis and Acklin, but also the end user of the system, the foreign claims department of Interpolis. The metaphor of actual communicating and reasoning entities using back-

model	function	domain
communication	validate messages, request identification request claim number, inform policy number	REQUEST-Protocol Green Card Traffic Interactions
competence	case identification, client identification, update file	transducer
self	determine role, instruct planner monitor requests	paying bureau, handling bureau monitor rules
planner	task selection, plan tasks	agent's agenda
environment	authorize agents	authorized agents

Table 4.2
The five models of the KIR agent split up in *function* and *domain*. The capabilities of the agent are decomposed into "functions". The elements in the "domain" column represent possible values and value ranges within the agent's domain related to the agent's capabilities.

offices (also called virtual employees) helped to explain the architecture of the system. Furthermore, it aided to show how and where design choices were made with respect to the functional and technical constraints.

The KIR agent is a specialization of the 5C model (see Table 4.2) and its accompanied message flows as described in Section 4.3. The communication model is instructed with the AIPs as described in Section 4.4.3 meaning that it validates incoming messages from other agents. If it does not understand the agent sends a NOT_UNDERSTOOD-message back. When it does not expect a message, the agent replies with a FAILURE-message. The self model has knowledge of the two roles of handling bureau and paying bureau. The planner model will select the appropriate task on the basis of a received message or an impulse from the back office system. The environment model holds a list of agents, i.e. the agents of 17 partners in the Euphoria network that are authorized to interact with the KIR agent. Furthermore the competence model has access to the transducer, from where it can retrieve and update information from the database of the back-office.

The interaction between the five models of the 5C model, in case of receiving a REQUEST-message is given in Figure 4.5. The process starts when the communication model receives an external request. The communication model asks the environment model if the sender of the request is authorized to consult this agent. On the basis of the register of authorized agent, the environment model responds with "positive". The self model receives the content of the external request from the communication model, which contains in this case a request to identify a client (cf. first step in Figure 4.3). On the basis of this request, the self model instructs the planner model to plan the goal "client identification". The planner model chooses a strategy to perform this goal and instructs the competence model to perform the job "client identification". The competence model will send a message to the transducer buffer and waits for an answer. The answer of the transducer is analyzed by the competence model and forwarded to the communication model. The communication model constructs an answer on the basis of the original external request and the result of the competence model and forwards it to the sender of the original external request.

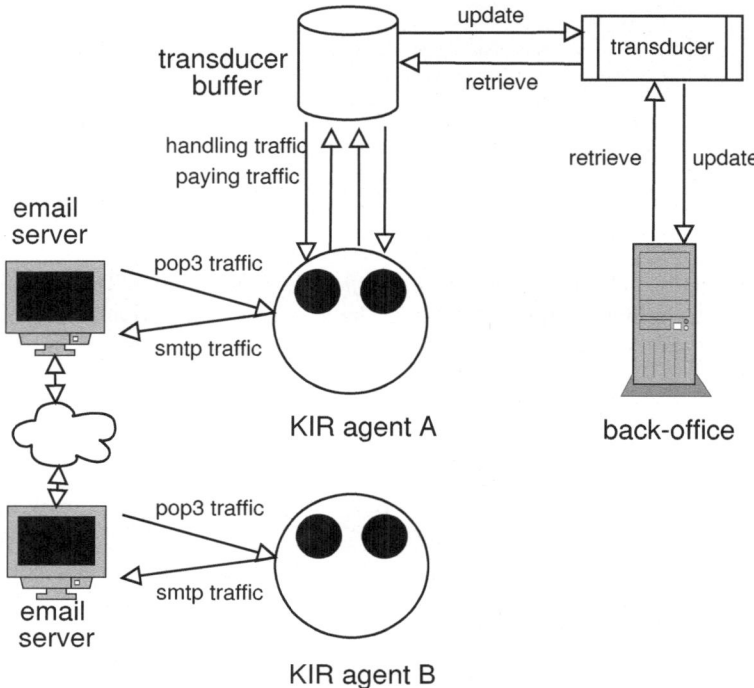

Figure 4.4
The architecture of the KIR system, showing two KIR agents and the coupling to the mail
server and the transducer.

4.4.6   Operationalization

The IT-department of Interpolis developed the transducer between the database of Interpolis and the agent within 30 days. The KIR agent was built in Java in less than 60 days.
The models are implemented as Java thread objects with asynchronous mailbox semantics, meaning that every model is a separate computational process with own control and
has a mailbox that it uses to communicate with other processes [Schmidt et al., 2000].
The mailboxes are implemented as databases with records representing incoming messages. Besides that, every variable is also stored in a model state database. Forwarding a
message from one model to another means that the sending model adds a record to the
mailbox database of the receiving model. This ensures that when the agent or a model (i.e.
Java thread) goes down, the state can be restored. Every action of a model is logged in a
log file, for both maintenance reasons and tracking and tracing of flows within the agent.
The use of databases ensures robustness and enables the requested daily startups and shutdowns. The arms length relationship constraint is handled in the environment model and
the self model. The environment model will filter out non-authorized messages, using a

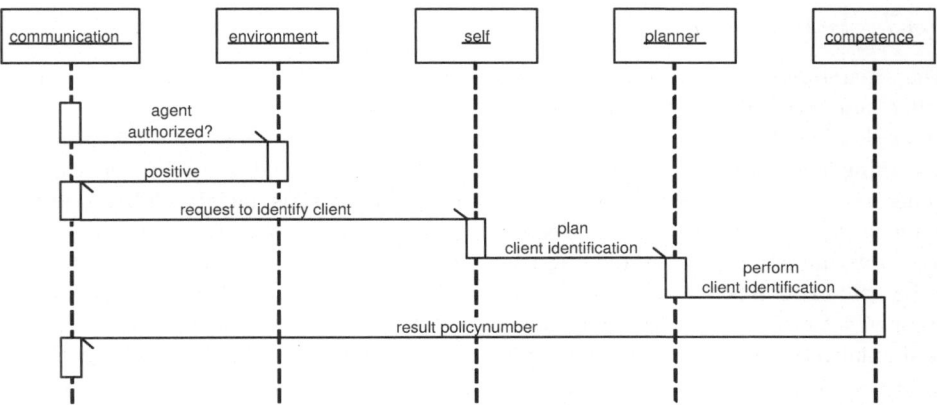

Figure 4.5

Sequence diagram that represents the interaction between the five models of the 5C model, implemented as Java threads, showing the process of receiving a REQUEST-message. This process starts when the communication model receives a message from another agent. When the sender of the request is authorized to consult this agent, the message is dispatched to the self model, which instructs the planner model to plan the goal "client identification". After choosing a strategy to perform this goal, the planner model instructs the competence model to perform the job "client identification". The competence model will send a message to the transducer buffer and waits for an answer, which is forwarded to the communication model. The communication model constructs an answer on the basis of the original external request and the result of the competence model and forwards it to the sender of the original external request.

(hard coded) list of authorized agent email addresses. The self model has a set of rules for alerting a claim handler, such as *"when an agent will ask for more than ten cases in the hour"* for identifying the querying of the database without an actual case, *"when an agent asks for more than three not existing cases or policies"* and *"when an agent sends a messages that cannot be read"*, for identifying possible hackers.

The insurance companies made the choice for e-mail as means of message transport between the agents. The reason was that e-mail functionality is present at all companies. Another option was the use of middleware, such as CORBA, but the state of the technology at several insurance companies prevented this. The format of the message is in a frame based like syntax for expressing feature-value pairs. Strict security is not applied to keep the hurdle of implementing the agency at a minimum. The system is relatively secure through the strict application of the format of subject and content, the small number of e-mail addresses in the system and the fact that the agent only communicates with agents it knows.

4.4.7   Extension

The separation of concern principle introduced in Section 4.3 appeals when we further refine and extend the application. For instance, the EU directive dictates that the procedures should not exceed the period of 3 months. If we want the agents to act consciously according to this principle, we need to refine the agent by providing it with more explicit goals (i.e. the goal to succeed with a procedure within 3 months) and the ability to reflect upon its own performance (i.e. to be conscious about how well it achieves its goals). Both functions can be realized by refining the agent's self model. If we also want the agent to be able to act when it observes that its goal is not met, we can then again extend the competence model to give the agent alternative methods for executing a job more rapidly. If alternatively we want to extend the payer role such that they can distinguish between different types of handlers, for instance handlers from insurance companies with whom there exists a special agreement to handle the claim in a less complicated manner, we can refine the environment model of the agent in order for it to be able to make this discrimination. In that case we also need to refine the agent's competence model as it needs to have knowledge of the alternative handling procedures as well. When adding an extra service (task or goal) to the agent, only the competence and self model have to be changed.

4.4.8   Evaluation

The KIR system presented is an industry-strength system based on the 5C model and techniques from the agent paradigm. The 5C model enabled the designers of the KIR system to focus on aspects of the software agent's intelligence separate from the rest of the agent's behavior and implementation taking into account functional and technical constraints. The KIR system showed that for the design of the two agent roles - the payer and the handler - the differences in agent capability is solely located in the competence model and self model; all of the other models are identical. In order to install an agent at an insurance company, only the transducer to the back-office had to be configured so that the agent has access to the right functionality and information. Furthermore, the authorization table of the environment model has to be filled properly.

The final implementation of the KIR system did not use an existing agent framework, such as JADE ([Bellifemine et al., 2001]), mainly because a large number of features in JADE were unnecessary for the KIR system. The functionality was too specific to use a general framework. Furthermore, existing frameworks at the time were not industry-strength. This means that there were no mechanisms for handling robustness, startups and shutdowns, and logging. Many of the existing frameworks rely on synchronous connections over TCP/IP. Insurance companies are very hesitant to let third parties make such connections from outside their internal networks, and some might even not be able to do so. The least common denominator used by every partner in the agency is e-mail. The introduction of the KIR system, immediately resulted in a work pressure release of three people at Interpolis and reduced the process of identification of client and claim from 6 months to 2 minutes. The 2 minutes here are an estimate of the time needed to send a number of agent messages using email. The bottleneck is the "polling" time of the involved email servers and the availability and latency of intermediate mail services.

4.5 Discussion

The 5C model can be used to understand and explain the added value of agent technology to a range of people involved, including software engineers and business managers. As such, the model can be a vehicle for designing and developing an intelligent software agent as a constituent of an agent application. The strength of the agent paradigm combined with the simplicity of the application design acted as an eye-opener. Firstly, the user (customer) has given the green light to develop and implement the KIR system at a European level. Secondly, the user has become a strong believer in the value of solutions in the insurance domain based on intelligent agents. Ultimately, we expect the 5C model to become the basis for an agent architecture and framework.

In developing of the KIR system, we made a first attempt to describe an agent model for designing intelligent agents. By "dissecting" the notion of "agent intelligence" into 5 dimensions and by listing the most common concepts, functions and learning opportunities of each of these, we presented a preliminary model of what it means for an agent to behave intelligently. The model can help to focus on individual characteristics of the agent's "intelligence" which are quite separated from the rest of the behavior. This explains why we formulated a conceptual model, rather then a technical framework. However, most of the issues we list along these 5 dimensions - e.g. "reflection" or "actor modeling" are not yet resolvable in general terms.

Given the current state of the art, most agents only need a communication model for interaction with other agents and a competence model to offer their services. The functionality of the other models is often hardwired. For example, there is not always a need to reason about the sender of a request. As with web services, most requests are accepted. Furthermore, simple agents do not need a sophisticated planning functionality, instead incoming request can be stacked on a traditional FIFO queue. The need to reason about own goals and identity is also not always necessary. On the basis of requirements of the overall system, the engineer can decide to combine functionality of the models into a limited set of models or to preserve the structure of the 5C model.

On the basis of the structure preservation guidelines (see Table 4.3) the designer can choose to preserve the structure of the 5C model or combine or merge functionalities into other models. The consequence of combining functionality of models into other models is that these models become extended. However, a lot of internal structures could be reused. Through the development of a series of agent applications along the lines prescribed by the 5C model, we observed the ease of reuse of different features of an agent implementation, facilitated through a separation sof concerns.

Thanks to its dissection of the notion of "intelligent agent behavior" the model tries to provides handles to focus on individual characteristics of the agent's intelligence quite separated from the rest of the behavior. For example, the functionality to receive a message, couple its content to a task and respond with a message containing the result of a task. Therefore, future research on the 5C model may include a library on reusable

model	consideration
communication	need to interact on the basis of protocols need to negotiate ability to speak an agent communication language ability to handle message content ontologies need to learn interpretation
competence	need to provide services need to execute tasks need to reason on domain knowledge need to connect to a legacy system need to learn skills
self	the agent plays a role in an organization need to instruct planner on the basis of explicit goals need to hold agent's state need to reason on identity need to monitor own actions need to reason on own competences
planner	need to behave autonomous need to deal with several tasks there are a lot of different jobs agent needs to operate in dynamic environment agent needs to learn from its errors
environment	other agents need authorization to get access to agent's services the agent community is not fixed need to manage contracts with other agents need to define new interaction protocols need to explore environment

Table 4.3
Preliminary guidelines for preserving models of the 5C model in a technical design.

model components.

Several agent architectures are comparable to the 5C model, however most of these architectures have a fixed structure. This means that all components (or models) are required in an architecture and that the interaction between the components is pre-determined. For example in the RETSINA agent architecture, there are four modules: *Communication and Coordination*, *Planning*, *Scheduling* and *Execution* [Sycara et al., 2003]. The Communication and Coordination module, which can be seen as a the 5C model's communication model, is responsible for interacting with other agents. The Planning module takes as input a set of goals and produces a plan that satisfies the goals, in the form of a task structure. This task structure is ordered by the Scheduling module. The Planning and Scheduling module show the same functionality of the 5C model's planning module. The Execution module monitors the task structure generation and ordering process and tries to ensure that tasks are carried out in accordance with computational and other constraints. This module resembles the 5C model's self model. It looks like the RETSINA model is designed from a planning and scheduling viewpoint. There is no functionality described for wrapping around legacy systems, which is handled in the 5C model's competence model. Furthermore, there is no explicit notion of an environment model. Finally, the RETSINA architecture is designed to operate within the RETSINA Multi-Agent System architecture[4]. It would take much time to compare all existing models with the 5C model. Therefore, we refer to existing surveys dealing with agent models and architectures[5].

Other research on agent models and architectures, such as SOAR and TAEMS[6] are integrated into research on multi-agent architectures which is typical technology-driven. This means that functionalities (e.g. the capabilities of the environment model) are embedded in the multi-agent system infrastructure, instead of in an individual agent. With the 5C model we have constructed a model from a representation-driven approach that can be used in isolation or on top of a multi-agent system infrastructure, such as a FIPA-compliant agent platform. For example in the KIR system, the agents operate in isolation without any multi-agent system infrastructure. In the IBROW system, see Section 5.3, the agents operate on top of the JADE platform.

---

[4]See http://www-2.cs.cmu.edu/~softagents/retsina_agent_arch.html.
[5]See www.cs.rmit.edu.au/agents, http://agents.umbc.edu and www.agentlink.org/resources/clearing-house.
[6]See www.isi.edu/soar and http://dis.cs.umass.edu/research/taems.

Chapter 5

Interoperation within a Complex Multi-Agent Architecture

This chapter is partly based on two deliverables of the IBROW project: D15 *Brokering in IBROW* and D10 *Interoperability* co-authored by B.J. Wielinga, A. Anjewierden and W. Jansweijer. The goal of the IBROW project (Intelligent Brokering on the Web, see http://ibrow.swi.psy.uva.nl) is to develop technologies for (semi-)automatic selection and configuration of new applications by reuse of existing services. Work on a multi-agent architecture capable of (semi-)automatic reuse of Problem-Solving Methods (PSMs) is discussed. Using the notion of separation of concerns, specialized agents are defined that operate within virtual environments. The agents within the architecture collaborate using specialized ontologies and collaboration patterns on top of an interoperability structure. A proof of concept is presented that explains the dynamics of parts of the architecture.

5.1 Introduction

This work addresses the problem of interoperation within a distributed architecture composed of heterogeneous components. The architecture supports the composition of applications from existing (web) services[1] that reside on the Web. These (web) services range from simple information retrieval from databases to knowledge-based consultation services. Such services can be seen as problem-solving methods (PSMs) for knowledge-based systems (KBSs) [Schreiber et al., 1999].

Most existing (web) services are distributed, heterogeneous and rigid, in the sense that they can not easily be configured. For example, the Semantic Web community has developed the view that it is unrealistic to assume that the content producers conform to a single standard and ontology. Different languages will be used for competence representations. Some service providers will use SOAP and WSDL as technical competence specification mechanism, others will use RDF(S) and OWL as ontology representation

---

[1] A web service is a software process that can be invoked remotely using web technology.

languages. The libraries of services (i.e. PSMs) of the future Semantic Web will be as heterogeneous as the current collection of search engines and other services that exist on the Web. Therefore, we need an approach that takes heterogeneity and distribution into account.

One way to deal with distributed and heterogeneous services is to apply intelligent software agents. Agents provide a natural way to describe distributed heterogeneous services [Genesereth, 1997]. For example, every service can be seen as an individual agent. Moreover, agent technology provides supporting technology and standards, including communication platforms, message transport mechanisms, message formats and white and yellow page services. Furthermore, the agent concept provides a metaphor to reason about processes and coordination [Bond and Gasser, 1988].

In our view, (web) services can conceptually be represented by agents. In order to exchange information between different services, agent wrappers can be built, so that these services can be unlatched to other services. The idea is that services can consult other services by using agents as intermediate. The rationale behind using agents is that they put an additional layer on existing services in order to have a common means for communication and coordination [Genesereth, 1997]. However, interoperability problems such as different communication languages, datamodels, infrastructures and coordination mechanisms still have to be solved.

Although web services and agents are already deployed in various domains, many of them tend to be inflexible: it is not possible to modify the underlying system, neither configure them for other domains, nor to integrate different services to produce new functionalities. Furthermore, most web services are heterogeneous and not designed to interact with other services. For example, Google provides a SOAP interface to its search services, which can be invoked from within an application[2]. However, the interface itself is not a service, it still needs to be embedded into another service.

In this chapter, we present an architecture that enables cooperation among agents capable of configuring and executing new applications composed of existing services present on the Web. Such an architecture could change the nature of using software from a centralistic compositional approach to a distributed (agent-based) plug and play process. The focus is on enabling interoperability among the agents that represent heterogeneous and distributed services.

This chapter discusses the outcomes of the IBROW project at several levels of detail. In Section 5.2 we discuss the IBROW approach in general. The Agent Architecture that supports the IBROW approach is presented in Section 5.3. In order to have the agents within the IBROW architecture interoperate, we outline the Interoperability Framework in Section 5.4. Section 5.4 discusses how we implemented the IBROW system. Finally, we present a proof of concept that explains the dynamics of parts of the IBROW system in Section 5.6.

---

[2]See www.google.com/apis/.

5.2 IBROW Approach

Reuse of knowledge and knowledge-based software components has always been an important goal of the knowledge engineering community. With the explosive growth of the Web, new opportunities for reuse arise: knowledge-intensive services and components can be offered on the Web. There are various PSMs, web services and resources available on the Web that could be linked together to form new applications. Several PSM libraries with corresponding operational components are now available [Fensel and Motta, 2001, Benjamins, 1993, Eriksson et al., 1995, Motta, 1999, Motta and Lu, 2000].

The goal of the IBROW project is to develop technologies for (semi-)automatic selection and configuration of PSMs[3] in order to compose new applications. The idea is that users interact with a service, specifying the task that an application should perform (i.e. goal specification). This service is called the *broker*, i.e. a service that mediates among demanding parties, such as users, and offering parties, such as PSM providers. Subsequently, the broker searches for PSMs on the Web and - if successful - configures an application that will solve the user's task [Benjamins et al., 1998].

In order to explain the IBROW approach, we divide its functionality into a number of *spaces*. A space is a virtual environment that clusters processes (such as agents and PSMs) and resources (such as libraries) that are distributed on the Web. Three spaces are defined: the *user space*, the *broker space* and the *execution space*, see Figure 5.1. The user interacts with the *user space* in order to formulate a goal for an application. A goal can be specified using the Universal Problem Modeling Language (UPML) framework [Fensel et al., 1999b].

The *broker space* is able to mediate between the user space and the many PSMs available on the Web, potentially capable of realizing the user's goal. The PSMs are organized in specialized PSM libraries, which provide competence descriptions to the broker space on request. These libraries are not part of the IBROW architecture, because these are offered by third parties. Therefore we did not define a *library space*. On the basis of the goal of the user, the broker space can configure custom-made applications using existing (heterogeneous and distributed) PSMs. For further reading on a centralized PSM broker we refer to [Benjamins et al., 1998].

The *execution space* is able to execute applications based on the output of the brokering process: the *application configuration*. Execution of applications involves invocation of PSMs and coordination over invocations of PSMs. The sequence of invocation and the coordination over it, is defined in a MAP (Multi-Agent Plan). This plan also handles the input/output mappings between the PSMs involved.

The problem now is that users, libraries and PSMs are distributed on the Web. Furthermore, the user, the broker and the execution spaces are too complex to build in one system. Therefore, we further separate the functions in each of the spaces into specialized agents.

---

[3]In the remainder, we use a very general notion of PSMs, consequently we see (web) services as PSMs.

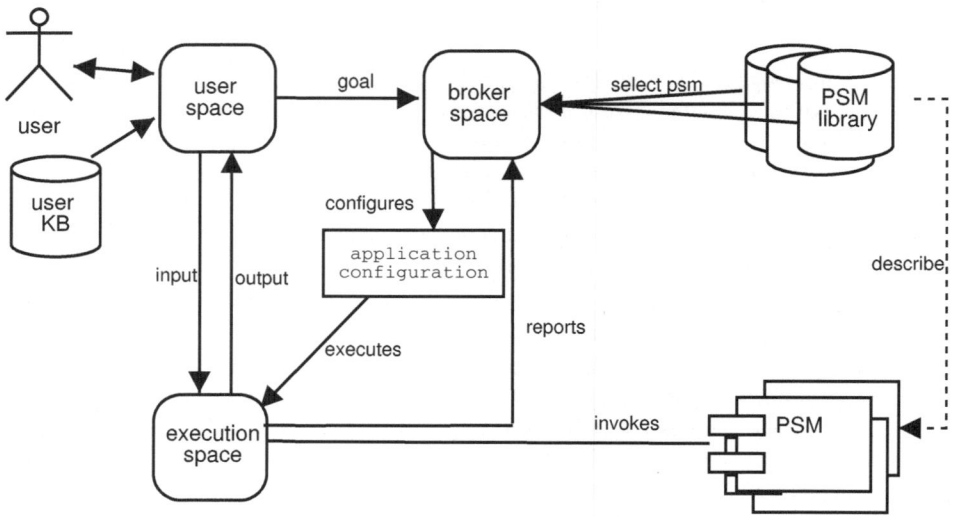

Figure 5.1
Features of the IBROW approach, showing the user space that mediates between the user and the broker space to establish a goal to be realized. Based of the goal specification, PSMs are selected from one or more PSM libraries and are configured into an executable application. The execution space will execute the application on the basis of input provided by the user KB.

5.3   Agent Architecture

In this section, we elaborate on the spaces defined above and define specialized agents that operate within the spaces. The idea is that the agents will not be integrated into one system. Rather the agents will be organized in a multi-agent architecture, see Figure 5.2.

The use of agents comes with a number of advantages. First, agents are capable of coupling distributed processes, without centralizing control. Using wrapping technology, an agent can form an interface between distributed processes, such as PSMs, and other agents [Genesereth and Ketchpel, 1994]. Secondly, specialized or generalized agents can easily replace existing agents. The reason for this is that agents do not share a common memory or common libraries of functions [Wooldridge, 2002]. Therefore, the replacement of one agent does not affect other agents. Finally, the control over the overall architecture is distributed. Every agent is responsible for a part of the overall functionality, because the required integration knowledge can also be distributed. For that reason, the agent is partially independent of other agents (i.e. autonomous). The remaining dependency between agents can be handled by coordination mechanisms where communication and flow of information is regulated.

We first discuss the agents that operate within the spaces. Next interoperation is

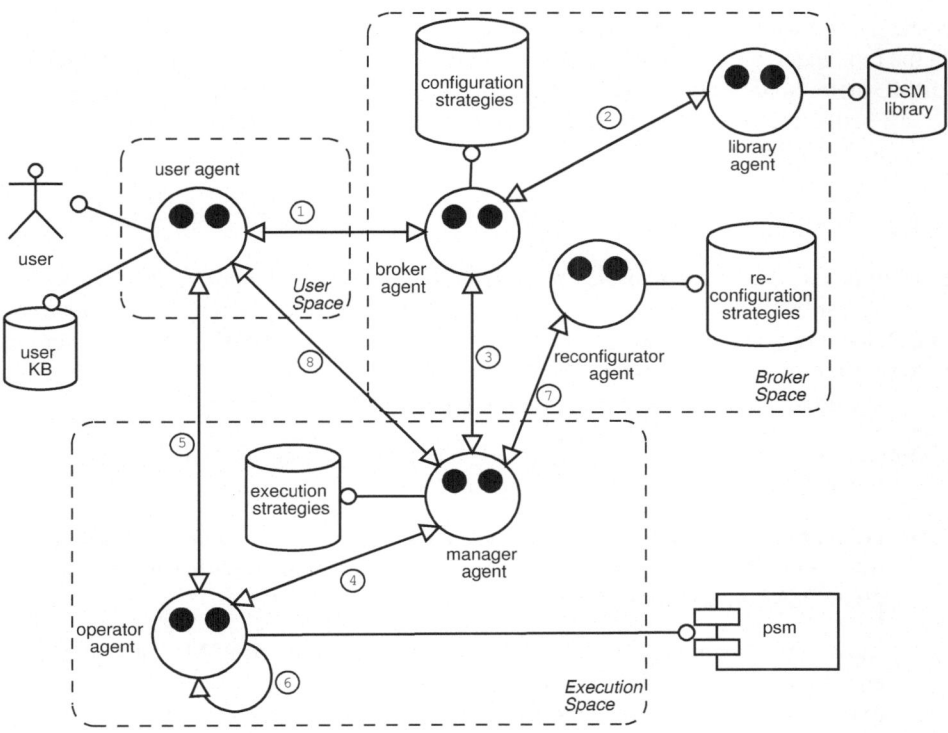

Figure 5.2
The IBROW multi-agent architecture showing the agents that operate within the user,
broker and execution space. The numbered lines (① - ⑧) represent collaborations between
agents, which are described in Table 5.3 (p.111).

discussed.

5.3.1 User Space

The end-users of the IBROW system interact with the user space. Since users are distributed on the Web, *user agents* are allocated to individual users. The user agent represents an end-user and hides the complexity of the overall system. Several variations on
the user agent related to the user's level of expertise are possible, ranging from novice to
expert user agents.

In order to acquire the goal specification and domain knowledge from the user, the
user agent uses an interface. For details on interfaces of the IBROW system we refer
to [Wielinga et al., 2003]. Furthermore, it passes goals to the agents in the broker space
and input to the agents in the execution space. The goal descriptions are in terms of
input and output roles, competence descriptions in terms of pre- and post-conditions, and

domain ontologies. The goal descriptions can be specified within the UPML framework. In the remainder, we do not discuss UPML in full detail. Details on UPML, including the UPML meta-model can be found in [Fensel et al., 1999b, Omelayenko et al., 2000].

Finally, the user agent presents results received from the agents in the execution space to the end-user.

5.3.2   Broker Space

PSM libraries and the actual broker process are located within the broker space. In order to locate PSMs, PSMs are clustered in specialized libraries. Every library agent represents one PSM library and provides PSM descriptions, expressed in UPML, to the broker on request. Library builders maintain the PSM libraries.

The broker space is responsible for the following tasks:

Maintain interaction with the user space. The user space delegates goals of users to the broker space.

Retrieve and select competence descriptions of suitable PSM candidates. PSM descriptions (in UPML) will be retrieved from PSM libraries, in order to select the appropriate PSMs to accomplish the user's goal.

Configure and adapapt the selected PSMs. Based on the selected PSMs, an application configuration is compiled. This configuration explains how the selected PSMs need to be configured. Possible configurations are the location of input and the required knowledge bases.

Delegate application configuration to the execution space. The broker space does not take care of the actual execution of the configuration. Therefore, it sends the application configuration to the execution space.

Inspect the outcome of execution space and reconfigure the application configuration. When the execution space has executed the application configuration, it reports to the broker space. Based on reconfiguration strategies (such as the Propose Critique Modify (PCM) algorithm), the broker space reconfigures the configuration (if necessary) and delegates it to the execution space.

The broker tasks can be with different levels of support to the user, ranging from giving interactive assistance in manual selection and configuration of PSMs, to the fully-automatic configuration of an intelligent problem solver. For example, manual selection and configuration of PSMs can be done with the Internet Reasoning Service[4], which supports the semi-automatic configuration of knowledge-based applications on the Web.

We have defined two types of brokers: the *Static Broker agent* and the dynamic broker agent: the *Reconfigurator*. The *static broker agent* defines the initial application configuration. After receiving a goal specification from the user agent, it contacts several

---

[4]See http://kmi.open.ac.uk/projects/irs.

library agents for PSM selection. From there, it constructs an application expressed in an application configuration. The application configuration is then delegated to the execution space.

The *Reconfigurator* helps the agents in the execution space to refine the configuration of the broker. This works as follows; the execution space reports (Propose) the output of an application configuration along with the application configuration itself to the Reconfigurator. The Reconfigurator evaluates (Critique) the output based on a set of criteria. The result of the evaluation is an altered (Modify) application configuration. The modified application configuration will be sent to the execution space. This process repeats until the set of criteria is satisfied. Examples of criteria are the quality and the quantity of the result set. When the Reconfigurator instructs a new configuration, the agents within the execution space take care of the execution. Otherwise, in case of acceptance, the agents within the execution space report the result set to the user agent.

5.3.3 Execution Space

The agents in the execution space are *Operators* and *Managers*. These two agent roles are based on the Operator and Manager roles as introduced in Section 2.2. Operators represent PSMs and are able to configure and invoke PSMs. The Manager is responsible for coordinating the Operators. The reason to use two agent types for the execution of an application configuration, is to separate the knowledge for invocation of the PSMs from knowledge for the coordination over the invocations of the PSMs. The advantage of this approach is that there is not one single complex agent responsible for the execution phase, rather a collection of specialized agents. Every agent can choose on an individual basis how to perform its activities in order to achieve its goals. This point is discussed in more detail below.

The main tasks of the execution space are:

Translate the application configuration produced by the broker, into a MAP. For every selected PSM, a PSM provider is selected.

Select a coordination strategy. A coordination strategy provides structures to follow the control structure of the application configuration (see also Chapter 3). Furthermore, it regulates the flow of inputs and outputs between PSMs. The coordination strategy is integrated in the MAP.

Negotiate with PSM providers. On the basis of the MAP, negotiation with PSM providers is initiated. A negotiation involves the configuration of a PSM. The idea is that PSM providers (i.e. agents) are relatively independent and have shielded off the functionality of the PSM, in such a way that PSMs cannot be directly invoked. Therefore, an explicit session with the PSM providers has to be started.

Execute the Multi-Agent Plan (MAP). Based on the steps in the MAP, the involved PSM providers are contacted in order to invoke PSMs. The flow of input objects and output objects is regulated according to the MAP.

Handle exceptions or failures raised by PSM providers or by loss of information. The
   execution environment takes appropriate steps in case something goes wrong. Possible situations of this type are a PSM provider that does not respond and unpro-
   cessable information.

Report the results of an execution to the Reconfigurator. The execution space waits for
   the reaction of the Reconfigurator.

In order to construct PSM providers we look at the problems involved in transforming a PSM into an agent, in such a way that it can be coupled to other PSMs providers
and Managers. First, most PSMs are not meant to be on the Web, they form a part of
a larger (centrally controlled) set of KBSs. Secondly, PSMs do not address issues like
communication, session management, multi-user support and web standards. Thirdly, the
interface to a PSM, i.e. the way to configure it and invoke it is not always specified or
clear. Fourthly, more advanced PSMs need configuration before they can be invoked. Finally, there are complex PSMs that require interaction with the user or other systems.

As a solution, only one agent type could be defined that is able to invoke all PSMs
defined in the application configuration. However, this is not possible because PSMs are
distributed on the Web and PSMs are heterogeneous[5]. Therefore, we need an addressing mechanism, in order to invoke the PSMs. Furthermore, there should be a transport
mechanism to establish a transaction with the PSM. Examples of transport mechanisms
are TCP/IP and IIOP. Secondly, the PSMs are heterogeneous, which means that for every
PSM a separate invocation mechanism has to be defined. An invocation mechanism can
be seen as a communication protocol above a transport mechanism, such as HTTP, SOAP
or CORBA. Finally, the PSMs behave differently, hence for every PSM a separate transaction mechanism has to be defined. Transaction mechanisms deal with how to encode and
decode information from one format to another. Examples of information transactions are
XML to plain text, RDF to SQL and so forth.

Another solution is to introduce a mediator, which is able to operate an individual
PSM and can communicate with other mediators. An (IBROW) Operator is a type of mediator that translates agent communication to proprietary instructions. In order to contact
a PSM, a *transducer* can be applied [Genesereth and Ketchpel, 1994]. A transducer can
map instructions from an agent to a service and vice versa. It can also map in the reverse
sense, that is, instructions from service to agent and results from agent to service. The
difference between the two mappings is that the former is part of a reactive behavior, the
latter is part of a pro-active behavior.

This approach has the advantage that the agent does not require knowledge of the
configuration and invocation of these services. The discussion on the use of annotation
languages, such as WSDL, DAML and OWL, and the use of other deployment techniques
for PSMs is not part of this work.

Given the fact that PSM invocation is complex and that for every PSM a separate
Operator has to be defined, we separated the actual *invocation* of PSMs, i.e. PSM con-

---

[5]These issues also lead to the conclusion that it is not trivial to define a single API (as in SOAP) for PSMs
that can be placed above PSMs.

model	functions	domain
communication	process MAP, report to reconfigurator instruct Operators, process reports	available message content ontologies
competence	MAP construction, operator negotiation, operate MAS, negotiate with reconfigurator	application configuration, current MAP coordination mechanisms, result set
self	life cycle management, instruct planner	"Manager role"
planner	task selection, plan tasks	agent's agenda
environment	search for operators consult DF	repository known operators, report-to relation with reconfigurator and user agent

Table 5.1
The five models of the Manager agent (according to the 5C Model, see Section 4.2 (p.76)) representing its capabilities split up in function and domain.

sultation, and the *coordination* over the PSM invocations. Invocation of PSMs is handled by Operators. Coordination is handled by the Manager. The Manager coordinates the execution of the application configuration by constructing a MAP. This MAP defines the sequence used to consult Operators that are able to invoke the required PSMs. The next step for the Manager is to start a negotiation with the involved Operator on the PSM configuration and the Operator's role in the MAP. The Manager starts the actual execution by consulting Operators. After the execution of the MAP, the Manager reports its result to the Reconfigurator.

The idea behind an Operator is that it provides an interface to a PSM. This interface is written in such a way that a PSM can be consulted as-is. This means that the Operator takes care of transport of information from and to a PSM, using the appropriate protocols and transactions. Deployment of PSMs can be done in two steps: (1) deployment of a competence description using UPML via PSM libraries or (2) deployment of PSM invocation via mediators (called Operators) that have access to PSMs.

The competences and states of the Manager are summarized in a 5C model (according to Section 4.2 (p.76)) agent design, see Table 5.1 (p.107). As shown, the communication model interacts with other agents in the IBROW system on the basis of the available ontologies. These ontologies are discussed in Section 5.4.3 (p.110). The competence model is able to execute four main tasks: *MAP construction*, *Operator negotiation*, *operate MAS*[6] and *negotiate with Reconfigurator*. The execution of these tasks for a specific domain is discussed in Section 5.6.2. The management of the agent's life cycles (cf. Section 3.4) is handled by the self model, which instructs the planner model. The specific states and transitions are described in Section 5.4.4. The planner model is responsible for planning the tasks required to follow the life cycles in the agent's agenda. Finally, the environment model is capable of searching (by consulting the agent platform's DF) for Operators and store them in a repository of known Operators. Information related to report-to relations with Reconfigurator and user agent are also stored in the environment model.

---

[6]MAS stands for Multi-Agent System.

5.4   Levels of Interoperability

In order to have the agents "smoothly" collaborate with each other, we discuss the problem of enabling Interoperability. Interoperability includes how the agents can communicate with each other, when they communicate and what message content they use. In order to study this problem, we apply four levels of interoperability: *technical*, *syntactic*, *semantic* and *coordination*. The first three levels correspond to traditional interoperability structures in agent communication such as [Haustein and Luedecke, 2000, Bellifemine et al., 2001, FIPA, 2002a]. In these structures the emphasis is on message transport, languages and ontologies. We added the coordination level in order to regulate communication patterns and flow of information. By this, we made a framework to abstract technique, representation, concepts and strategy to enable interoperability.

Level	Element	Standard	Examples
coordination	responsibility execution conversation control	organizational role behavior interaction protocol	manager, broker, librarian reactive, pro-active REQUEST-INFORM
semantic	task-method ontology message content ontology	UPML XSD	PSM, Competence method, type=xsd:string
syntactic	message content language message envelope	XML FIPA-ACL	`<primitive step/>` sender, receiver, content
technical	message transport	HTTP	GET, POST

Table 5.2
The interoperability levels with elements, standards and examples.

Within the framework, we made the assumption that interaction between agents is based on message passing, meaning that the agents are not capable of, for example, invoking methods at other agents but have to explicitly state a question in a message (cf. [Wooldridge, 2002]). In order to enable agents to exchange messages, they need to agree on using the shared network protocols and message transport mechanisms. These decisions can be handled in the *Technical interoperability* (or transport) level. For example, all or a selection of agents can agree to use HTTP as information exchange protocol and TCP/IP as information (message) transport mechanism. Decisions related to envelope-encoding and message content languages are covered in the *syntactic interoperability* level, such as agents using XML and FIPA-ACL. *Semantic interoperability* means that agents use shared ontologies such as domain ontologies [Fensel et al., 1999b]. Finally, *coordination interoperability* implies agents using the shared procedures, such as "every service has to register", and sharing the notion of organizational roles, such as Manager and Librarian (cf. Section 3.4). The interoperability levels are summarized in Figure 5.2.

Although some topics seem trivial, they are briefly mentioned to indicate the required steps to enable interoperation. We describe the technology and methods involved in enabling interoperation in multi-agent systems, to show the complexity of having agents interact with each other. However, the point is, when using standards, agent designers only have to deal with the coordination level, which should realize smooth collaboration between the agents.

5.4.1 Technical Interoperability

Although it is possible to have a multi-agent system running on one machine, most multi-agent systems will be distributed over a network of machines. These agents have to exchange messages with each other, which involves sending and receiving parties. For that, an addressing mechanism and a message transport mechanism are required. In the IBROW architecture, we applied the FIPA agent communication standard [FIPA, 2002b]. FIPA uses HTTP over TCP/IP for message transport, meaning that agents use the standard Internet protocol, available on any web-enabled machine. Using "GET" and "POST" commands, "MIME encoded" information can be transported. The addressing mechanism is based on standard URL and IP addresses. For example, the Manager can be addressed using `Manager@gaper.swi.psy.uva.nl`. For more details, we refer to the FIPA specifications [FIPA, 2002b].

The use of standards is important, because standards decrease the amount of new technology that has to be introduced to agents and agent wrapper builders. Furthermore, standards such as HTTP, TCP/IP and URLs are well tested and have matured to reliable and robust means for information and data exchange. A survey on detailed technical agent communication issues can be found in [Huhns and Stephens, 1999, Labrou et al., 1999, Bellifemine et al., 2003].

5.4.2 Syntactic Interoperability

When having enabled message transport between agents within a network (i.e. message *sending*), we look how agents can *compose* and *parse* agent messages. First, the format of the message exchanged will have to be known by senders and receivers. Secondly, the agents need to have agreed on a standard format. Such a format is defined by FIPA, which provides a vocabulary for message formats. This vocabulary is called FIPA-ACL (Agent Communication Language) which is loosely based on KQML [Huhns and Stephens, 1999, FIPA, 2002b]. A message written in FIPA-ACL is composed of two levels: message content and message meta information.

The message meta-information contains the addressing, such as sender and (intended) receivers. Furthermore, it provides information on the actual content of the message, such as what language was used for the content and what (message content) ontology is to be used to couple meaning to the terms used . Several content languages are allowed, such as RDF, XML and SL [FIPA, 2002b]

In the IBROW architecture, XML is used as content language, because the brokering service (i.e. a Prolog process) and the Reconfigurator use XML to reason about application configurations.

The actual content of messages can contain coordination information, such as instructions and reports, and information, such as input, support and output objects. These objects can be encoded and annotated using "MIME-types". Instructions and reports are expressed in the XML language. An example of a message is given in Figure 5.17 (p.133).

5.4.3 Semantic Interoperability

In order to provide semantics to agent communication, ontologies can be used [van Aart et al., 2002a]. Ontology-based communication is discussed in detail in Section 6.3. Also the use of ontologies and agents is motivated by the development of DAML-Services[7]. The difference between our approach and that of DAML-S, is that we do not commit to a single representation language.

On the basis of ontology-based communication, a number of specialized ontologies are defined that are able to manage the diversity of information transportation within the IBROW system. An alternative is to define one central ontology that is able to cover all information flows. If all agents would have to commit to this single ontology, the agents would be equipped with knowledge they do not need to perform their activities. For example, an Operator would not need to reason about how to retrieve PSM descriptions from a PSM library. Furthermore, it is unlikely that agents that are built by different institutes will commit to a single ontology. This point is further stressed by Hendler, who has predicted that there will not be large centralistic ontologies, rather a lot of specialized ontologies [Hendler, 2001]. The use of a specialized ontology also adheres to the notion of separations of concerns. Light weighted and dedicated agents can be built, which can be easily maintained and even replaced if necessary.

In order to investigate what ontologies are required, we discuss an analysis of interactions between the agents within the IBROW architecture. The interactions are required to accomplish tasks within the IBROW system, such as "select PSMs from PSM libraries". For this particular task an ontology is required that is able to express information related to PSM competences such as pre- and post-conditions. An interaction has an initiator (i.e. sender) and one or more responders (i.e. receivers). Within an interaction, messages are exchanged that use terms from ontologies. The result of the analysis is given in Table 5.3.

The ontologies are discussed in detail below. Some of these ontologies are based on the UPML framework. UPML provides a frame in which information related to competences and behavior of PSMs can be stored.

---

[7]See www.daml.org/services.

R.	Initiator	Responder	IBROW Task	Ontology	Exemplar terms
①	user agent	broker agent	delegate user goal	task	pre and post condition, input and output roles
②	broker agent	library agent	select PSMs	task-method	pre and postcondition, pragmatics
③	broker agent	manager agent	delegate configuration	process	primitive step, role, PSM
④	manager agent	operator agent	coordinate execution	operations	consume, produce,
⑤	operator agent	user agent	acquire input	domain	input
⑥	operator agent	operator agent	transfer intermediate objects	domain	intermediate objects
⑦	manager agent	reconfigurator	reconfigure application	process	step, role, PSM
⑧	manager agent	user agent	report results	domain	outcome

Table 5.3
Interactions between agents, associated tasks and ontologies. The relation numbers (① - ⑧) corresponds with the collaborations from Fig 5.2 (p.103).

Task ontology The user agent is responsible for assisting the user in formulating goal specifications. The goal specification is delegated to the broker agent, using the *task ontology*. The interaction between the user agent and broker is represented by directed line ① in Figure 5.2. Within the interaction between the user agent and broker agent, the user agent uses concepts such as *input* and *output roles* and *pre-* and *post-conditions* to specify the goal of an application. The broker agent uses the goal specification as input to configure an application. For details on goal specification we refer to literature on UPML [Fensel et al., 1999b, Fensel et al., 1999a]. On how an application is configured, we refer to [Wielinga et al., 2003].

Task-method ontology In order to configure an application, the broker agent selects PSMs from PSM libraries. The library agents provide the broker agent with PSM descriptions. The interaction is represented by the directed line ② in Figure 5.2.

The *pre* and *post conditions* concepts are required, to reason about the competences of individual PSMs. *Pragmatics* are required to reason about availability, performance and the configuration of PSMs. These competence descriptions are maintained by library agents, which can be queried by the broker using the *task-method ontology*.

The difference between the task ontology and the task-method ontology is that the task ontology describes the expected behavior of an overall system, the related domain and the data required to execute the system. The task-method ontology deals with domain independent competence descriptions, possible configurations and pragmatics of individual PSMs.

Process ontology When the broker has completed an application configuration, it is delegated to the Manager, see the directed line ③ in Figure 5.2. An application configuration is expressed in terms of primitive steps, roles and PSMs. A sequence of primitive steps defines the application configuration. A primitive step represents the work to be done. The work means invoking a PSM using *support roles* and feeding input. *Support roles* are used to express PSM configuration, e.g. what knowledge base to use. The input and output exchanged between steps are expressed by *intermediate roles*. In fact, *intermediate roles* are used as transport objects between different PSMs.

The input of the application is expressed by *input roles* and the output by *output roles*. Every primitive step refers to the configuration of a single PSM. The first primitive step within the application configuration, defines one or more required input roles. The output roles of the application are defined by the last primitive step in the primitive step sequence. The primitive steps between the first and last primitive steps use intermediate roles (i.e. transport objects) to exchange input and output roles. The terms used in an application configuration are covered by the *process ontology* (see Figure 5.3).

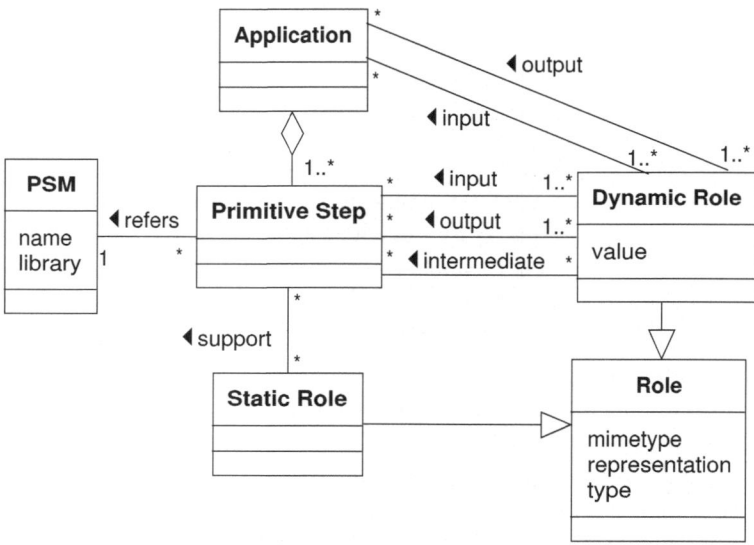

Figure 5.3
Process Ontology, i.e. the application configuration schemas.

Operations ontology Based on the application configuration, the Manager constructs a MAP. Terms such as input roles and output roles are translated to input objects and output objects. These terms are captured in the operations ontology, which is based on the task-method ontology for coordination defined in Figure 3.3 (p.48). The involved Operators are instructed according to the MAP, see the directed line ④ in Figure 5.2 (p.103). After instruction, the Manager coordinates the application execution.

An instruction, exchanged between the Manager and Operators, contains the terms *consume_from* to expresses what *objects* i.e. roles to consume from which *Operator(s)*. The instructions are part of a coordination strategy as discussed in Section 3.2. When applying direct supervision, the Manager instructs the Operators to report (i.e. forwarding output objects) directly to the Manager. In standardization of work, the Operators are instructed to report to another Operator. The term *distribute_to* expresses what *objects* to distribute to which *Operator(s)*. These terms are covered by the *operations ontology*. After reception of the instructions, the Operators configure the PSM they represent.

When the Manager starts the actual execution, the Operators call the required inference functions. The outcome of the inference functions will be forwarded according to the Manager's instructions.

Domain ontology In order to execute the application, the Operators need initial information in terms of input objects from the user agent. The *domain ontology* describes the mapping between input objects and information related to the user domain. The information is stored in the user's knowledge base (KB). The input objects are transported using agent interaction as denoted by the directed line ⑤ in Figure 5.2.

When multiple Operators are involved, the Operators transfer intermediate objects to other Operators. These transactions are denoted by the directed line ⑥ in Figure 5.2. When the execution is finished, the last Operator reports to the Manager as denoted by the directed line ④ in Figure 5.2. From there, the Manager reports the outcome to the Reconfigurator (directed line ⑦). When the Reconfigurator is satisfied, the Manager will report the *output* to the user agent (directed line ⑧). A part of the trace of the interactions is illustrated in Figure 5.19.

The discussed ontologies are relative small in the sense that they contain a limited number of concepts and relations. The advantage is that the agents involved only have to be equipped with dedicated knowledge to reason about their domain. The price of this decision is that there is redundancy between the ontologies. This could cause additional effort for the maintenance of the ontologies.

5.4.4 Coordination Interoperability

Above we have analyzed the possible interactions between the agents and the means to enable these interactions. We will now discuss how the agents can work together in harmony.

The idea behind coordination interoperability is that agents have agreed to play organizational roles within a multi-agent system. Examples of roles are Manager, Operator and Broker. Accompanied with a role is the type of behavior. Among behaviors is reactive behavior, i.e. the agent will wait until another agent starts an interaction, and pro-active behavior, which means that the agent will take the initiative to start an interaction in order to fulfill its responsibilities.

We discuss the coordination between the agents in the execution space, i.e. the Manager and the Operators. Furthermore, the external behaviors of the Manager and Operators will be presented.

5.4.4.1   Manager Operator Coordination

The role of the Manager is to coordinate the Operators, including telling Operators how to perform their work in detail, such as getting the input objects, how to transform input to output, and to whom to distribute the output. These instructions are part of the MAP that the Manager composes on the basis of the available Operators and the received application configuration. We will look at how the Manager and Operators collaborate, see Figure 5.4.

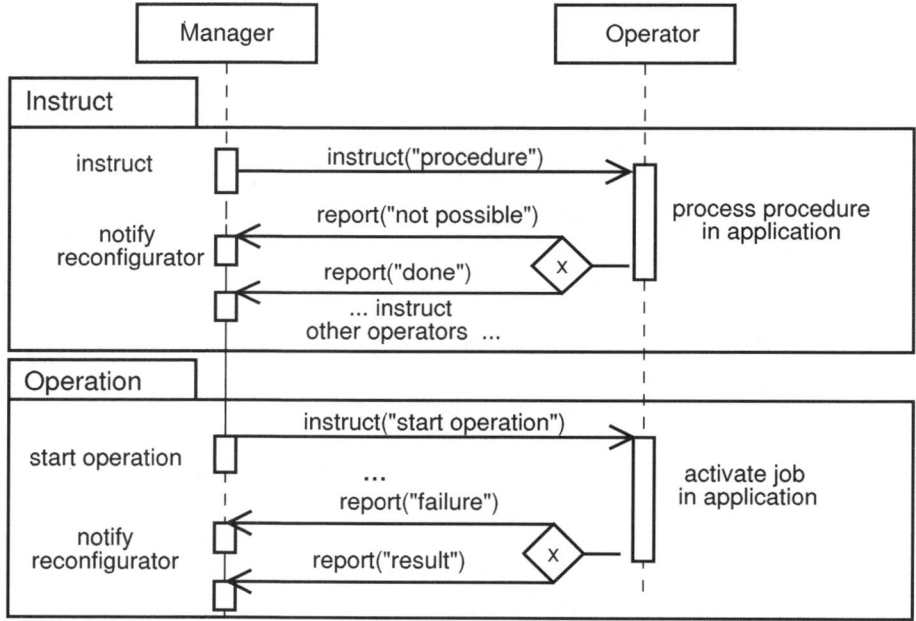

Figure 5.4
Sequence diagram showing the collaboration between the Manager and an Operator.

The idea is that the Manager first instructs the Operators with the use of an `instruction`. With an instruction, the Manager can implement a coordination mechanism. Next the Manager will request for actual invocation of PSMs. The two packages in Figure 5.4 show these two steps, i.e. *instruction*, and *start operation*.

The first step is *instruction*, which has as the intention to configure the PSMs and the data flows between Operators. This works as follows. The Manager will send a **request** to an Operator containing an *instruction*. Such an instruction contains the following four items.

1. From what agent to consume its input. For example, Operator B needs input from Operator A.

2. What PSM to invoke. For example Operator A will have to invoke a PSM which can be a Prolog function.

3. Configuration of the PSM, i.e. the coupling to a domain, which is in most of the cases a knowledge base.

4. To what agent to distribute its output. In case of centralized coordination, this will be the Manager. In case of decentralized coordination, it will be another Operator.

When the Operator has received the Manager's instructions, it will try to configure its PSM. The Operator can respond with a report containing:

1. **not_possible**, which means that the Operator cannot get access to the requested PSM or the PSM is not available.

2. **done**, meaning the instructions are processed and the PSM is configured.

The next step of the Manager is to start the actual application execution, i.e. the MAP operation. For this the Manager will send a **request** to the Operator containing the *job* to be performed and the required *input*. The Operator can respond with:

1. **failure**[8], meaning that the execution of the job failed, i.e. an exception raised by the PSM itself. For example, there could be something wrong with the received input.

2. **result**, containing the output of the PSM.

The collaboration described above is of a simple kind. More elaborate collaborations where the Manager and Operators go in negotiations are subject for further research. The aim of this collaboration is to show how the four interoperability levels fit on each other.

The next two sections will describe the individual behaviors of the Operator and Manager that implement this collaboration.

5.4.4.2 Operator Behavior

In Section 3.4.1, we introduced the behavior of an Operator, which consists of a composition of three life cycles, i.e. the *platform life cycle*, the *application life cycle* and the *execution life cycle*. For the Operators in the IBROW architecture, we adjusted the three life cycles to: *platform life cycle*, the *application life cycle* and the *PSM invocation life cycle*. The *PSM invocation life cycle* is a specialization of the *execution life cycle*. The behavior of the Operator is illustrated by means of a pseudo state diagram in Figure 5.5.

---

[8]The difference between the "not_possible" and "failure" report is that "not_possible" means that it is not possible to invoke a PSM. The term "failure" indicates that it is possible to invoke a PSM, however that in execution time, the PSM has triggered an error message.

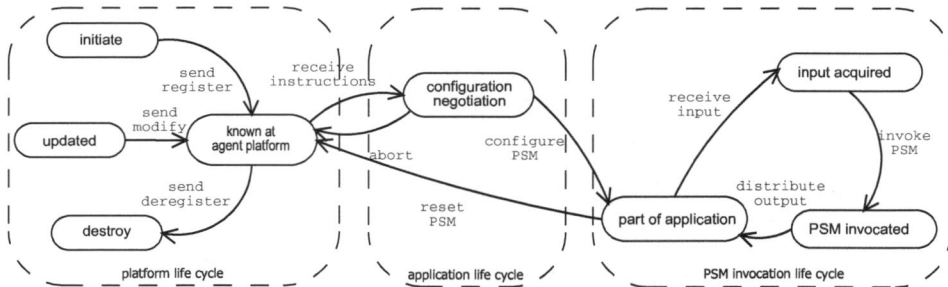

Figure 5.5
Pseudo state diagram showing states (rounded boxes) and transitions (arrowed lines) of the three life cycles of the Operator's behavior within the IBROW architecture. This diagram is a specialization of the diagram in Fig. 3.15 (p.63).

The *platform life cycle* is the same as the *platform life cycle* described in Section 3.4.1.

The *application life cycle* starts when the Operator receives instructions from the Manager. The Operator will move to the `configuration negotiation` state. From this state, the Operator will try to configure the PSM, the Operator represents. If successful, the Operator will be part of a (larger) application and will wait until it can enter the *PSM invocation life cycle*. If the configuration fails, the negotiation will be aborted and the Operator will leave the application life cycle. Otherwise, the Manager will report to the Operator that the application execution is terminated. In this case the Operator will reset the configuration of the PSM and leave the application life cycle.

The *PSM invocation life cycle* will start, when the PSM is successfully configured and when the Operator has acquired input for the PSM invocation. An Operator can acquire input on a re-active and pro-active manner. These two modes depend on the instructions received by the Manager. Given the acquired input, the Operator will invoke the PSM it represents. The result of the PSM will be distributed according to the instructions of the Manager. After output distribution, the Operator will go back to the `part of application` state.

5.4.4.3   Manager Behavior

In Section 3.4.2 (p.64), we introduced the behavior of a Manager, which consists of three life cycles, i.e. the *platform life cycle*, the *configuration life cycle* and the *execution life cycle*. For the Manager in the IBROW architecture, we adjusted the last two life cycles to: *MAP configuration life cycle* and *MAP execution life cycle*. The pseudo state diagram for the behavior of the Manager is illustrated in Figure 5.6

The *MAP configuration life cycle* starts when the Manager receives an application configuration from the Broker. The Manager will recruit Operators by consulting the agent platform's AMS and DF to search for relevant Operators. When a set of candidate

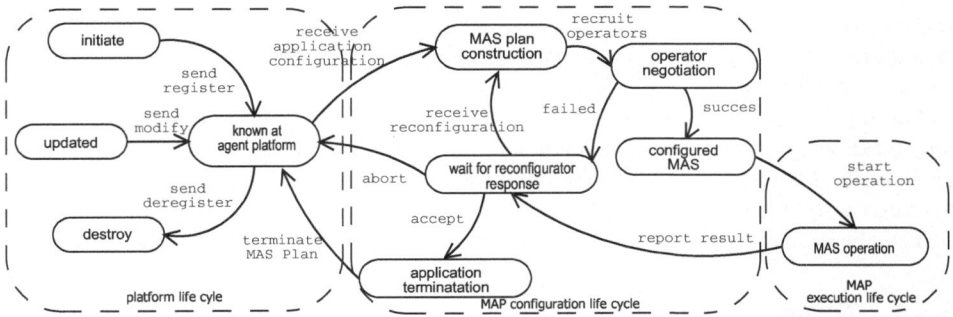

Figure 5.6
Pseudo state diagram showing states (rounded boxes) and transitions (arrowed lines) of the three life cycles of the Manager's behavior within the IBROW architecture. This diagram is a specialization of the diagram in Fig. 3.16 (p.64).

Operators is found, the Manager will start negotiations with the Operators. In case of success, the Manager will enter the *MAP execution life cycle*. Otherwise, the Manager will report to the Reconfigurator. From the `wait for Reconfigurator response`, the Manager can leave the MAP configuration life cycle or can receive a new configuration.

In the *MAP execution life cycle* the Manager will start from the `configured MAS` state of the *MAP configuration life cycle* and will start MAS operation by sending job requests to involved Operators. When the MAS operation has been finished, the Manager will report the results of the multi-agent system (MAS) to the Reconfigurator.

When designing a 5C agent, using the internal and external behavior, the self-model would contain the role and the goals of the agent. The planner model would contain reactive and pro-active behavior in order to follow the life cycles. Interaction between the agents, including the technical, syntactic and semantic interoperation, could be handled in the communication model. The environment model would contain models of the roles of other agents.

5.5 Implementation

In this section, we discuss how the agents within the execution space are implemented. Given the conceptual description of the agent components and behaviors we discuss how pieces of the agent architecture can be implemented. With this implementation, we have performed a number of experiments, which will be discussed in Section 5.6.

The main challenge is to implement agents that can operate in a distributed environment. However, this is not the only challenge we have to face. In fact, we also need to address the problems related to agents running on several machines that are distributed within a (possible) large scale network. Another challenge is set by the need to test and debug the agents, separately and in combination. For example, there is no possibility of a desktop GUI for every individual agent. In the remainder, we first discuss the applied technology set, i.e. the tools and technology that are used as the basis for the IBROW system. Next, we present the implementation of the basic IBROW agent, which is the parent agent of the Manager and Operators. After that, we discuss the agent log, which is used to store communication traces and agent activity log. Finally, we present inspection tools that can be used to post-mortem inspect the dynamics of the agents within the system.

5.5.1   Technology Set

Below, we describe the basis of the IBROW implementation and we discuss the technological solutions we have applied, in order to address two important problems: the development of agents and the development of PSMs.

5.5.1.1   Agent Development

An important enabling factor for the development of multi-agent systems is constituted by the existence of a number of agent-oriented toolkits[9] that natively provide basic services such as communication, life cycle management, yellow pages and so on.

In the IBROW system, we applied a popular agent toolkit: JADE (Java Agent DEvelopment framework) [Bellifemine et al., 2001]. JADE is a software framework that simplifies the implementation of multi-agent systems through middleware that complies with the FIPA specifications, a library of classes that developers can use or extend while creating agents and a set of tools that support the debugging and deployment phases. JADE agents communicate by exchanging messages in compliance with the FIPA ACL language. Furthermore, JADE supports the AMS (Agent Message Service) and the DF (Directory Facilitator), which represent the white and yellow page for agent (service) discovery.

Given the already existing basic agent libraries, we have built the IBROW agents on top of the JADE toolkit. The agents were developed in Java (JDK 1.3) and deployed as Linux services. This means that the agents can be remotely started, suspended and stopped.

5.5.1.2   PSMs

Several PSMs are available as Java libraries (i.e. Java packages). Examples are data transfer, database access, parsers and composers and content grabbing. PSMs for data transfer include FTP, HTTP, EMAIL clients and repositories. Amongst PSMs for Database access are standard JDBC (i.e. Java version of ODBC) couplings for several commercial and open source database implementations. Several packages are available for parsing and composing, such as *javacc* and *Document Object Model (DOM)*[10]. With these packages,

---

[9]See www.agentlink.org/resources/agent-software.html.
[10]See www.sun.com/products/JavaCC and http://xml.apache.org/xerces2-j.

parsers for RDF and XML can be applied. In order to fetch information from web pages, WebL can be used[11]. WebL is a scripting language that enables Java programs to extract information from web pages. For example, a WebL script to extract information from the search engine Google is given in Figure 5.7. In fact, WebL is an example of a wrapping technique and is more useful than the interface that Google offers, because it can easily be altered to query other web services.

```
var result;
var page = GetURL("http://www.google.com/search",
        [. q=searchterm, bntG="Google+Search", hl="en", num=5.]);

// Check no div
var testDiv = Elem(page,"div");
if Size(testDiv)>0 then

  // Links are the first A inside any P inside the first (and only) div tag
  var paras = Elem(page, "p") directlyinside Elem(page, "div")[0];

  // Process the anchor tags
  every para in paras do
    var hrefs = Elem(para, "a") directlyinside para;
    result.append(hrefs[0]["href"]);
  end;
end;
return result;
```

Figure 5.7
Example of a wrapping technique: WebL script to query the search engine Google within an application. The script uses the variable searchterm as input, which is a search query. The variable result contains a list of urls found .

The problem is that many PSMs are distributed and heterogeneous in terms of input, output roles and behaviors. In order to have an Operator representing one of more available PSMs, the Operator should have access to it. A solution is using *PSM wrappers* and *PSM transducer* (cf. [Genesereth and Ketchpel, 1994]), which can mediate between a PSM and other agents. The transducer is capable of accepting messages from agents, translating them into the PSM interaction protocol and consulting the PSM. After the response of the PSM, the PSM transducer translates the response into the agent communication language and sends the resulting message to other agents. The advantage is that no knowledge of the PSM other than its interaction behavior is required and is therefore useful when the code for the PSM is unavailable to the Operator builder or too difficult to modify.

When the code (i.e. methods and calls) and state (i.e. data structures and knowledge bases) of a PSM are available, a *PSM wrapper* can be applied to directly examine and manipulate the PSM. Wrappers are more efficient than transducers, because there is less serial communication. Both methods are supported within the IBROW system.

An example of wrappers and transducers for a specific domain is given in Figure 5.18 (p.134).

---
[11]See http://research.compaq.com/SRC/WebL.

Several off-the-shelf components are used as the basis for the implementation of the IBROW system. The most important reason is that when pursuing web and agent standards, components that already comply to these standards should be used.

5.5.2   Agent Implementation

All agents within the IBROW system are extensions of the IBROW agent. Within the IBROW system, there are agents developed in Prolog, mainly as transducer of PSMs written in Prolog, and agents developed in Java. In the remainder we focus on the Java agents, which are extentions of the JADE agent class. The JADE agent offers basic message handling, such as message receiving and sending. Furthermore, it offers a basic planning mechanism allowing the scheduling of agent behaviors. The IBROW agents offer services that are related to interoperability, such as life cycle management and message content ontology handling.

In the next three sections, we overview the internals of the IBROW agent, the Operator and the Manager.

5.5.2.1   IBROW Agent

Message transport is concerned with sending and receiving messages. Sending messages involves the construction of ACL messages as Java objects. ACL messages are represented by the Jade class, jade.lang.acl.AclMessage. An example is given in Figure 5.8.

```
...
ACLMessage msg = new ACLMessage(REQUEST);
msg.setSender(this.getAID());
msg.addReceiver( new AID("receiver", "foreign-platform") );
msg.setLanguage("FIPA-SL");
msg.setOntology("Operations-Ontology");
msg.setEncoding("String");
msg.setProtocol("fipa-request");
msg.setContent(contentObject.encode("FIPA-SL", "Operations-Ontology") );
agent.send(msg);
...
```

Figure 5.8
Simplified Pseudo code for configuration of an ACLMessage object.

A message is not sent directly to an agent, rather to the ACC (agent communication channel), which is to be seen as a message transport bus [FIPA, 2002a]. The ACC first tries to read the ACL part of the message. If the message is not correct, the sending agent receives a Failure message back. Otherwise, the ACC tries to deliver the message according to the receiver slot.

Every agent makes use of *behaviors*. A *behavior* is a separate process that performs one or more tasks. Behaviors are implemented by behavior objects, which are used

```
public class Scheduler extends Thread {
  ...
  public void run() {
    while (state==running) {
      for every behavior {
        behavior.action();
      }
    }
  }
  ...
}
```

Figure 5.9
Basic behavior scheduling in simplified Java code.

by the **scheduler** thread[12]. In Figure 5.9[13], the basic scheduler process of an agent is given. As shown, every behavior is activated in a simple round robin scheduling method. Behaviors can be added and removed during runtime. In Figure 5.10 and Figure 5.11[14] two examples of behaviors are given.

```
public class PlatformLifeCycle extends Behavior {
  private int state = 1;
  private boolean finished = false;

  public void action() {
    switch(state) {
      case INIT: agent.addBehaviour( new AMSRegistration() );
      case AMSREGISTERED: agent.addBehavior( new DFRegistration() );
      case DFREGISTERED: agent.addBehavior( new DFRegistration() );
      ...
      case MODIFIED: agent.addBehavior( new DFModify() );
      case DESTROY: agent.addBehavior( new DFDeregistration() );
      case DFDEREGISTERED: agent.addBehavior( new AMSDeregistration() );
      case AMSDEREGISTERED: finished = true;
    }
  }
  public void update(int newState) {
    this.state = newState;
  }
  ...
}
```

Figure 5.10
State machine implementing the platform life cycle.

---

[12]A thread is an active object with its own locus of control. Multiple threads can run at the same time.

[13]This pseudo code is extracted from the original Java code. "{" represents "**begin**" and "}" represents "**end**".

[14]In Java the else statement is not used in a conditional statement.

In the IBROW agent, we have implemented life cycle management as a composite state machine. The platform life cycle state machine is given in Figure 5.10. In every action, the behavior inspects the current state, and acts accordingly. An agent has a set of initial behaviors that take care of AMS and DF registration. For examples of the AMS behavior, the DF behavior and example messages, we refer to [van Aart and Jansweijer, 2003, Bellifemine et al., 2003]. When a behavior wants to change its state, it uses the function update.

5.5.2.2 Operator

An Operator is implemented as a subclass of the IBROW agent, which means that its competences are implemented as behaviors. We discuss one of these behaviors in detail.

As described above, the Manager can choose to follow several coordination strategies. The behavior for an Operator for Standardization of Work is given in Figure 5.11. This behavior is composed of three functions, action, processProcedure and processInput. In the function action the Manager checks if a message is received. If so, the content of the message is inspected. If the message contains an instruction in the form procedure (according to Figure 3.3 (p.48)), the Operator has to adjust its configuration, using the function processProcedure. As shown, the "member"[15] activity contains the name of the activity the Operator has to perform in the current configuration. Furthermore, the member distribute_to contains the address of the agent to whom the Operator has to send its output to. With this simple mechanism, the Manager can configure Operators to coordinate themselves following a sequential MAP.

If the message contains an object, the Operator has to perform an activity using the object, which is handled by the function processInput. In this function the Operator produces an output on the basis of the activity selected by the Manager. Next, the output is sent to the agent as specified in distribute_to.

5.5.2.3 Manager

Given a broker configuration, the Manager configures a MAS plan. The implementation of this process is shown in Figure 5.12. the Manager starts a loop over the of primitive-steps in the received ApplicationConfiguration object. For every primitive step, the Manager first determines the type of service requested, in this case using the name of the service. Next the Manager looks for an Operator that offers the service requested in the primitive step, using the platform's DF. In this case, we assume that the Operator will cooperate without negotiation with the Manager. In other cases the Manager will need to negotiate on attributes like price, delivery time and duration of the execution of the service. Finally, the Manager adds the service combined with the selected Operator to the Multi-Agent Plan (MAP).

Given the MAP, the Manager can choose between several coordination strategies, see also Section 3.3 (p.49). The generateMAP function will be part of a coordination strategy. As an example, we give the implementation of direct supervision in Figure 5.13.

---

[15] A "member" in Java can be seen as an "attribute" of an object or a "slot" of a concept.

```
class StandardizationOfWork extends Behavior {
  private String distribute_to;
  private String activity;
  ...
  public void action() {
    ACLMessage msg = agent.receive();
    if ( msg != null ){
      if ( msg.contains(procedure) ) processProcedure(msg.content);
      if ( msg.contains(object) ) processInput(msg.content);
      ...
    }
  }
  public void processProcedure(Procedure p) {
    this.distribute_to = p.distribute_to;
    this.activity = p.activity;
  }
  public void processInput(Object input) {
    Object output = performActivity(activity, input);
    ACLMessage msg = new ACLMessage(INFORM);
    msg.addReceiver(distribute_to);
    msg.setContent(output);
    agent.send(msg);
  }
  ...
}
```

Figure 5.11
Simplified Java code for basic Operator behavior for Standardization of Work. A procedure is a type of instruction according to Figure 3.3 (p.48).

When the direct-supervision behavior is instantiated, the constructor init is called. In this function, the member of the behavior is configured using the generateMAP function, which fills the MAP object.

Next, the delegateNextJob function is called, where the "current" activity is selected, in this case the first one, combined with the selected Operator. Using the activity and Operator information a Job is constructed, which is sent to the Operator. From here, the Manager waits for an answer from the Operator. If it contains a report, the function ProcessReport will be called, that replaces the current-object with the Output object received from the Operator. Next, the processReport function is called. This process repeats until all activities from the MAP are delegated to Operators.

5.5.3 Agent Log

In order to be able to gather data about the behavior of the agents within the system, we implemented an agent log as a centralized database (or a blackboard) where remote agents (i.e. agents that are not located on the same machine) can store information. This information, such as communication traces and state transitions, can be used to study

```
...
public MAP generateMAP(ApplicationConfiguration appConf) {
  MAP map = new MAP();
  for every ( primitive-step in appConf ) {
    String service = primitive-step.getPSM().getName();
    Agent operator = DFService.lookup(service);
    map.add(service, operator);
  }
  return map;
}
...
```

Figure 5.12
Simplified Pseudo code for Multi-Agent Plan (MAP) generation on basis of an Application Configuration.

the dynamics of the system. The database is developed in MySQL[16] and is hosted on an agentcities server in Amsterdam[17]. This dual Pentium-III server runs a Linux distribution.

The technique of logging is also applied to software services, such as web servers, that run on servers, which are located in remote locations. Using remote login techniques, log files can be inspected. For example, the web server package Apache[18] makes use of an access log and an error log. The access log records all legal transactions regarding the web content. The error log records all failed transactions.

The IBROW agents log two types of information: information related to communication and information related to state transitions. Communication information consists of incoming communication (i.e. messages received) and outgoing communication (i.e. messages sent). The state transaction information contains data on state transitions recorded by individual agents. Every log entry is accompanied by a timestamp. There are several techniques to fill an agent log, such as sniffing. In the sniffer approach, an external process monitors all communication and external behavior of agents. The problem with this approach is that not all events, such as state transitions can be externally monitored. Furthermore, agent engineers might not like to have an external process "spying" their agents.

Alternatively, (authorized) agent within the system access the agent log themselves. On the basis of remote connection techniques, the agents have access to the agent log database, where the agents themselves can choose what to record in the log. Others who want to inspect the dynamics of the multi-agent system can login to the database and perform queries on it. Examples of queries are "is every sent message also recorded by the sending party", "how many messages did the Manager send to Operators?" and "did every agent follow the life cycles?".

The log database contains two main tables, the message table and the state table.

---

[16] See www.mysql.org.
[17] See http://gaper.swi.psy.uva.nl.
[18] See www.apache.org.

```
public class DirectSupervision extends Behavior {
    private MAP map;
    private Object current-object;
    private boolean finished = false;
    ...
    public void init(ApplicationConfiguration appConf, Object input) {
        this.map = generateMAP(appConf);
        this.current-object = input;
        delegateNextJob();
    }
    public void action() {
        ACLMessage msg = agent.receive();
        if ( msg != null ){
            if ( msg.contains(report) ) processReport(msg.content);
            ...
        }
    }
    public void processReprort(Report r) {
        this.current-object = r.getOutput();
        delegateNextJob();
    }

    public void delegateNextJob() {
        Activity a = map.nextActivity();
        if ( a== null ) { finished=true; return; }
        Agent operator = map.getOperator(a);
        Job job = new Job(a,operator);
        job.setInput(current-object);
        ACLMessage msg = new ACLMessage(REQUEST);
        msg.addReceiver(operator);
        msg.setContent(job);
        agent.send(msg);
    }
    ...
}
```

Figure 5.13
Simplified pseudo code for Manager behavior when applying Direct Supervision.

The **message** table is modeled after the format of ACLMessages. It contains fields such as **sender, receivers, language, ontology, protocol** and **content**. Other fields include the direction (i.e. incoming and outgoing) of the messages and timestamps (i.e. when the message was sent or received). For every message sent, a record is added by the sending agent and records are added by the receiving agents. By inspecting the table, communication traces can be followed. An example of a message trace is illustrated in Figure 5.14. The **state** table is modeled after a simplified model of a state machine. Every record in the table represents a state transition. For that, the table contains the following fields, **begin-state, end-state, transition, timestamp, agentname**. The **transition** contains the name of the event that triggered the shift from **begin-state** to **end-state**. Agent can log state

timestamp	direction	sendername	receivername	performative	content
2003-05-01 17:15:36	out	useragent	brokeragent	REQUEST	<?xml version="1.0" encoding="UTF-8"?> <consult> <applicationname>Classify Documents
2003-05-01 17:15:36	out	brokeragent	useragent	AGREE	<null>
2003-05-01 17:15:37	out	brokeragent	manager	REQUEST	<?xml version="1.0" encoding="UTF-8"?> <broker_output> <primitive_step id="ps21"> <inp container="kb">extract_features.xml</obtain_from> </support_role> <support_role id="sup
2003-05-01 17:15:38	in	brokeragent	manager	REQUEST	<?xml version="1.0" encoding="UTF-8"?> <broker_output> <primitive_step id="ps21"> <inp container="kb">extract_features.xml</obtain_from> </support_role> <support_role id="sup
2003-05-01 17:15:38	out	manager	brokeragent	AGREE	<null>
2003-05-01 17:15:38	in	brokeragent	manager	REQUEST	<?xml version="1.0" encoding="UTF-8"?> <broker_output> <primitive_step id="ps21"> <inp container="kb">extract_features.xml</obtain_from> </support_role> <support_role id="sup
2003-05-01 17:15:38	out	manager	docobtainer	REQUEST	<?xml version="1.0" encoding="UTF-8"?> <instructions> <consume_from>manager</consu
2003-05-01 17:15:38	out	manager	featextracter	REQUEST	<?xml version="1.0" encoding="UTF-8"?> <instructions> <consume_from>manager</consu
2003-05-01 17:15:38	out	manager	docclassifier	REQUEST	<?xml version="1.0" encoding="UTF-8"?> <instructions> <consume_from>manager</consu
2003-05-01 17:15:38	out	docobtainer	manager	AGREE	<null>
2003-05-01 17:15:38	out	manager	docobtainer	REQUEST	<?xml version="1.0" encoding="UTF-8"?> <instructions> <consume_from>manager</consu
2003-05-01 17:15:38	out	docobtainer	useragent	REQUEST	<?xml version="1.0" encoding="UTF-8"?> <input_role> <representation>directory</represe
2003-05-01 17:15:38	out	docclassifier	manager	AGREE	<null>

Figure 5.14
Screenshot o fthe Agent Log showing the results of an query performed on the agent log.
The query is: "SELECT TIMESTAMP, DIRECTION, SENDERNAME, RECEIVERNAME, PERFORMATIVE, CONTENT from MESSAGE;".

transitions, so that their internal behavior can be monitored. The moment of transition can be stored in **timestamp**. The identification of the agent is stored in **agentname**.

The agent log is a database where information related to communication and state can be stored and retrieved. In the remainder we discuss a selection of tools that make use of the agent log. These tools are part of the *agent console*.

5.5.4 Inspection Tools

The agent console is a web service that offers a collection of inspection tools. There are two types of tools, textual and graphical tools. The textual tools present data retrieved from the agent log in the form of tables. For example, Figure 5.14 is generated from the tool that enables users to query the agent log, using own SQL statements.

The graphical tools make use of an external web service, *webdot*[19]. This web service

---

[19] See www.graphviz.org/webdot/.

can generate image files (i.e. Portable Network Graphics (PNG[20]) files) that can be presented in a web browser. The agent console and webdot communicate with a simple graph language. Displayed objects, such as boxes and ellipses can be equipped with hyperlinks, meaning that if a user clicks an object, he is referred to a page with more details.

5.5.4.1 Communication Diagram

The communication diagram is a graphical representation of agents exchanging messages. Using the **message** table of the agent log, diagrams can be generated that show message interchange between a set of selected agents. Agents are expressed by ellipses and messages by boxes. Every message contains information on the sequence number of the message, the performative and a description of the content.

In Figure 5.15 a screen shot of a communication diagram is given. As shown, the user can specify a number of parameters that helps to narrow the size of a diagram. The boxes i.e. messages, are hyperlink sensitive, which means that they point to another web page. In this case the objects refer to another inspection tool, the *message inspector*. The message inspector shows (textually) all fields of a single record within the **message** table, in this case by the user selected.

Several observations can be made from inspecting communication diagrams. Deadlocks can be spotted, when a message is sent to an agent, but no outgoing messages follow. One expects the agent to reply to incoming messages to the sender or to other agents. If not, the communication trace ends at this agent, because the agent is down or it cannot do anything with the message. Otherwise, the sending agent has sent messages to the wrong agent, or with the wrong content. One way to resolve dead ends within a communication trace is having agents always responding to messages, even when they are not the intended receiver of a message or understand the content (cf. [FIPA, 2002h]).

A life lock can be identified when two or more agents send failure messages stating that they cannot understand the message. It means that these agents send failure messages in a loop. These situations can be corrected by using the **number-of-hops** attribute of ACLMessages. This attribute counts the number of messages that are sent within a conversation. When this number exceeds a threshold, resolving actions can be taken by the agents involved. When an agent does not send or receive any message, this agent could be superfluous. In a multi-agent system design, several agents are identified, but in the execution of the system, agents can be unrequired. A reason can be that the competence of these agents is not required for the tasks and environment at execution time.

5.5.4.2 State Diagram

The state diagram is a graphical representation of the internal behavior of an agent. Simplified state machines can be drawn, based on the entries of the **state** table. The boxes represent states, the arrowed annotated lines represent state transitions. The annotation represents the identification of the transition. An example is given in Figure 5.16.

---

[20]See www.libpng.org.

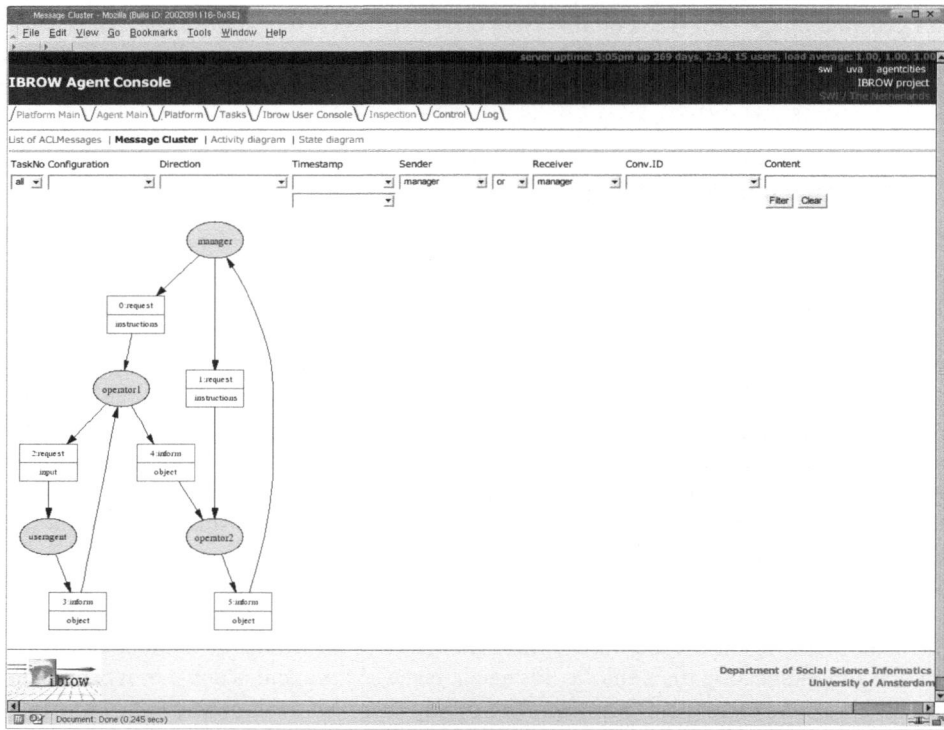

Figure 5.15
Screenshot of a part of the communication between the the Manager and the Operators. The user can specify a number of parameters that helps to narrow the size of a diagram. The boxes, i.e. messages are hyperlink sensitive, where the hyperlinks refer to a page that contains containing detailed information related to a message.

From a state diagram, parts of the internal dynamics of an agent can be studied. For example a deadlock can be identified. A deadlock can be discovered by looking at the last state of a state diagram. If this state does not represent an end state, it means that the agent stopped processing at that point.

Bottom Line   The discussed selection of tools has the purpose to assist agent engineers to inspect the dynamics of distributed systems. The graphical tools make use of webdot. However, webdot is a limited graphical engine. UML notation is limited too. Furthermore, the layout cannot entirely be controlled. The algorithm behind webdot tries to minimize the number of crossed lines. The use of link sensitive graphical objects (i.e. objects as hyperlinks) enables the user to "browse" traces within the agentlog.

The deployment of inspection tools as a web service can assist multiple (distributed)

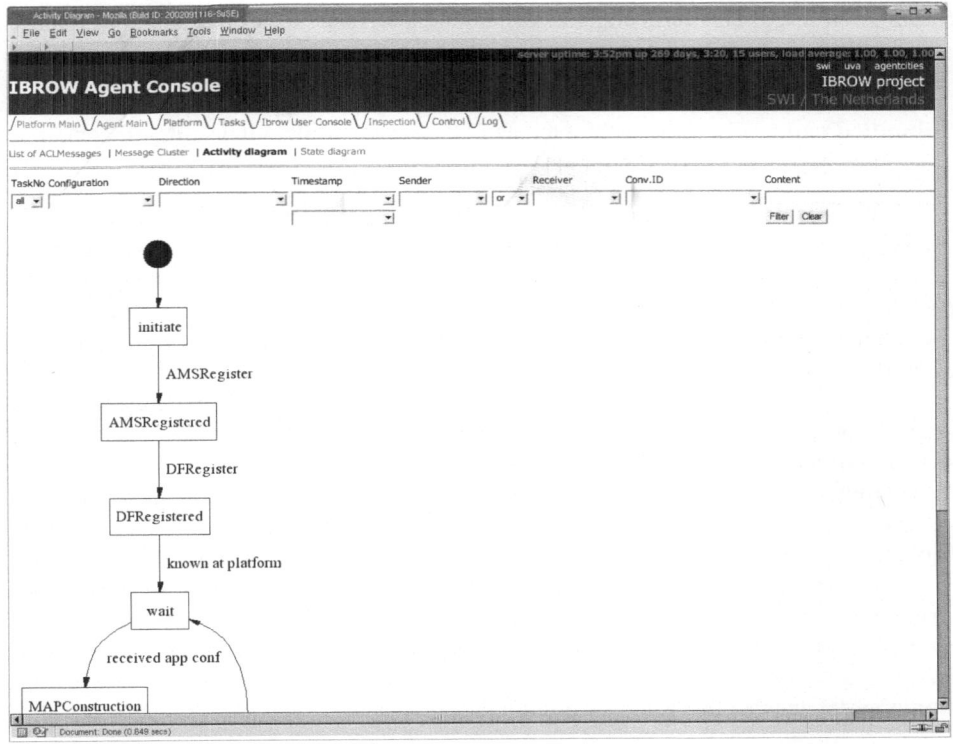

Figure 5.16
Screenshot of a part the Manager's State Diagram.

agent designers to inspect the dynamics of systems at the same time. Another advantage of a web service is that agent designers do not need to install special software in order to monitor the behavior of agents.

5.6 Classification of Conference Submissions

Document classification is an interesting domain for reuse of knowledge-intensive services and components. In this section, we will discuss a proof of concept that deals with classification of conference submissions. The focus of the discussion will be on the agents in the execution space.

A conference the size of ECAI2002 received over 600 submissions. The problem is that the program chair (PC) had to classify the submissions by hand in order to distribute them to reviewers. The idea is, to automate this process using a collection of configured PSMs. A submission for a conference consists of two parts:

Submission form This form contains the administrative details of the submitter (name, address, etc.) as well as information about the submission itself: title, abstract and keywords.

Submitted paper The paper submitted as PDF. For scientific articles, it will contain a title, abstract, body and references.

The goal of the application is to determine for each submission to which "area" it belongs. An area is a sub-discipline within the field of the conference. For example, *Machine Learning* would be a sub-discipline of *Artificial Intelligence* and each Machine Learning paper should be distributed to the reviewer(s) responsible for this area. A sub-discipline may itself be further decomposed (indefinitely), e.g. *Case-Based Reasoning* is a sub-discipline of Machine Learning.

The PC (i.e. end user) has developed an ontology of the sub-disciplines it considers relevant for the conference and assigns keywords to these. The authors of papers enter a selection of these keywords in the submission form. Ideally, the keywords are sufficient to determine the correct area of a submission. In practice, authors often enter multiple keywords that are inconsistent (i.e. keywords that belong to more than one area) either because the content of the paper warrants it or to increase the probability of acceptance.

The strategy of the application is to look at multiple information sources to determine the area of a submission. Information sources are: title, keywords (as entered by the author), abstract and the paper itself. Obviously, reading the paper is more time-consuming than reading the abstract and if it is possible to derive the area from the keywords and/or abstract this is highly preferred.

The agents in the execution space start their operation using an application configuration. For that, we will briefly discuss the activities in the brokering space. Next we will show outcomes of the agents in the execution space.

5.6.1 Brokering

In order to configure the application, PSMs from three libraries were selected: the *data transport library*, the *document analysis library* and the *classification library*. After identification of these libraries, the broker retrieves PSM specifications. These PSM specifications can be matched with the goal specifications using different matching strategies, such as *keyword match*, *simple task-PSM matching* (on the basis of specification), and *theorem proving based matching of competence*. In our experiment, we restricted ourselves to the ECAI broker, which is described in [Wielinga et al., 2003].

The data transport library contains PSMs for P2P and web based file transport, i.e. download routines based on web and Operating System (OS) standards. The document analysis library provides PSMs that can perform various tasks related to documents (analysis, extracting features, reformulation, tokenizing, parsing, identifying phrases) [21]. The PSMs have been designed in such a way that the output of one PSM can be used as

---

[21] See www.swi.psy.uva.nl/usr/anjo/home.html.

the input to another component provided that the ontologies match. The PSMs can handle various representations, such as PDF, HTML, XML and plain text. The classification library (the IRS[22]) contains PSMs that can perform classification. These PSMs can be configured with a classification ontology, such as the AI classification taxonomy. Every PSM from the library is equipped with a PSM wrapper or PSM transducer, with which Operators can consult the PSMs.

Step	PSM	Library	Features	Description
1	select-submission	data transport	input=**location** output=document language=JAVA coupling=wrapping	select a submission from location
2	extract fields	document analysis	input=document output=fields language=Prolog coupling=transducing	select relevant fields and values
3	extract-features	document analysis	input=fields output=features language=Prolog coupling=transducing	construct features
4	classify	classification	input=features output=**class** language=Prolog coupling=transducing	classify features into a class

Table 5.4
Application Configuration for the ECAI application. This table is extracted from the original application configuration produced by the Broker, expressed in XML, in order to increase the readability. The bold values in the features column represent the initial input (in row 1) and the final ouput objects (in row 4).

The remainder of this work will describe how Operators are organized and managed in order to classify a bulk of scientific submissions for the ECAI 2002 conference in appropriate categories based on an AI classification taxonomy. We will not discuss how the broker has constructed a configuration, rather how the configuration is translated into a MAP, how this MAP is executed and the negotiation with the Reconfigurator. The configuration for the ECAI application as constructed by the broker is given in Table 5.4.

5.6.2 Execution

In order to illustrate the dynamics of the agents in the execution space, we have organized this section according to the states in the *MAP configuration life cycle* and *MAP execution life cycle*. The steps in the MAP configuration life cycle are *MAP construction, Operator negotiation, configured MAS, MAS operation* and *wait for Reconfiguration response*.

---

[22]See http://irs.kmi.open.ac.uk/.

5.6.2.1   MAP Construction

Based on the application configuration, the Manager will construct a MAP, using the function as described in Figure 5.12. For every primitive step, the Manager will look for a suitable Operator, using the agent platform's DF, construct instructions and put these in the MAP. The selected Operators and instructions are captured in the MAP (see Table 5.5).

Step	Operator	PSM	Operator Instruction
1	document-obtainer	select submission	activity=select-submission input=url consume_from=useragent output=XMLdocument distribute_to=field-extractor
2	field-extractor	extract fields	activity=extract_fields input=XMLdocument consume_from=document-obtainer output=fields distribute_to=feature-extractor
3	feature-extractor	extract features	activity=extract-features input=fields consume_from=field-extractor output=features distribute_to=classifier
4	classifier	classify	activity=classify input=features consume_from=feature-extractor output=class distribute_to=manager

Table 5.5
Multi-Agent Plan for the ECAI application. The original Multi-Agent Plan is expressed in XML.

In our experiment, we have chosen to let the Manager coordinate the multi-agent system using "standardization of work". Using this coordination strategy the Manager can delegate the control over the operation to the Operators (see also Section 3.3 (p.49)). Given the MAP, the Manager will start negotiations with the Operators.

5.6.2.2   Operator Negotiation

As described in Section 5.4.4.1, the Manager will start negotiations with Operators after construction of the MAP. Given the MAP, the Manager will inform the involved Operators on the basis of instructions how to act. After reception of the instructions, the Operators will adjust their behavior according to these instructions.

The Operators use the instructions to configure their internal behavior, as described in Figure 5.11. The *distribute-to* term tells the Operator from which agent, what object to expect. For example, the agent *document-obtainer* will have to use the object *location* of the type URL as input for its PSM wrapper to invoke the PSM *select-submission*. The output (i.e. an XML document) of the PSM wrapper of the PSM will be sent to the agent as specified in the *distribute-to* slot. An example message is given in Figure 5.17.

```
(REQUEST
 :sender   ( agent-identifier  :name manager)
 :receiver  (set ( agent-identifier  :name document-obtainer))
 :encoding String
 :language FIPA-SL
 :ontology Operations-Ontology
 :protocol fipa-request
 :content   ((action
  (agent-identifier :name document-obtainer)
  (Instruction
   :activity "Select Submission"
   :consume (agent-identifier :name useragent)
   :distribute (agent-identifier :name field-extractor)
   :domain "http://ibrow.org/documentClassification.rdf")))
```

Figure 5.17
Example message, involving the Manager sending a message to document-obtainer containing an instruction. The instruction explains to the the document-obtainer that it should get its input (i.e. a URL referring to an PDF document) from the user-agent, that it should configure the PSM to the domain *DocumentClassification* and that it should distribute the output (i.e. a XML document containing the features of the PDF document) to the field-extractor.

5.6.2.3 Configured MAS

The Configured MAS is illustrated in Figure 5.18, which is arranged cf. the MAP in Figure 5.5. This diagram also includes the Operator negotiation, as described in the previous section. The lines of communication between Manager and the Operators as illustrated by numbered line ④ in Figure 5.2 resemble the lines of communication in the sequence diagram for Standardization of Work in Figure 3.11 (p.58). As shown, the type of interface between the agents and the PSMs is wrapper or transducer cf. Table 5.4.

5.6.2.4 MAS Execution

The next step of the Manager is to start the execution by sending the message "start operation" to the Operator: document-obtainer. The document-obtainer will ask (using a REQUEST message) the user agent to have the user to specify a location. The user agent responds (using an INFORM message) with the answer "URL". Document-obtainer will use its PSM wrapper to invoke the PSM select-submission, using the object *URL*. The response of the PSM wrapper is a collection of documents that contain submissions[23].

---

[23]In order to illustrate the process, the list only contains one url.

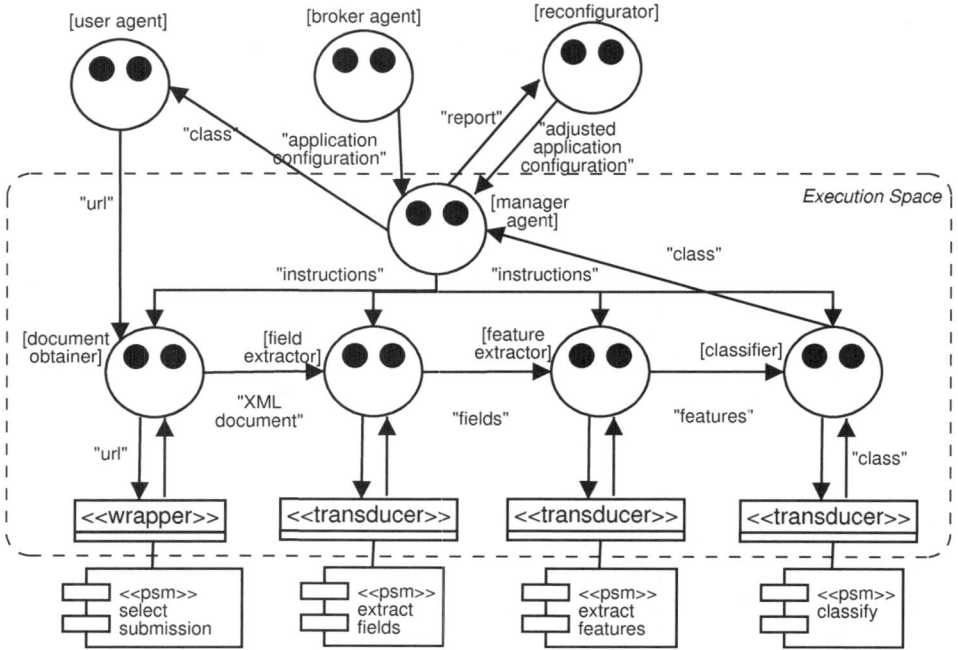

Figure 5.18
(Pseudo) Deployment diagram of the execution space (see also Figure 5.2 (p.103)), show-ing agent configuration according to the Multi-Agent Plan described in Table 5.5 (p.132). The labels annotated with [...] represent agents and "..." represent objects.

The document-obtainer will send the documents one by one to the *field extractor*. The *field extractor* will activate its PSMs and send its results to the *feature-extractor*. The *feature-extractor* will forward its results to the *classifier*, which will on its turn forward its results to the Manager. The Manager will collect all results from the *classifier*.

The communication traces of the states *Operator negotiation* and *MAP execution* are illustrated in Figure 5.19.

When all documents are classified, the Manager will construct a report containing the application configuration and the result set.

5.6.2.5   Wait for Reconfiguration Response

Given the result set, the Manager will start a negotiation with the Reconfigurator. This negotiation is an instantiation of the FIPA ContractNet protocol. The Manager will PRO-POSE the report (i.e. the broker configuration and result set) to the Reconfigurator.

The Reconfigurator can respond with an ACCEPT-PROPOSAL or REJECT-PROPOSAL. An ACCEPT-PROPOSAL means that the Reconfigurator is satisfied and

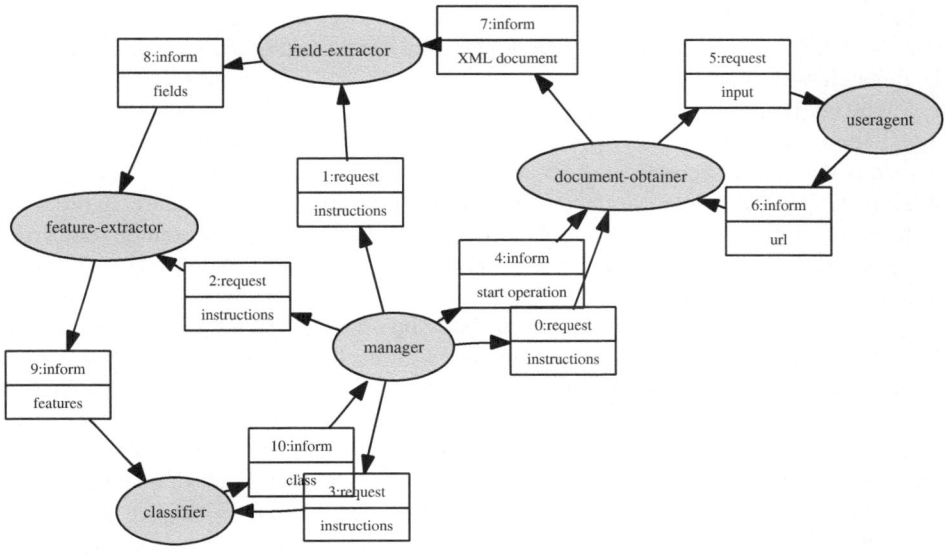

Figure 5.19
Communication Diagram from the Agent Log showing interaction traces between the agents within the execution space. The ellipses represent agents, the boxes represent messages and the arrowed lines represent the direction of the messages. The messages shown here are equipped with a sequence number, the speech act (or intention) and the actual content.

that the Manager can report the results to the user. A REJECT-PROPOSAL means that the result set did not meet the criteria of the Reconfigurator and the Reconfigurator will instruct the Manager with an adjusted application configuration. Then the Manager will reconstruct a new MAP, and the execution process starts over again.

The results of the classification of the ECAI submissions are described in [Wielinga et al., 2003]. Several runs were required for the Reconfigurator to find an optimal configuration. We tried to describe the dynamics of the agents using the inspection tools of the agent console. As shown, the agents behave according to the "standardization of work" coordination strategy.

5.7 Discussion

In this work, we discussed a complex architecture in terms of service discovery, life cycles, coordination strategies and service invocation. The notion of separation of concerns was applied to focus on different aspects of the architecture. Every developed agent offers its own expertise such as PSM provider (i.e. library agent), invoker of PSM (i.e. Operator), coordinator (i.e. Manger), configurator (i.e. the static broker) and reconfigurator (i.e. the dynamic broker agent).

The intelligent agent metaphor enabled us to describe the services and their cooperation within the architecture as agents when represented by roles and behaviors. A lesson learned is that using separation of concerns instead of integration into one large monolithic system helped us to cluster heterogeneous services into one architecture. In order to enable the services (i.e. agents) to interact with each other, we applied common standards and available technology, such as FIPA compliant communication and procedures, agent toolkits and web technology.

We described the technology and methods involved in enabling interoperation to show the complexity of having agents interact with each other. When using standards, agent designers only have to deal with the coordination level of the interoperability framework. In the coordination level, designers only have to specify collaboration between agents. Therefore, they do not have to fill in all the levels of the interoperability structures. However, the collaboration diagrams discussed in this work are of a simple kind. More elaborate collaborations where the agents can negotiate are a subject for further research. The design of ontologies for ontology-based communication is discussed in the next chapter.

There are several alternatives to our approach: one monolithic system, distributed objects and web services. Using a monolithic system approach all necessary components and services are integrated into one system. A number of the advantages are: there is a minimal need for interoperation and there is a central point of success and failure. The disadvantages are: all components need to be centrally gathered, which is not always possible, the application will become very complex, components written in different languages need to be translated or rewritten and only a small number of engineers can work on the system, due to integrity constraints. When using distributed objects, there is need for middleware, such as CORBA. The advantage is that objects can call methods of distributed object themselves, without explicit communication. The disadvantages are that standardization is achieved on a low level and there is a need for control processes that coordinate the distributed objects, because objects lack their own control. Finally, every component can be represented as a web service. The advantage is that SOAP is becoming a standard that is supported by many development kits. The reason for this is that SOAP is a light weight protocol that works with existing standards, such as XML and HTTP. The disadvantages are that web services lack interaction protocols, coordination mechanisms and the notion of (hierarchical) roles, such as Manager and Operator.

In the submission classification scenario we showed how an application configuration is translated into a MAP. The execution of this MAP showed how PSMs from different libraries can interact with each other. We had three libraries of PSMs to our disposal, i.e. data-transport, document analysis and classification. We did not investigate configuration and execution of services from other libraries, because the libraries were not available (i.e. only described on paper) or were not accessible (due to technical or semantic problems).

Using the agent console, we could inspect parts of the dynamics of the IBROW architecture. Despite the limited expressive power of the graphical inspection tools, we could gain insights into the communication and internal behavior of agents. However, the control over the agents is still a problem. When testing or debugging a multi-agent system, it is still difficult to start, restart, stop or suspend agents.

Although we showed some overall behavior (such as configuration and execution) of the architecture, most of the knowledge and behavior of the individual agents is hard-wired. In order to have a flexible system, the agents should also be able to detect possible failures and find individual means (such as applying another strategy) or group means (consulting other agents) to overcome these failures.

In spite of the use of common standards (such as XML and FIPA) and technology we encountered most of the problems in the technical and syntactic interoperability layers. A possible improvement could be having less strict parsing technology. If a user makes a typing error, the user agent should be able to detect it and correct it. Furthermore, failing network connections, server failures and failing communication are inevitable in a distributed environment. Therefore, the agents should have error handling and fail-over mechanisms as found in grid computing. For example, if a PSM fails for some reason, an Operator should be capable to reschedule the execution to another Operator.

We foresee an *agent-based market place* consisting of provider agents, customer agents and broker agents. The broker agents deliver an intelligent service that enables third party knowledge-service reuse, where suppliers provide libraries of knowledge services adhering to some standard, and customers can consult these libraries to configure a knowledge system suited to their needs by selection and adaptation. A customer in this context is a person/company who wants to solve a particular problem. Users who use the brokering service simply get results for their requests. It is not of interest for users how the brokering service acquired the result.

Chapter 6

Message Content Ontologies

In this chapter we address the problem of how agents can handle message-based communication. Our approach is to look at ontology-based communication, in which the meaning and intention of messages is specified in message content ontologies. The idea is that agents can share semantics by committing to shared message content ontologies. We discuss a theoretical framework for message-based communication, in which we sketch an ideal world where an agent is capable of various ontological operations. A pragmatic approach is presented, which enables the creation and use of ontologies to support message-based communication between agents.

A tool is described that assists agent engineers in designing message content ontologies and export it to Java source code. A case study on Legal services illustrates conversations between agents based on a message content ontology. The work presented is partly based on the paper *Creating and Using Ontologies in Agent Communication*, published in Proceedings of the Workshop on Ontologies and Agent Systems at AAMAS 2002. The co-authors are R.F. Pels, G. Caire and F. Bergenti. The case study described is based on an Agentcities grant project (see www.acklin.nl/agentcities). The "Bean Generator" tool described is designed by the author and is used by various institutions and companies that work with the JADE toolkit (see http://gaper.swi.psy.uva.nl/beangenerator).

6.1   Introduction

In this section, we present a layered framework containing a Reference Model for ontology-based agent communication. Using ontologies in agent communication enables agents and agent engineers to add semantics to agent conversations.

A traditional distributed system interoperates with other systems by giving these other systems access to its information retrieval functions. One technique to interoperate, for instance to transfer information between distributed systems, is Remote Methods Invocation (RMI). Giving systems direct access to other systems' information retrieval functions leads to tightly coupled systems. However, multi-agent systems are loosely coupled distributed systems, where agents do not have direct access to each others functionalities (services). By exchanging messages, agents can access other agents' services. The messages are not only used to exchange information, but also to communicate on a higher level, such as negotiation about price, instructions and sharable knowledge [Genesereth and Ketchpel, 1994, Huhns and Stephens, 1999].

Message-based communication can be described on several levels of detail: message transport, message encoding, communication languages, message interpretation and composition [Labrou et al., 1999]. Message transport is involved with agent addressing and communication protocols. Whether a message is encoded in binary, string or other format is of concern at the message encoding level. Several agent communication languages exist, for example KQML or FIPA-ACL.

We focus on the ideas motivating the FIPA standardization, because it is supported in the agent community[1]. On top of the agent communication language, FIPA has adopted the idea of ontology-based communication from [Neches et al., 1991], where the meaning and intention of message contents is specified in message content ontologies. In order to share semantics, agents commit to shared message content ontologies. The agent engineer is free to design and implement the communication model of the agent around message content ontologies. The only requirement is that the content of messages exchanged commit to one or more message content ontologies. In this case, agents can interact without having to negotiate about message structure and message content. A similar approach can be found in Open-EDI [Weigand and Hasselbring, 2001].

The problem addressed in this chapter is defined by [FIPA, 2001] as:

"Despite its crucial importance for guaranteeing the exchange of content information among agents, (...) a suitable "Reference Model" for ontologies needs to be established."

The assumption is that agents share a common Reference Model that provides the proper semantics in message-based communication. Specific message content ontologies will be based on this Reference Model. The question is, what such a Reference Model could look like and how agents can generate and interpret messages that commit to such a Reference Model.

In the remainder, we give a brief introduction on ontologies. Next, we discuss a layered framework containing a Reference Model for message content ontologies, in which we sketch an ideal world, where agents are capable of various ontological operations. Then, we discuss a pragmatic approach to the Reference Model based on the current state-of-the art in agent technology, which is applied in a case study on legal services. We conclude this chapter by a discussion on the two approaches and issues arising from this work.

6.2   Ontologies in a Nutshell

An ontology is defined by [Studer et al., 1998] as:

---

[1] An alternative to FIPA is the Rosetta initiative(www.isi.edu/expect/projects/agents/rosetta.html) and available technology (See, www.agentlink.org/software). In contrast to FIPA, the Rosetta architecture is based on middleware, which represents most of the agent's environment. This means that an agent should be equipped with an interface to the Rosetta architecture. The drawback of this approach is that the agents are not loosely coupled to the agent environment.

An ontology is a formal, explicit specification of a shared conceptualization. A "conceptualization" refers to an abstract model of some phenomenon in the world by having identified the relevant concepts of that phenomenon. "Explicit" means that the type of concepts used, and the constraints on their use are explicitly defined. (...) "Formal" refers to the fact that the ontology should be machine-readable. "Shared" reflects the notion that an ontology captures consensual knowledge, that it is not private to some individual, but accepted by a group.

According to van Heist and colleagues, ontologies can be classified according to the *subject* of conceptualization [van Heijst et al., 1997]. A *domain ontology* specifies facts and constraints related to a specific domain. Many domain ontologies exist, such as *engineering ontologies* [Borst, 1997], *mathematical ontologies* [Gruber and Olsen, 1994], chemical ontologies [Fernández-López et al., 1999] and *medical ontologies* such as Galen[2].

A *generic ontology* is similar to a domain ontology, however the concepts defined are generic across many fields. Generic ontologies are also seen as upper-level ontology or top-level ontology [Guarino, 1998]. Examples of generic concepts are object, event, and action. Upper-level ontologies are produced by the *standard upper ontology IEEE working group*, *Upper Cyc* and *Sensus*[3]. An *application ontology* conceptualizes information that can be used for a particular application. In Section 6.3.2.1, we describe a number of application ontologies. This ontology is composed of concepts from domain ontologies and generic ontologies. A *representation ontology* provides primitives that can be used to represent other ontologies. It provides a framework without making claims about the world. An example is "Open Knowledge Base Connectivity (OKBC)"[4], which provides a uniform model of knowledge based systems based on a common conceptualization of classes, individuals, slots, facets, and inheritance. OKBC forms the basis of the ontology construction tool Protégé 2000[5] [Noy et al., 2000]. Another example of a representation ontology is the Frame Ontology, which defines concepts in the form of frames or objects, allowing to describe hierarchies of classes with slots [Gruber, 1993].

For methodologies related to ontology engineering we refer to [Gomez-Perez, 1999, Noy and McGuinness, 2001].

In the remainder of this chapter, we focus on specific subjects that are relevant for agent communication. A number of agent communication ontologies are defined that model these subjects.

---

[2] See www.opengalen.org.

[3] http://suo.ieee.org, www.cyc.com/cyc-2-1/cover.html and www.isi.edu/natural-language/resources/sensus.html

[4] Details on Open Knowledge Base Connectivity can be found at www.ai.sri.com/~okbc/.

[5] See http://protege.stanford.edu.

6.3   Message Content Ontology Framework

In this section, we discuss a theoretical approach to establish a Reference Model (cf. [FIPA, 2001]) for message content ontologies. The framework consists of a collection of ontologies, which we refer to as agent communication ontologies. The basis of these ontologies is the *speech acts* theory [Labrou et al., 1999, Shoham, 1993, Bond and Gasser, 1988]. Messages exchanged between agents are annotated with speech acts, giving messages specific meanings. The theory originates from linguistics [Searle, 1969, Austin, 1976], where it is used to analyze human speech and text. A speech act is composed of three components: *locutionary act, illocutionary act* and *perlocutionary act*. The *locutionary act* is concerned with the material generation of utterances. The *illocutionary act* is concerned with carrying out a speech act. An illocutionary act itself is composed of an *illocutionary force* and a *propositional content*. An *illocutionary force* can be seen as a performative, such as questioning, negotiating, ordering and asking to do something. The *propositional content* is the object of the illocutionary force, such as problem, price, product or activity. The *perlocutionary act* is concerned with the effect an illocutionary act has on the state of the receiver. We focus on the illocutionary force, which we refer to as *performative*.

Linguists have made a difference between explicit and implicit performatives [Austin, 1976]. Agent Communication languages such as KQML and FIPA-ACL make use of explicit performatives [Labrou et al., 1999]. Here, every agent utterance (i.e. the sending of a message) is seen as a speech act, which is composed of a *propositional content* and a *performative*. The structure of a speech act is then of the form $E(I(A))$, where E is the explicit performative, I the implicit performative and A the arguments of the directive[6]. For example, a message containing an explicit performative is: promise(deliver(cd)), where promise is the performative (in this case a "commissive, because the speaker has committed him to a future course of action, c.f. [Searle, 1969]), deliver the intended transaction and cd the argument.

Most human communication does not explicitly express one of these types of speech acts. For example, one does not ask a question in the form of:"I direct you to the give me the price of a CD", or "I assert the price of a CD to 30 EURO". In order to come close to human communication, we will make use of implicit performatives. This means that we directly make use of a specific performative, without declaring the type of performatives. The form of an utterance is in the form of $I(A)$. For example, an utterance such as (Buy (CD :name "Mahler 1")) is to be read in a first-person present declarative form [Labrou et al., 1999]. Hence, this message can be read as "hereby, I declare that I want to buy the CD with the name Mahler 1".

Concepts such as CD can be found in an existing ontology, cf. [Cranefield and Purvis, 1999]. Therefore we can reuse existing concepts and relations of these ontologies into our agent communication ontology[7]. There are several

---

[6]In more, detail $E(I(A))$ is the logical representation of a speech act. The actual representation of an utterance depends on the languages of agent communication (ACL). For example, in SL it is possible to express multiple performatives in one utterance.

[7]By reuse, we mean reusing one concept and related relations or the reuse of an entire branch of an ontology.

methods to reuse and share ontologies, divided into syntactical and semantic methods [Gomez-Perez, 1999, Pinto and Martins, 2000]. An example of a syntactical method (which operates on the symbol level) is the translation of an ontology into another ontology representation language. Semantic methods (which operate on the knowledge level), includes merging of one ontology with another and mapping of one concept to another.

Another important communication theory is *conversational interaction* [Geis, 1995], which reasons on the use of performatives by conversation members. In every conversation there is at least one initiator and one other participant. Furthermore, there are rules that restrict the use of performatives. For example, the manager and operators in the IBROW architecture (see Section 5.3) engage in interaction in order to collaborate. In the agent community, these rules are called *protocols*. Every participant in a conversation should follow these protocols. In our framework, we couple protocols to roles. In communication theory this is called *role-taking*[8] [Levinson, 1991]. A protocol can dictate that for every question asked, an answer has to be given. For example in the IBROW architecture, if the broker asks a question to a librarian, both the broker and the librarian know what role to take and what performatives to use. So the broker as questioner sends ask(needed competences) to a librarian. The librarian as agent questioned, responds with reply(candidate PSMs).

6.3.1 Agent Communication Meta Ontology

The *Agent Communication Meta Ontology* defines generic concepts necessary for agent communication: *conversation domain concept, performative, protocol* and *agent role*. The elements of this ontology are not explicitly used in the messages exchanged between agents. Rather, these elements are used as reference by agents and agent engineers. Agents can use it to reason about interactions with other agents. For example, when an agent decides to consult another agent, it can select the appropriate vocabulary, performatives, protocol and role. When an agent engineer is designing an agent he can configure the functions of the communication model of the agent.

In order to bind the concepts together, a number of relations are defined: allowed concept, allowed performative and allowed protocol. The relation allowed concept means that every performative should contain one or more instances of domain concept. The relation allowed performative denotes that every protocol contains an ordered number of performatives. Finally, the relation allowed protocol tells that agent roles (part of the agent role ontology) should commit to one or more protocols. The subject represented by metaclasses and relations are illustrated in Figure 6.1.

6.3.2 Reference Model

The four subjects of agent communication are defined into four agent communication ontologies: *conversation domain ontology, performative ontology, protocol ontology* and

---

[8]Other terms used are *feed forward* and *empathy*.

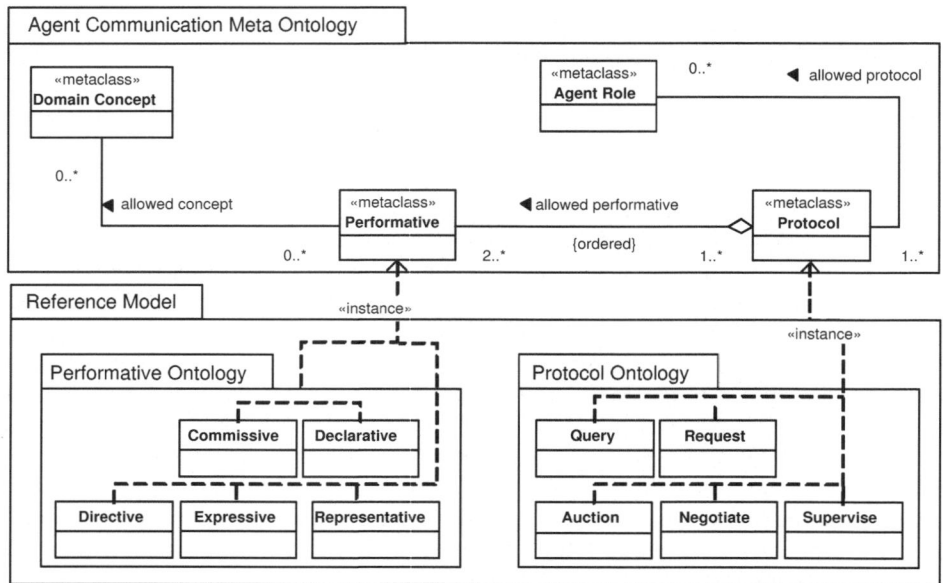

Figure 6.1
Agent Communication Meta Ontology and a part of the Reference Model, showing the
four subjects of agent communication: **domain concept, performative, protocol** and
agent role. The relations **allowed concept, allowed performative** and **allowed protocol** bind the subjects together. The relation **allowed concept** means that every performative should contain one or more instances of **domain concept**. The relation **allowed
performative** denotes that every protocol contains an ordered number of performatives.
The Ordered relation enables to describe the allowed sequence of performatives in a
protocol. The relation **allowed protocol** tells that agent roles (part of the agent role ontology) should commit to one or more protocols. The relation between the **performative**
and the Performative Ontology and **protocol** metaclasses (from the Agent Communication Meta Ontology) and the Protocol Ontology (from the Reference Model) are of type
<<instance>>. The elements of the Performative Ontology are discussed in Table 6.1.
In Table 6.2, the elements of the Protocol Ontology are discussed.

the *agent role ontology*. These four agent communication ontologies form the Reference
Model. The relations between the ontologies are illustrated in Figure 6.2.

The *Reference Model* is an instantiation of the Agent Communication Meta Ontology. The relations between the Agent Communication Meta Ontology and the Reference
Model are illustrated in Figure 6.1. Below, we discuss the agent communication ontologies in detail.

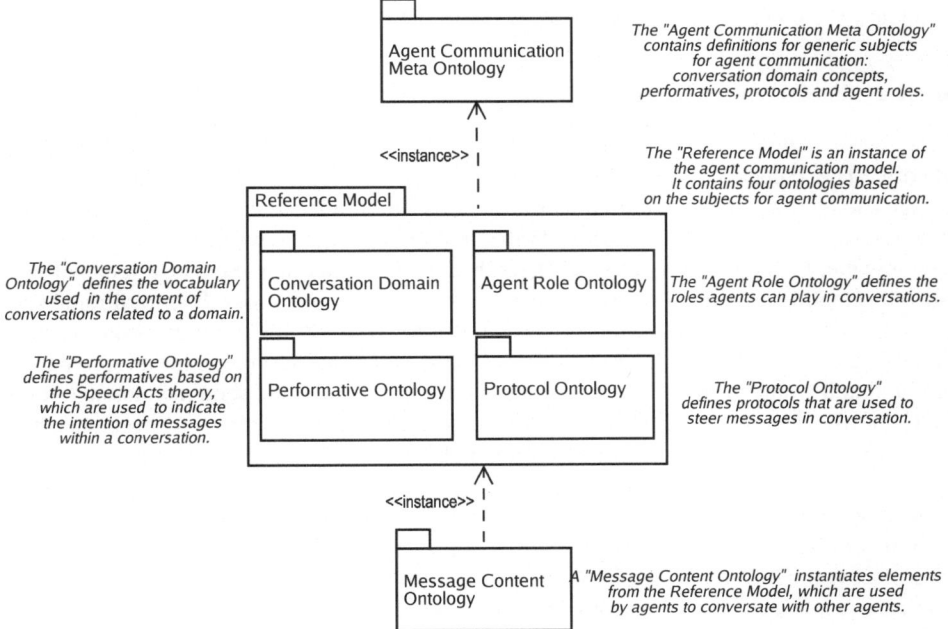

Figure 6.2
The agent communication ontologies represented by UML packages. The dependencies (i.e. the dashed arrowed lines, which are to be read as "source depends on destination") show the relations between the ontologies. The Agent Communication Meta Ontology defines the subjects for agent communication ontologies: conversation domain concepts, performatives, protocols and agent roles. The Reference Model is an `instantiation` of the Agent Communication Meta Ontology. The Reference Model makes use of the four agent communication ontologies. Finally, the Message Content Ontology instantiates elements from the Reference Model.

6.3.2.1   Conversation Domain Ontology

A *conversation domain ontology* defines the vocabulary used in the propositional content of conversations related to a domain. Examples are price, product, answer, question, proposal, offer, name, person and address. Furthermore, it defines the structure of a domain, for example a product has a price, a question has zero or more answers, an offer is related to one product, a person has a name and an address.

Several ontologies are available that can be used in the design of conversation domain ontologies. Elements of existing ontologies can be imported, adapted or translated into other ontologies. Several ontologies exists for identifying products in an electronic commerce applications through product descriptions,such as S95, the United Nations

Standard Products and Services Codes, E-cl@ss, and RosettaNet[9].

6.3.2.2 Performative Ontology

The *performative ontology* defines performatives that are based on the Speech Acts theory. The Speech Acts theory is introduced into Agent Communication Languages to design agent communication as close to human communication as possible [Labrou et al., 1999]. In traditional information exchange between systems, messages are only pieces of data [Weigand and Hasselbring, 2001]. In order to create a social effect, such as creating an obligation, performatives are added to messages. In a traditional setting one service would send a message (CD :name "Mahler 1") to a musicshop service, intending to *buy* a CD. Both services "know" that when one service sends a reference to a CD, that it wants to buy a CD. In agent systems, an agent would send the message (buy (CD :name "Mahler 1")), where the buy performative can be seen as a speech act (the message is an attempt to perform a transaction between a buyer and a seller).

The idea behind Speech Acts is that sentences can be categorized into particular types. We follow the classification as suggested by [Searle, 1969], see table 6.1. In this classification there are five basic categories of performatives (illocutionary forces): Representatives, Commissives, Directives, Declaratives and Expressives. Representatives are speech acts that represent some state of affairs. For example, asserting facts about a domain, such as telling the price of a CD.

Commissives are speech acts that commit the speaker to some future course of action. In an economic setting, this can be used to have agents committing to a contract. For example, promising to perform a job in the future, such as: "at noon, I will buy a CD". Directives are speech acts whose intention is to get the addressee to carry out some action. For example, asking a question related to a domain, such as "what is the price of CD X?". Declaratives are speech acts that themselves bring about a state of affairs and which are spoken by a recognized authority. In order to give a Manager control over Operators, an Operator has to see a Manager as an authority. For example, an Manager instructs an Operator how to perform its activities. Expressives are speech acts that indicate the speaker's psychological state or mental attitude. For example, one agents "thanks" another agent for its services.

Several variations of the categorization of Searle exist, see [Austin, 1976, Singh, 1998, Ferber, 1999]. Also in the Agent Field, specializations of Speech Acts have been reported. A number of explicit performatives are specified by Haddadi and FIPA, which can also be used as implicit performatives. Haddadi has defined a library of communication types [Haddadi, 1995]. A selection of these types is: Require, Order, Reject, Ask and Reply. FIPA has specified: Accept Proposal (which can be seen as an instance of a "representative"), Call for Proposal (directive), Confirm (commissive), Inform (representative), and request (directive) [FIPA, 2002d]. These performative or communicative types are either representatives, directives or commissives [Singh, 1998]. For example, the performative *inform* is supposed to give information and *request* cor-

---

[9]See www.s95.info, www.unspsc.org, www.eclass.de and www.rosettanet.org.

Performative	Description	Examples
Representative	inform the addressee of some state of affairs	*asserting, concluding, describing* "The price of every CD is 30 EURO."
Commissives	commit the speaker to future course of action	*promising, threatening, offering and vowing* "If you buy 10 CDs, the price is 23 EURO."
Declaratives	"representatives" spoken by a recognized authority, such as a director or president	*marrying, naming, and firing from employment* "I allow this shop to sell CDs."
Directives	attempts by the speaker to get the addressee (or receiver) to do something	*requesting, questioning and commanding* "What is the price of a CD?" "Can I buy this CD?"
Expressives	express a psychological state	*greeting, thanking and congratulating* "Thank you for buying this CD!"

Table 6.1
Five basic categories of performatives (illocutionary forces), cf. [Searle, 1969].

responds to a demand for information. In order to allow authority, which is needed to construct organizational relations such as a Manager-Operator relation, "Declaratives" are needed. Furthermore, to allow learning based on feedback, the speech act "Expressive" is needed. For example, a Manager can give positive or negative feedback on the activities performed by an Operator in order to learn the Operator coordination pattern.

6.3.2.3 Protocol Ontology

Next to individual message exchange, agents engage in conversations. Conversations can be seen as a shared sequence of messages that agents follow [Labrou et al., 1999]. We have expressed the notion of sequencing between allowed type of messages by the `Ordered` relation in Figure 6.1. In order to guide conversations, (interaction) protocols can be used that restrict the allowed sequence of performatives. Examples of shared sequences are negotiations [Chavez and Maes, 1996] and auctions [Rodríguez-Aguilar et al., 1998]. The shared sequences of performatives are defined in the *protocol ontology*. For example, a directive, such as a question, should be followed by an representative to answer the question. The Protocol Ontology of the Reference Model, contains a number of generic protocols, which can be seen as a Reference Model for conversations see Table 6.2.

FIPA has defined a number of interaction protocols. For example the FIPA-REQUEST protocol specifies that a request performative should be followed by a refuse, or an agree [FIPA, 2002h]. After the agree performative, the performative failure and inform are allowed.

Other interaction protocols deal with the Contract Net [FIPA, 2002e] and Auctions, such as the English auction [FIPA, 2002g] and the Dutch auction [FIPA, 2002f]. In addition, Haddadi has defined a library of message patterns [Haddadi, 1995]. Examples are, that an order performative has to be followed by a report performative, require has to be followed by agree or reject, and propose has to be followed by request, require or reject.

In Table 6.3 we have placed the performatives as given in Table 6.1 against the

Protocol	Description	Example utterance	exchanged between two or more agents
FIPA-Query	asking	A to B (directive):	"What is the price of a CD?"
	for information	B to A (commissive):	"Agree to answer the question."
		B to A (representative):	"The price of a CD is 30 EURO."
FIPA-Request	requesting to	A to B (directive):	"Can you order a CD?"
	perform an action	B to A (commissive):	"Agree to perform the action."
		B to A (commissive):	"The CD will arrive next week."
FIPA-Auction	bid on	A to B, C (directive):	"Who wants to buy this CD?"
	object	B to A (commissive):	"I bid 20 EURO."
		C to A (commissive):	"I bid 18 EURO."
		A to B, C (representative):	"Sold to A, for 20 EURO."
Negotiate	negotiate on	A to B (directive):	"What is the price of a CD?"
	object	B to A (commissive):	"I offer the CD for 30 EURO."
		A to B (representative):	"I reject, price too high."
		B to A (commissive):	"I offer the CD for 25 EURO."
		A to B (representative):	"I accept."
Supervise	coordinate	M to A (declarative):	"Follow my instructions."
	an agent or process	A to M (commissive):	"Agree."
		M to A (directive):	"Find a CD shop."
		A to M (representative):	"I found a CD shop."
		M to A (directive):	"Try to buy a CD for less then 28 EURO."
		A to M (representative):	"I bought a CD for 25 EURO."
		M to A (directive):	"Send CD to address X."
		M to A (expressive):	"You did a good job."

Table 6.2
A selection of types of protocols and descriptions. The *FIPA-Query*, *FIPA-Request* and *FIPA-Auction* protocols originate from the FIPA standards (cf. [FIPA, 2002h, FIPA, 2002h, FIPA, 2002e]) and are extended with speech act categories and examples related to the musicshop domain. The *Negotiate* and *Supervise* protocols are added to illustrate the variety of possible protocols. In the example column, the letters "A", "B", "C" and "M" represent names of agents.

protocols as given in Table 6.2, in order to illustrate the **AllowedPerformative** relation. As shown, a number of performatives are required (+) or optional (*). The three existing protocols, *Query*, *Request* and *Auction*, allow the **agree** performative that confirms a directive. We see the **agree** performative as a commissive, which is optional. The idea is that agents "agree" on how to negotiate. Examples of agreements are the number of negotiation rounds, number of participants, object of negotiation and rule setting.

A negotiation protocol is also called the "rule of encounter", which enables agents to share allowed sequences of performatives in a negotiation [Lomuscio et al., 2003]. In our negotiate protocol, directives are used to ask a participant of a negotiation for an offer, such as the price. In response, a commissive is used to offer a bid. Next, representatives are used to react positively or negatively on a bid.

In our supervision protocol, directives are used by an agent with a manager role to instruct its subordinates, such as an operator. The operator responds with representatives to report the result of the instructions. The use of the expressive performative can play a role in learning situations, because it enables a feedback, such as rewarding. Taking a

Performatives / Protocols	Representative	Commissives	Declaratives	Directives	Expressives
Query	+	+		+	
Request	*	*		+	
Auction	+	+		+	
Negotiate	+	+	*	+	*
Supervise	+	*	*	+	*

Table 6.3

Examples of the **Allowed Performative Relation** relation, on the basis of the Performatives as given in Table 6.1 and protocols as given in Table 6.2. In this relation, performatives are required (+) or optional (*).

situation where a manager supervises an operator, the manager could use feedback in the form of expressives, to teach the operator how to perform its activities. In the end, the operator could operate without direct supervision of the manager.

Ontologies that can be used as the basis of protocol ontologies are the Enterprise Ontology [Uschold et al., 1998] and the Toronto Virtual Enterprise [Gruninger and Fox, 1994][10].

6.3.2.4   Agent Role Ontology

The *agent role ontology* defines the roles that agents can play in conversations. An agent role defines the responsibility and allowed behavior of an agent. In the Reference Model, we modeled responsibility and allowed behavior of an agent as the protocols and agent is allowed to use. This is represented by the **allowed protocol** relation in Figure 6.1.

We already discussed a number of agent roles: Operator and Manager (see Section 2.2 (p.11)), Broker and Librarian (see Section 5.2 (p.101)) and an agent platform's Directory Facilitator (DF) and Agent Manager Service (AMS) (see Section 3.4.1 (p.63)). Furthermore, in an e-commerce setting there are roles, such as supplier, producer, partner, and consumer [Weigand and Hasselbring, 2001].

6.3.3   Message Content Ontology

Message content ontologies can be used by agents to discuss about facts, beliefs, hypotheses and predications related to specific domains. Hence, a message content ontology makes use of a conversation domain, performative, protocol and agent role ontologies. When agents want to communicate, the appropriate message content ontology is selected.

Based on the type of conversation, the required domain concepts and relations, performatives and protocols, and agent roles are referred to (i.e. instantiated). In our framework, a Message Content Ontology instantiates elements from the Reference Model (cf. Figure 6.2).

---

[10]See www.aiai.ed.ac.uk/∼ entprise/enterprise/ontology.html and www.eil.utoronto.ca/tove/toveont.html.

Several examples of message content ontologies can be found in the agent literature and agent programming manuals: *Agent Management Ontology, Currency ontology* and *Cinema Service Ontology*. We briefly discuss these ontologies and relate them to our agent communication ontologies.

The FIPA Agent Management Ontology is a message content ontology used for conversations between (visiting) agents and the agents on a FIPA compliant agent platform (cf. [FIPA, 2002c]): the AMS (agent management service) and the DF (directory facilitator). In order for a (visiting) agent to work on an agent platform, it has to behave according to an agent life cycle (as discussed in Section 3.4) [FIPA, 2002c]. Every (visiting) agent that wants to join an agent platform should register itself with the AMS and the DF. The AMS maintains a register of physical agent addresses, and the DF maintains a register of agent service descriptions. If the agent decides to leave the agent platform, it should deregister itself.

This ontology is composed of a number of performatives: register, deregister, search and modify. Within our framework, the performatives register, deregister and modify are of type "directive", because visiting agents use them to *change* the DF's register. For example, the performative modify is used when an agent wants to change its address or service. In case the agent wants to locate other agents, it can use the performative search. This performative is of type directive, because it can be used to *question* the DF's register.

Examples of the relations between speech acts and domain concepts are: the performatives register *requires* the concept agent-description, which contains other properties such as name to identify the agent, address to locate the agent and services to describe the services the agent offers. Furthermore, the performative search *requires* the concept service, and the performative modify *requires* the domain concept agent-description. Allowed sequences of performatives are not specified in the ontology.

There is a notion of *visiting agent, DF* and *AMS*. The role of a visiting agent is to register itself on a platform and it can make use of the search, modify and deregister performative. However, these roles in relation to protocols are not specified.

The Cambia Currency Ontology is a message content ontology used by an agent that provides a service to make currency conversions between a number of currencies[11]. An agent should specify source and destination currency as well as the date, to determine the correct exchange rate, and the amount. The ontology contains the performative convert, which requires four domain concepts: from, to, rate and dateC. This performative is of type directive, because it is used to request the currency agent. The concept from is used to denote the source currency code (e.g. "USD") and the amount. To specify the target currency code (e.g. "EUR"), the concept to is used. The concept rate specifies the type of conversation, this can be

---

[11] See http://zurich.agentcities.whitestein.ch/Services/Cambia.html.

"cash", "inter-bank" or "credit card". Finally, the concept dateC contains the date of conversion. There is no notion of role or protocol.

The Tilab Cinema Representation Service Ontology is a message content ontology used by the cinema broker agent that provides information concerning a selection of cinemas of the cities of Turin and Paris[12]. One of the specified performatives is: provide-cinema-info (of type directive) which can be used to question the cinema broker. The domain concepts are Show, Cinema and CinemaPreference. The concept Show contains attributes related to time of a show and price. The concept Cinema describes the address and contact details of a cinema. The preferences of a user, such as time and price are described in the concept CinemaPreference.

There is a notion of two roles: user agent and cinema broker. A user agent uses the performative provide-cinema-info combined with the concept CinemaPreference to ask the cinema broker, to acquire a list of available shows and cinemas. The relation between the user agent that can use the performative provide-cinema-info and the cinema broker agents, is not specified in the ontology.

In the three examples, we can identify the notion of performative and domain concepts, and the relation between the performatives and the allowed domain concepts. Roles, protocols and relations between roles, protocols and performatives are not specified. The reason for this is that these ontologies are applied in relative simple agent systems, with a limited number of agents, reasoning capabilities and possible interactions. Furthermore, these ontologies are designed "ad hoc". Another message content ontology that is used by agents in an agent-based supply chain management system, can be found in Section 2.5.4 (p.33).

6.3.4 Message Content Ontology Creation

In our approach, there are two steps for defining a message content ontology: *identification of conversation specific concepts* and *specification of conversation specific concepts*. This process is illustrated in Figure 6.3.

In the first step: Identification of Conversation Specific Concepts, the required conversation specific concepts for the Message Content Ontology are defined. This step takes as input the Agent Communication Meta Ontology and the ontologies of the Reference Model: the Conversation Domain, Agent Role, Performative and Protocol Ontology (see Figure 6.1). On the Agent Communication Meta Ontology level, the classes of the Reference Model are seen as instances[13]. The result of this step is (technically) an object diagram that shows the needed concepts for a conversation (see Figure 6.4). On the level of the Reference Model, the instances of the object diagram are seen as classes.

In the second step: Specification of Conversation Specific Concepts, the defined conversation specific concepts will be specified in detail. The step takes the object

---

[12]See http://jade.cselt.it/AgentCities/CinemaRepresentativeServiceDescription.htm.

[13]To define a class based on a metaclass, one has to make an instantiation of a metaclass.

diagram and a selection of external ontologies as input. The attributes for the classes are defined in the Reference Model and linked to other, possibly already existing, classes. The result is a message content ontology represented as a class diagram(see e.g. Figure 6.5).

The idea is that the conversation specific concepts can make use of classes imported from other ontologies.

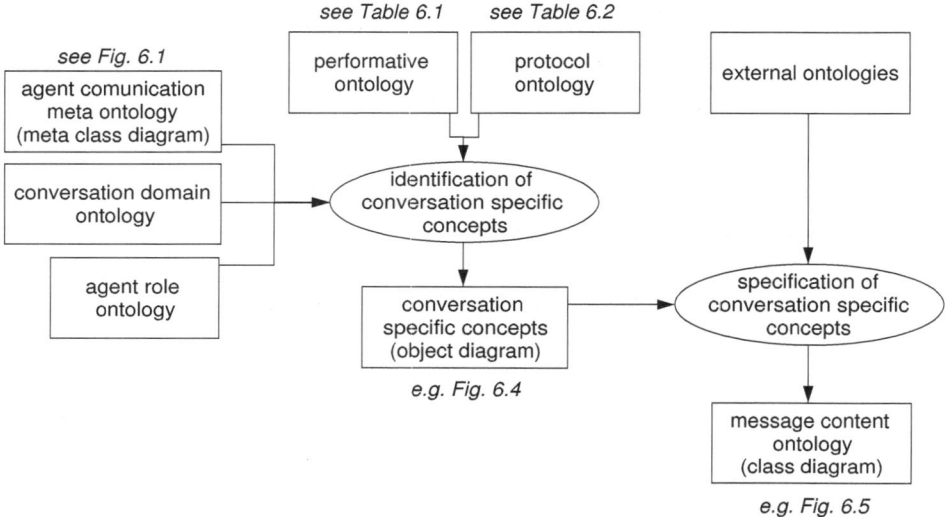

Figure 6.3
Inference diagram showing the process of message content ontology creation. The step Identification of Conversation Specific Concepts takes as input the agent communication meta ontology, conversation domain, agent role, performative and protocol ontologies. The result of this step is (technically) an object diagram that shows the needed concepts for a conversation. The step specification of conversation specific concepts takes the object diagram and a selection of external ontologies as input. The result is a message content ontology represented as a class diagram. Where applicable, links to figures, tables or examples in this chapter are given.

In the next two sections, we discuss *identification of conversation specific concepts* and *specification of conversation specific concepts* in detail.

6.3.4.1   Identification of Conversation Specific Concepts

Conversation specific concepts are defined based on generic classes of the Agent Communication Meta Ontology. In order to illustrate the process of creating the required classes of a message content ontology, we define an example in an electronic commerce domain, because it is a popular domain for agent systems [Luck et al., 2003]. Agents can represent parties that want to do business, such as buying and selling items. Both the buying agent and the selling agent will try to negotiate in order to get the best deal. An example of a negotiation is bargaining for the price of a CD in a musicshop.

In our example, we start with defining roles needed for CD bargaining: buyer and seller. The buyer role has as goal to buy a CD for a reasonable price. The role of seller is to sell as many CDs as possible. In order to have the two roles negotiate with each other, we defined two protocols: cdNegotiationBuy and cdNegotiationSell. The first protocol is coupled to the buyer and allows the performatives: ask, buy, reject and abort. The second protocol is coupled to the seller and allows the performatives: offer and abort. The performative ask is used by the buyer to start a negotiation by asking for the price of CD. The seller can offer a price, which the buyer can accept by using buy or continue the negotiation by using reject. Both roles can break off the negotiation by using the performative abort. The domain concepts involved are CD and price. The concept CD refers to the item subject of negotiation. The concept price refers to the argumentation used in the negotiation.

The instantiation of the required conversation specific concepts is illustrated in Figure 6.4. This object diagram shows the required conversation specific concepts for the musicshop example, as instances of the Agent Communication Meta Ontology (e.g. the object CD is an instance of the metaclass Concept). The name of an object is composed of the identification of an object, followed by the name of the metaclass (e.g. Concept, Directive, Negotiate and AgentRole). For example, the object Buy is an instance of the metaclass Representative. The relations between the objects are inherited from the Agent Communication Meta Ontology. As illustrated in Figure 6.1, the relation between AgentRole and Negotiation (which is of type Protocol) is allowed protocol. The relations between the Protocols and the directives, commissive and representative (which are of type Performative is allowed performative. The relation between the Performatives and the Concepts is of type allowed concept.

6.3.4.2 Specification of Conversation Specific Concepts

In order to make the switch from the metalevel to the domain level, we map the defined instances of the Reference Model onto classes. For example, the instances defined in Figure 6.4 are mapped on the classes in Figure 6.5. The purpose of this step is to elaborate (i.e. make the generic classes specific) on the definition of the conversation specific concepts in terms of properties (or attributes) and relations. We refer to [Noy and McGuinness, 2001] for ways to define the properties of these classes. The resulting class diagram is illustrated in Figure 6.5.

For our example, the concept CD is equipped with the attributes title, artist and content. The attribute content is described using the concept Track for individual track identification. The concept Track is imported from the ontology for a catalog system for a classical music compact disc publisher [Cranefield and Purvis, 1999]. We refer to this ontology by "CDCatalog". Other ways to identify products in an electronic commerce setting are defined in Section 6.3.3. An alternative to the CDCatalog is the Music Domain Ontology, which contains concepts that can be used to describe music and/or songs on

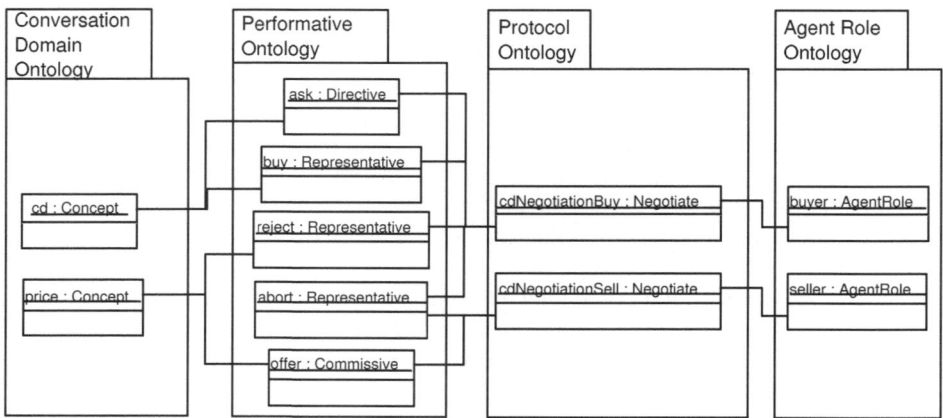

Figure 6.4
Object diagram showing the conversation-specific concepts as instances of the agent communication meta ontology. The placements of the object resemblances the sequence of
metaclass place placement in Fig. 6.1. From left to right, the sequence is Concept, type
of Performative, type of Protocols and AgentRole. The name of an object is composed of
the identification of an object, followed by the name of the metaclass. The object CD is
an instance of metaclass Concept. The relations between the objects are inherited from
the agent communication meta ontology, see Figure 6.1.

the basis of composer, musical instruments, musicians and style[14].

The concept price contains the attributes value and currency. The currency attribute is of type CurrencyCode, which is imported from the currency ontology that specifies the "three letter currency codes" as defined by ISO 4217[15]. Given this attribute, the
agents involved could use the above described currency conversation service.

The performative Buy makes use of the attribute payment of type Money-Tender-
Type, which is imported from the Cyc upper level ontology[16]. This concept defines types
of the payment form, such as credit card, cash and cyber coin. When the buyer wants to
actually buy a CD, the buyer can also negotiate on the way of payment.

In order to summarize the process from Agent Communication Meta Ontology to
message content ontology, we have described a "trace" in Figure 6.6. As shown, the class
buy is an instantiation of the class Representative from the Performative Ontology.
The class Representative is an instance of the metaclass Performative from the Agent
Communication Meta Ontology. The class Buy makes use of the class Money-Tender-
Type of the external ontology Cyc, to describe the attribute payment.

---

[14]See www.daml.org/ontologies/276.

[15]See www.daml.ecs.soton.ac.uk/ont/currency.daml.

[16]The Cyc upper ontology is reused in the HPKB-UPPER-LEVEL ontology. The Cyc ontology can be found
at www.cyc.com.

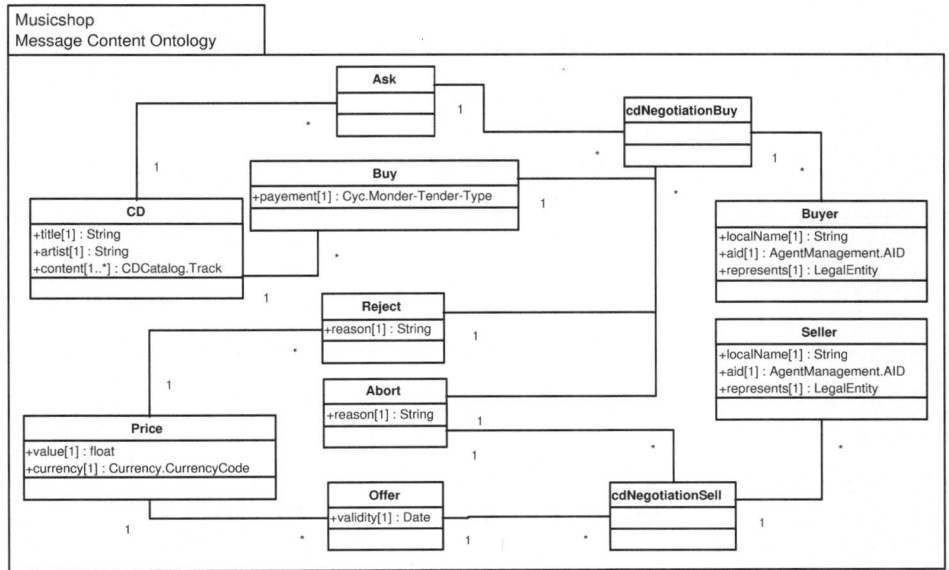

Figure 6.5
Class diagram showing the design of the Musicshop Message Content Ontology. The attribute types which contain a dot refer to imported types. For example, in class CD, the member content is of type Track imported from the ontology CDCatalog. There is no explicit relation defined between the concepts CD and Price, because they are not coupled within conversations. This means that the two concepts are not used within one utterance. The two concepts are implicitly related via the performatives Ask, Buy, Offer and Reject.

6.3.5 Message Content Ontology Application

In order to discuss a message content ontology in action, we show how agents apply the musicshop ontology. In an ideal world, we can assume that all agents are capable of handling imported parts of message content ontologies. Problems related to ontology integration include mapping between different types of languages, versions of ontologies and levels of detail. For a discussion on the use of ontologies we refer to [Uschold and Grüninger, 1996]. Furthermore, we assume that the agents are FIPA-Compliant, meaning that they have registered themselves at an agent platform and know how to consult a platform's DF (directory facilitator, i.e. an agent platform's yellow pages).

Below a part of a conversation is given, which is composed of four stages. The conversation in the third stage makes use of the Musicshop message content ontology. In the first stage, where agent B consults the DF to find an agent that represents a CDshop, the FIPA Agent Management Message Content Ontology (see also Section 6.3) is used. Then,

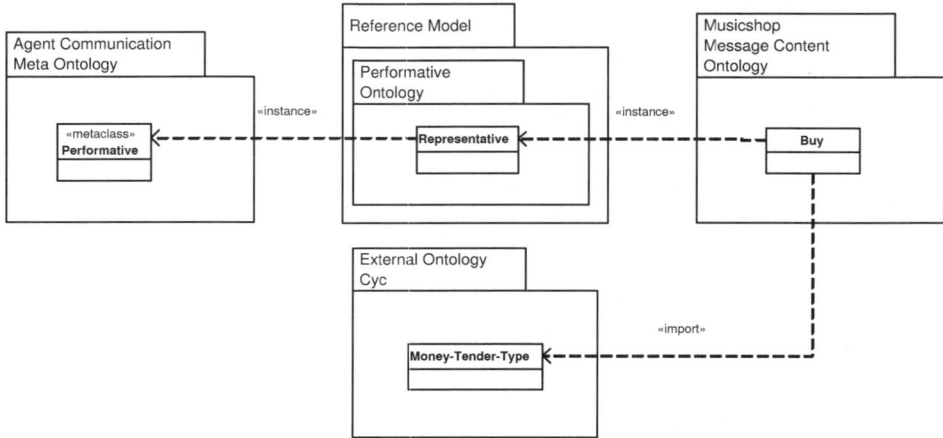

Figure 6.6
The process from Agent Communication Meta Ontology to Message Content Ontology.
As shown the class buy in the Message Content Ontology is an instantiation of the class
Representative from the Performative Ontology. The class **Representative** is an in-
stance of the metaclass **Performative** from the Agent Communication Meta Ontology.

agent B starts a negotiation with agent S (the agent suggested by the DF) on how to follow
the message content ontology. This part of the conversation is based on the negotiation
protocol and makes use of the *Execution Negotiation Message Content Ontology*. Next,
the agents start the actual negotiation by arguing on the price of a CD on basis of the
Musicshop ontology and the negotiation protocol. Finally, the agents argue on the actual
payment using the *Payment Negotiation Message Content Ontology*. We added the Execution Negotiation and Payment Negotiation Message Content Ontologies to illustrate
how agents can switch between multiple message content ontologies.

1: service location (using the FIPA Agent Management Message Content Ontology)
① agent B to DF: (Search (service-description :type "CDShop"))
② DF to agent B: (Agree (Search (service-description :type "CDShop")))
③ DF to agent B: (Result (AID name: "agent S"))

2: execution negotiation (using the Execution Negotiation Message Content Ontology)
① agent B to agent S: (Ask (Ontology))
② agent S to agent B: (Answer (Ontology name: "Musicshop"))
③ agent B to agent S: (Tell (Role name: "buyer"))
④ agent S to agent B: (Tell (Role name: "seller"))

3: actual negotiation (using the MusicShop Message Content Ontology)
① buyer to seller: (Ask (CD :title "the best of" :artist "Paolo Conte"))
② seller to buyer: (Offer (Price :value "19.90" :currency "EUR") :validity "18/02/2004")
③ buyer to seller: (Reject :reason "price too high")
④ seller to buyer: (Offer (Price :value "18.50" :currency "EUR") :validity "18/02/2004")
⑤ buyer to seller: (Reject :reason "price too high")

⑥ seller to buyer: (Offer (Price :value "18.00" :currency "EUR") :validity "18/02/2004")
⑦ buyer to seller: (Buy (CD :title "the best of" :artist "Paolo Conte") :payment "credit-card")

4: payment negotiation (using the Payment Negotiation Message Content Ontology)
① seller to buyer: (Ask (CreditCard))
② buyer to seller: (Offer (CreditCard :number "1111 2222 3333 4444" :validity "1203"))
③ seller to buyer: (Reject :reason "credit card not valid")
④ buyer to seller: (Offer (CreditCard :number "2222 3333 4444 5555" :validity "0105"))
⑤ seller to buyer: (Accept :comment "CD will be delivered within 1 week")
. . .

In the first stage, agent B sends message ① to the agent platform's DF to search for an agent that offers services belonging to the "CDshop" domain. After a lookup in the DF's repository, the DF suggests to contact agent S with message ②. The conversation between the DF and agent S, are based on the Agent Management Ontology, see Section 6.3.3 and [FIPA, 2002c]. The applied protocol in this conversation is the Request-Protocol.

In the second stage, agent B and agent S start a discussion on how to perform the negotiation. Two decisions are made: one on the message content ontology (see messages ① and ②) to apply and on the division of roles (see messages ③ and ④). From here on agent B plays the role of "buyer" and agent S plays the role of "seller". More work on ontology negotiation can be found in [Bailin and Truszkowski, 2001]. Here we assume that the imported ontologies used in the musicshop ontology are available (e.g. via an online ontology repository). If not, the agents should be capable of finding a substitute ontology or can decide to stop the negotiation. In addition, version problems have to be solved. For example, agent A and agent S make use of different versions of the music-shop ontology or one or more of the imported ontologies. We assume that the agents are capable of detecting version problems and are capable of resolving it, by upgrading to a common version. There can also be problems related to the level of detail of the imported ontologies. For example, one attribute can be of a type in an upper ontology and another in an application ontology. In this case, we assume that the agents are capable of building mappings or bridges between levels of detail. The applied protocol in this conversation is the negotiation-protocol.

In the third stage, the buyer begins the actual negotiation, based on the Musicshop ontology and the negotiation-protocol. The negotiation starts with message ① using the action Ask combined with the concept CD to ask for an offer of the seller. The seller responds with message ②, which has the action Offer including a validity attribute and the object Price. The validity attribute is used to refer to the validity of the offer for this particular CD. Next, the buyer sends message ③ containing the action Reject and a reason, in order to reject the offer. The seller responds with message ④ containing a new Offer, which is rejected by message ⑤. The offer in and ⑥ is accepted by the buyer, and sends message ⑦ to the seller, which contains the action Buy.

Finally, in the fourth stage, the seller and buyer try to settle the payment, which is based on the negotiation-protocol. As shown, the seller asks the buyer for details on the selected payment form, i.e. "credit card". The first answer of the buyer is rejected due to an invalid credit card. The second answer of the buyer is accepted and a delivery date is

model	function	domain
communication	execution negotiation, actual negotiation, payment negotiation	FIPA Agent Management, Execution Negotiation, MusicShop and Payment Negotiation Message Content Ontology
competence	decide on offer, make payments	current offer, available payment forms
self	determine role, instruct planner	buyer role
planner	task selection, plan tasks	agent's agenda
environment	search for sellers, manage contracts	known agents

Table 6.4
The five models of the buyer agent (according to the 5C Model) representing the its capabilities split up in function and domain.

offered.

6.3.6   Agent Design

In Table 6.4, a 5C model of the buyer agent is shown. In order to perform the conversation described above, the communication model has to be able to interact with other agents, such as sellers, based on available message content ontologies. The environment model will search for other agents (such as the seller agent), store details on known agents and manage contracts (such as the promise to buy a CD) with other agents. The self model contains the role of the agent, i.e. Buyer and instructs the planner model to behave accordingly. The planner model will select the appropriate taks based on the instructions of the self model. Finally, the competence model decides on offers from the seller and can make payments. Furthermore, it has details on the current offer and on available payment forms.

As shown, all 5 models of the 5C model are needed for agents interacting on the basis of the Reference Model. One of the reasons for this overhead is due to pre-negotiation discussion. Agents first have to decide what message content ontology to use and how to divide the agent roles (as illustrated in phase 2 in the conversation discussed above). This possibility is appealing for a system based on "Mutual Adjustment", see Section 3.3.3 (p.59). When using this coordination strategy, the agent role ontology will contain explicit notion of roles, which are necessary, when agents are capable of changing roles.

6.4   Operationalization of Ontology-based Communication

In the previous section we presented a framework containing a Reference Model. In this section, we argue that not all parts of the Reference Model are always required for agent communication. For example, the agent role ontology is meant to model more elaborate roles, such as Manager and Operator. One of the reasons to distribute the task of a system is to separate responsibilities, which are connected to roles. Given, the current state of the art in agent technology, agent designers often choose to have agents commit to one role, e.g. Broker, Librarian, Manager or Operator. Therefore, given the current state of the art, the use of agent roles can be seen as superfluous. Consequently, the relation between protocols and agent roles can become redundant. For example, in the case of the FIPA Agent Management Ontology, visiting agents already know the existence of the AMS and the DF. Even registration procedures (with the AMS and the DF) are hardwired in agent tool kits as two separate agents [Bellifemine et al., 2003].

Most agents at this moment are relatively simple, in terms of reasoning power. One reason for that is that implementing agents with traditional AI languages is problematic [Labrou et al., 1999][17]. A lot of existing tools such as JADE are designed in Java, because of its popularity and of the availability of reusable components. Furthermore, more low level standardization has to be realized [Luck et al., 2003].

The role of a Reference Model is to provide means for agents and agent engineers to reason about ontology-based agent communication. Therefore, we propose to use a *Minimal Ontology*, which only defines conversation specific concepts. The *Minimal Ontology* is discussed in detail in Section 6.4.1.1. When designing relative simple agents using the current state of the art, the Minimal Ontology can be applied.

In the remainder of this section, we answer the following two questions: *How can ontologies for message content be designed?* and *How can messages be generated and interpreted, both on the basis of a* Minimal Ontology*?* The first question is related to ontology modeling. Typical issues related to ontology modeling are, domain of interest, knowledge to be stored in the ontology and the maintenance of the ontology [Noy and McGuinness, 2001]. The second question is related to the application of the ontology. In this case, ontologies are used to support relatively simple conversations between relative simple agents. These conversations are built up out of multiple messages, which can contain questions, answers, offers and so forth.

6.4.1 Message Content Ontology Implementation

In this section we present the minimal agent communication ontology. Followed by a method to define message content ontologies based on the Minimal Ontology. Next, we discuss how message content ontologies can be mapped onto an implementation language. Finally, we discuss issues related to message content ontology creation.

6.4.1.1 Minimal Agent communication ontology

The minimal agent communication ontology[18], presented, is preliminary and contains only basic concepts and relations based on the Agent Communication Meta Ontology. The idea is, that when we gained enough experience with this Minimal Ontology, and possible conversations, extensions in the direction of the Reference Model can be made. The trade-off is between expressive power and usability. A Minimal Ontology that is very

---

[17]Although this claim originates from 1999, little is known on agents with considerable reasoning power, such as learning and reasoning on different types of ontologies and knowledge.

[18]In the remainder we refer to "minimal agent communication ontology" by "Minimal Ontology".

expressive may not be easy to use. For example, a Minimal Ontology could demand that the state of an agent and the overall goals of the system have to be specified. The idea could be that the sending agent, specifies its internal state and denotes for what goal a message is sent. This could lead to an overload of information, where the agents spend more time on processing information than on its actual task.

As mentioned above, FIPA has specified ontology-based communication, in which the semantics of message contents is specified in message content ontologies. The JADE toolkit has implemented the FIPA specifications[19]. The ontology handling functionalities within this toolkit are extended to explicit ontology handling. JADE is Java oriented, therefore ontology specifications have to be expressed in Java code. This code will be part of the agent.

Every concept in an ontology has to be defined as a *Java Bean*. A Java Bean is a special type of a Java class, which adheres to a specific design. A Java Bean has members (i.e. attributes) that can be written with a `set` operation and be read with a `get` operation or an `is` operation[20]. An example of a Java Bean is given in Figure 6.7.

One of the content languages FIPA has described and for which tools are available is FIPA-SL0[21] [FIPA, 2002i]. The SL0 representation of this class is (CD :name "the best of" :artist "Paolo Conte"). We focus on the creation of the ontologies and use the SL0 format to describe examples of the content of messages.

For every sent message, a translation from the internal Java instances to SL0, has to be made. For every received message, a translation from SL0 representation to internal Java instances has to be made. A more elegant alternative functionality is to manipulate ontologies as external resources expressed in SL0. However, no concrete implementation of a SL0 knowledge base is available.

The JADE toolkit offers limited ontology manipulation, we follow its (limited) view on ontologies. The reason for this is that a lot of agent engineers use the toolkit to develop agents in. Within the JADE toolkit, there are a limited number of basic ontological classes[22] with corresponding concepts that can form the basis of a Minimal Ontology. The candidate elements of the Minimal Ontology are *Concept* and *Action*, because they correspond with the *domain concept* and *performative* from our Reference Model. We neglect the notion of role and protocol in order to keep the ontology minimal.

A *Concept* is a superclass of the domain concepts that are subject of discussion, such as good, price, person, and address. This element refers to the conversation domain ontology. A Concept has *properties* that can have values. For example, a CD can have the properties *title* and *artist* instantiated with the values "the best of" and "Paolo Conte".

An *Action* is a superclass of the intentions (or performatives) that can change the world. This element refers to the performatives of the performative ontology. Examples of actions are sell, offer, ask, tell, propose and buy.

Every Action contains at least one *Concept*. This means that every action is coupled

---

[19]It has successfully passed so called interoperability tests held by FIPA, see http://jade.cselt.it.

[20]The `is` operation is used to check the value of boolean typed members.

[21]SL0 is a subset of FIPA-SL. The syntax of SL is based on *s-expressions* used in LISP, which are balanced parenthesis lists [Labrou et al., 1999].

[22]These elements (i.e. Java classes) can be found in the jade.content package.

```
public class CD extends Concept{
    private String artist, title;
    private Collection tracks = new Collection();
    public void setArtist(String s) { artist = s; }
    public String getArtist() { return artist; }
    public void setTitle(String s) { title = s; }
    public String getTitle() { return title; }
    public void addTrack(Track t) { tracks.add(t); }
    public List getAllTracks() { return tracks; }
    public void removeTrack(Track t) { tracks.remove(t); }
    public void clearAllTracks() { tracks.clear(); }
}
    ...
    CD theCD = new CD();
    theCD.setTitle("the best of");
    theCD.setArtist("Paolo Conte");
    ...
```

Figure 6.7
Java bean class definition of the concept "CD" and a possible initialization. The first part of the code is the bean definition, showing its members and set and get methods. The second part shows how parts of the bean are filled.

to one or more objects in the world. For example, Buy is connected to a CD and offer is connected to a price. Therefore, we include the relation AllowedConcept in the Minimal Ontology, to relate Concepts to the Action class.

An example message content ontology related to a musicshop is illustrated in Figure 6.8. As illustrated the conversation specific concepts are defined as abstract classes (i.e. the classes printed in italic letters) and not as meta classes. The reason for this is to keep the creation of message content ontologies less complicated compared to the Agent Communication Meta Ontology. We can already see, a drawback of the Minimal Ontology, because, it does not include the possibility to define axioms and rules. For example, the rule that the seller has to respond with the action Offer after receiving an action Ask, cannot easily be modeled in the ontology.

In the remainder of this section, we discuss a tool that is a first attempt to automate agent coding. With the use of Protégé message content ontologies can be defined based on the Minimal Ontology. The ontologies defined within Protégé can be translated to Java code, which can be used for buildings agents with the JADE toolkit.

6.4.1.2 Defining Message Content Ontologies

Defining a message content ontology means specializing the elements of the Minimal Ontology. In order to be able to use the current ontology editors to design our Minimal Ontology we decided to comply with the OKBC knowledge model, used in Protégé 2000, Protégé 2000 is a commonly used ontology editor, which enables engineers to graph-

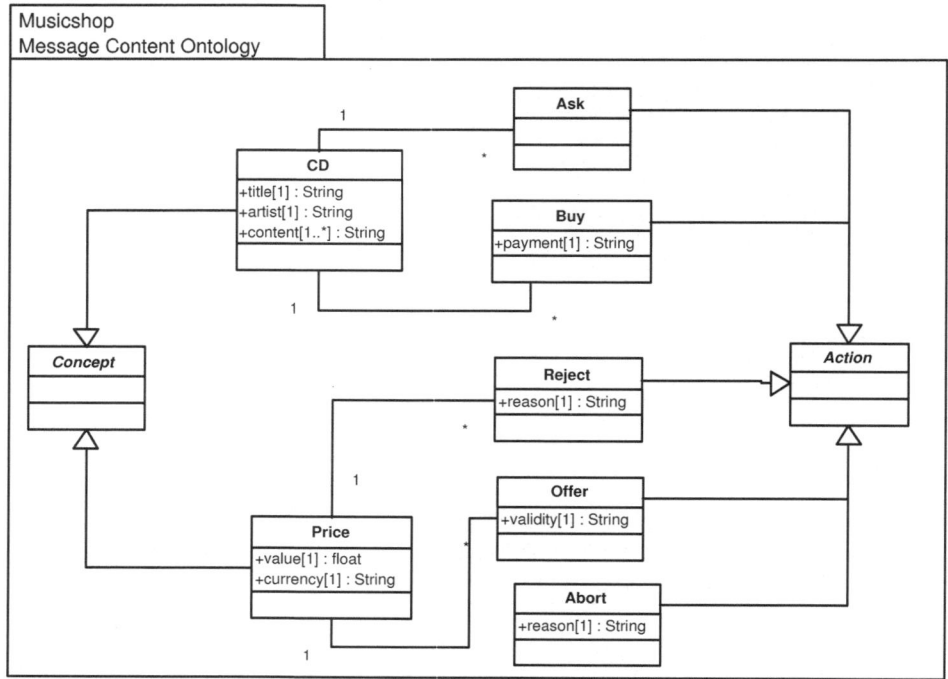

Figure 6.8
Musicshop Message Content Ontology for a conversation in a CD shop (see also Figure 6.5 (p.155)), based on the Minimal Ontology. The first class citizens of the Minimal Ontology are represented as abstract classes, which are printed in italic letters. The associations between classes of type **Action** and **Concept** are of type **AllowedConcept**. There is no explicit relation defined between the concepts **CD** and **Price**, for the same reason described in the caption in Figure 6.5 (p.155).

ically model ontologies. Furthermore, additional functionality and storage formats can be "plugged in" into the system. An ontology within Protégé is based on a frame-based (OKBC) knowledge model [Noy et al., 2000]. Therefore, ontologies modeled with this tool, can be mapped onto Java structures.

The ontology model of Protégé consists of classes, slots and slot facets [Noy et al., 2000]. Classes are concepts in the domain of discourse, with which a taxonomic hierarchy can be constructed. Slots describe properties or attributes of these classes. A slot in itself is a frame that has a type. This can be a primitive class, like String, Integer and Float, or an instance of another class. Furthermore, a slot has a value. Slot facets (see Table 6.5) describe properties (or constraints) of slots.

The design of the musicshop ontology is given in Figure 6.9 and Figure 6.8. As shown the concept CD has three slots: **title**, **artist** and **tracks**. The slots **title** and **artist**

Facet	Description	Examples
cardinality of a slot	the number of values the slot can have, i.e. 0,1,N.	class *person* can only have one father, $c = 1$, class *father* can have multiple children, $c = N$.
allowed values	restriction of the value type of a slot.	Integer, String, Instance of a class.
numeric boundaries	the minimum and maximum value for a numeric slot	the slot *age* is between 0 and 150.
required or optional	whether a slot is required or not	the slot *name* is required for the class *person*.

Table 6.5
Facets of the slots part of ontologies within Protégé including description and examples.

are modeled as String, are required and the cardinality is single. This means that every instance of CD, such as the Paolo Conte's CD, needs exactly one title and artist. We also added the slot tracks, to define the content of a CD. The slot is defined as multiple instances, which means that the slot refers to a collection (sequence) of instances of the type Track. Each class Track has the slots title and duration.

The concept Price has two slots: value and currency. The slot value denotes the amount of the price and currency the corresponding currency. In order to comply with the currency slot with international standards, the values of this slot could be restricted to an ontology that has defined internal currency codes. The International Organization for Standardization (ISO), a worldwide federation of national standards bodies, has specified the *ISO 4217 standard*, which contains global currencies and the three-character currency codes that are generally used to represent them[23]. In order to keep the ontology simple, this step is omitted by only considering EUROs, which is represented by "EUR".

In order to have the agents discuss on CDs in a musicshop setting, four Action types were modeled: Buy, Ask, Reject and Offer. These actions can be used to negotiate on the price of CDs. The actions correspond with the implicit performatives defined in Section 6.3.4.

One of the advantages of the Protégé tool is that other ontologies can be imported. Repositories of existing ontologies ranging from Biological domains to market place product and service descriptions, can be found at the Protégé community page and at the DAML site[24]. The languages used to represent these ontologies can range from XML, RDF, DAML-OIL, XMI, SQL to UML.

6.4.1.3 Mapping from Ontologies Design to Java Beans

To support the agent engineer in creating and using message content ontologies, we developed a plug-in for the Protégé 2000 environment called the *Bean Generator*. With this plug-in, a domain ontology within Protégé can be developed and exported to Java beans.

The translation from Protégé knowledge base to Java Beans works as follows: Every class in the Minimal Ontology, i.e. `Concept` and `Action` is the basis for the generation

---

[23] See www.xe.com/iso4217.htm.
[24] See http://protege.stanford.edu/ontologies.html and www.daml.org/data.

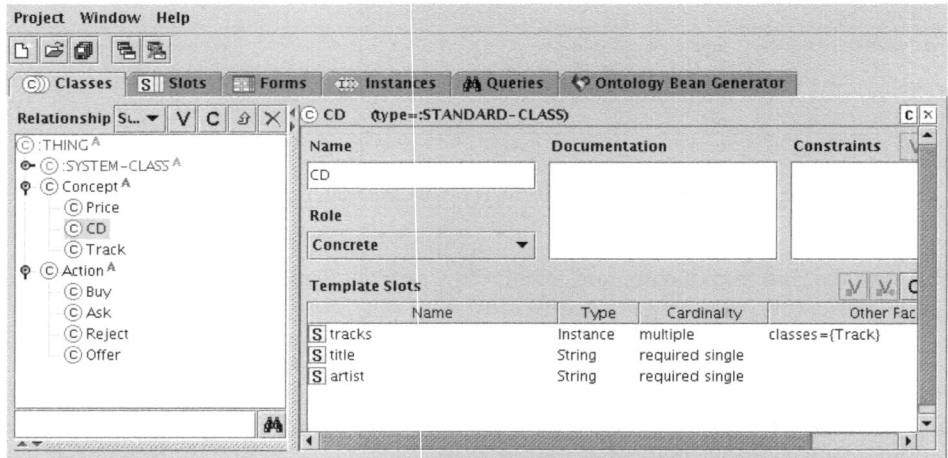

Figure 6.9
Screenshot from Protégé containing the Musicshop Message Content Ontology based on
the Minimal Ontology.

of a Java class. The taxonomic structure (i.e. inheritance relations) of the domain model
is mapped on the inheritance capabilities of Java. Therefore if `S1` is a super-schema of
`S2` then the class `C2` associated to schema `S2` must `extend` the class C1. Slots of a
Class are associated with data members of the Java Bean associated with the Class. If the
type of the slot is a primitive class, like String, Integer or Float, then the Bean Generator
maps them onto their Java equivalents, otherwise the member of the class is defined as an
instance of the corresponding Java class. If the cardinality is higher than one, a class of
type `Collection`[25] is used.

The methods for generating Java classes from an ontology design is given in Figure 6.10. In Protégé an ontology is represented as a knowledge base, i.e. the collection
of classes, slots and facets. Starting from this knowledge base, the method **generate** is
called. This method first generates an ontology mapping file, as given in Figure 6.11.
Next, it adds schemas to the ontology-mapping file and generate beans for every subclass
of the classes Concept and Action.

The **addToSchema** method adds the definition of a class in terms of a Schema.
Next, it adds fields to the schema that define the slots and their facets. As shown in Figure 6.11, the schemas for the concepts **Track** and **CD** are added. Furthermore, the fields
for the cdSchema are specified including their type, cardinality and whether they are
mandatory or not.

The **generateBean** method creates a file (i.e. a Java bean) according to the class
name. The file is filled with a bean definition and the slots of the class. This definition

---

[25] The class *Collection* is only an interface. The class java.util.ArrayList actually implements the class Collection.

```
public class BeanGenerator {
  private String ontologyName, package;
  private File ontologyMapping;
  ...
  public void generate(KnowledgeBase kb) {
    ontologyMapping = generateFile(ontologyName + ".java");
    ( for every superclass in { Concept, Action } ) {
      ( for every candidate in kb.getCls(superclass).getSubClasses() ) {
        addToScheme(candidate);
        generateBean(candidate);
      }
    }
  }
  public void addToScheme(Cls cls) {
    ( for every slot in Cls.getDirectSlots()) {
      String attributeType = translateFromProtegeToJava(slot.getType() );
      addScheme(ontologyMapping, slot.getName(), attributeType);
      addSlotToScheme(ontologyMapping, slot.getName(), attributeType);
    }
  }
  public void generateBean(Cls cls) {
    File f = generateFile(cls.getName + ".java");
    generateBeanDefinition(f, cls.getType());
    ( for every slot in Cls.getDirectSlots() ) {
      String attributeType = translateFromProtegeToJava(slot.getType() );
      addMember(f, slot.getName(), attributeType);
      addSetter(f, slot.getName(), attributeType);
      addGetter(f, slot.getName(), attributeType);
    }
  }
  ...
}
```

Figure 6.10
Simplified Java code for generating the "ontology mapping file" and accompagnied Java beans.

expresses the inheritance relation of the bean. For example, the inheritance relation between the class CD and the class Concept, is expressed in Java by class CD extends Concept as illustrated in Figure 6.7.

For every slot in the class, a translation from Protégé type to Java type is made[26]. Next, the attribute definition and its associated getter and setter are added. For example for the slot "title", the member specification String title is added and the method getTitle() and setTitle().

---

[26]Most types, such as String and Float can be mapped directly. However, the ANY type is mapped onto object and symbol is mapped on String.

```
public class MusicShopOntology extends BasicOntology {
   // vocabulary
   public static final String CD_ARTIST="artist";
   public static final String CD_TRACKS="tracks";
   public static final String CD_TITLE="title";
   public static final String CD="CD";
   public static final String TRACK="track";

   ...
   public MusicShopOntology() {

     ...
     // concepts
     ConceptScheme trackScheme = new ConceptScheme(TRACK);
     add(trackScheme, musicshop.Track.class);
     ConceptScheme cdScheme = new ConceptScheme(CD);
     add(cdScheme, musicshop.CD.class);
     ...
     // fields
     cdScheme.add(CD_TITLE, getScheme(STRING), MANDATORY);
     cdScheme.add(CD_TRACKS, trackScheme, 1, UNLIMITED);
     cdScheme.add(CD_ARTIST, getScheme(STRING),MANDATORY);

     ...
   }
}
```

Figure 6.11
Part of the "ontology mapping file" (expressed in Java code) for the Musicshop Message
Content Ontology, generated by the Beangenerator. The first part of the file defines
the vocabulary of the ontology. Next, the schemas for the concepts Track and CD are
added. Finally, the members for schemas are specified including their type, cardinality
and whether they are mandatory or not.

Discussion   On the basis of the generated Java beans and the ontology-mapping file,
agents can translate internal Java instances into message contents and vice versa. Therefore, the agents do not need an inference engine that can reason about message content.
This can make agents simple and small (i.e. a light footprint[27]). One way to look at this,
is that many agents will not have to be able to reason on the knowledge level, because
they have to perform relatively simple tasks, such as information retrieval and gathering.

One of the disadvantages of this approach is, that the ontology handling is rather
static. If something in an ontology changes (e.g. due to maintenance), the internals of
the agent have to be altered. Furthermore, it is rather complex to insert new ontologies at
runtime. This means that the internals of the agent have to be altered in runtime, with for
example reflection. An alternative would be that the agent is equipped with an inference
engine and a ontology knowledge base that can be altered at runtime.

---

[27]Actual size of the agent expressed in bytes.

6.4.2 Message Content Ontology Application

In this section, we discuss how agents can generate and interpret the content of messages. Content generation is described using the *content encoding* process. Content interpretation is described using the *content decoding* process.

6.4.2.1 Content Encoding

There are two basic reasons for an agent to send a message. First, to start a conversation, such as asking for the price of a CD. Secondly to participate in a conversation, such as responding to a question. In both cases, the agents have to make translations from its internal state (i.e. collection of java instances) to an ACL languages, such as SL0. Translations can be made with an *encoder*.

An encoder is a service that can translate a piece of information from one format to another. The algorithm of the *encoder* that takes care of Java instances translation to an ACL is given in Figure 6.12. As described, the method generateFrames generates a (sub) frame for every member of the object. For example, for an instance of the action, Offer, a frame (in this case expressed in SL0) is generated which takes the form (Offer (Price :value e :currency c) :validity v). In order to fill the values of the slots of the frame, the method fillFrame is called. This function checks whether a member is of a primitiveType, such as String, Float and Boolean, or a complex type. For every complex type, such as Price, a new (sub)frame is generated.

Based on the language, represented by currentLanguage, and the ontology mapping file, represented by currentOntology, the appropriate parts of the content are written. When using SL0, the Price concept is represented by (Price :value "19.90" :currency "EUR"). Using XML, the concept Price is represented as <Price value="19.90" currency="EUR"/>.

6.4.2.2 Content Decoding

When an agent receives a message, the content has to be translated into the internal model of the agent. For example, when receiving a message filled with the content: (Offer :id 1 (Price :value "19.90" :currency "EUR")) the appropriate instances have to be generated. In this case, instances of the class Offer and Price are generated. The service that takes care of the translation from content language to internal models, is called the *decoder*. The algorithm of the decoder is given in Figure 6.13.

As shown, the method decode takes a String representation of the content of a message as input. It first parses the content into elements, such as frame definition, slot definition and slot value. Then it calls the method generateObjects. This method generates an Object belonging to the first frame definition in the content. For example, for the frame definition of Offer, an object Offer is instantiated. Next, the member of this object is filled with the method fillAttribute.

The method fillAttribute, takes a slot and an object as input. The method checks whether the slot is of a primitive type, such as String, Float and Boolean, or of a complex

```
public class Encode {
  private Ontology currentOntology;
  private Language currentLanguage;
  ...
  public String encode(Object obj) {
    return generateFrames(obj);
  }
  public String generateFrames(Object obj) {
    String result = currentOntology.generateFrame(obj.getClass());
    (for every member in obj) result.append( fillFrame(member) );
    return result;
  }
  public string fillFrame(Member member) {
    if (member.getType() in currentOntology.primitiveTypes) value = member.getValue();
    else value = generateFrames( member.getValue() );
    return currentLanguage.translate(value);
  }
  ...
}
```

Figure 6.12
Simplified Java code for generating (i.e. encoding) the content of a message.

type. When the slot is of a complex type, the method **generateObjects** is called, in order to acquire a reference to one or more new objects. Finally, the appropriate getter method is invoked, to fill the value of the slot with either a value or references to other objects.

Discussion   The above described encoding and decoding methods are necessary for agents that are not equipped with an inference engine. If the agents were equipped with an inference engine, the state of the agent could be stored in an explicit knowledge base. The operations on this knowledge base necessary for communication take care of message composition and decomposition.

The question remains, when to apply the described encoding and decoding mechanism and when to equip an agent with an inference engine. Several criteria can be considered, such as speed, size and flexibility. Speed can be seen as the time needed to develop an agent and the time needed to perform a communicative act.

An agent equipped with an inference engine and an explicit knowledge base is likely to be larger then an agent equipped with the ontology mapping process. These criteria can be considered when working with mobile agents and agents on mobile devices. In agent transport, one wants to keep the footprint of agents as small as possible. On mobile devices, there is only a limited size for storage and limited speed for operation.

When compiling an ontology into the actual agent, it is harder to alter the ontology. This means stopping the agent, generating a new ontology, compile and deploying the agent, and restarting. A knowledge base is easier to manipulate and it can be transported to other agents.

```
public class Decode {
  private Ontology currentOntology;
  private Language currentLanguage;
  ...
  public Object decode(String content) {
    Elements elements = currentLanguage.parseLine(content);
    return generateObjects(elements);
  }
  function Object generateObjects(Elements elements) {
    Object result = currentOntology.generateObject(elements.next() );
    ( for every slot in elements) fillAttribute(slot, result);
    return result;
  }
  public void fillAttribute(Slot slot, Object result) {
    if (slot.getType() in primitiveTypes) slotValue = slot.getValue();
    else slotValue = generateObjects( slot.getValue() );
    invokeMethod(result, "set" + slot.getName(), slotValue);
  }
  ...
}
```

Figure 6.13
Simplified Java code for interpreting (i.e. decoding) the content of a received message.

6.4.3 Application of Bean Generator

The use of the Bean Generator has been reported in a number of publications and applications. One of them is the Financial Speller service, which provides financial reports (in textual form) containing predictions concerning deposit or credit/investments, taking into account a fixed interest rate and payments, and three operations to calculate depreciation charges over the calculating interval[28].

The Budapest Library Agent deals with book search and scans in the National Szchnyi Library [Varga and Hajna, 2003]. The agent holds a register of user preferences in the form of interest records. On a daily basis, the agent checks if there are new books in the library and compares them to interest records. If there is a match the agent sends an email to the user of the interest record. The main concepts are interest record, bibliographic record and bibliographic query. the main actions are related to registering and manipulating user interest, searching the library and scanning for new material.

The German research program "Intelligent Agents in Real-World Business Applications" is concerned with the application of agents for business and economic related tasks[29]. One of the domains modeled with the use of the is manufacturing logistics [Dinkloh and Nimis, 2003]. Typical concepts in the manufacturing logistics domain are material, operations, machines and cycle and assembly times[30] [Frey et al., 2003].

---

[28] See http://sas.ilab.sztaki.hu/wsid.
[29] See www.realagents.org.
[30] See www.ipd.uka.de/KRASH/index.html.

Other not (yet) reported domains include information exchange at the Rotterdam Harbor, hospital logistics, ontology negotiation and crisis management.

6.5 Legal Advisor

In this section we show the application of the message content ontologies and the above described approach in the domain of European Competition Law. We choose another domain then the Musicshop in order to show the variety of message content ontologies.

European Competition Law focuses on determining what law system(s) and rules are applicable in case of international business. Law systems include for instance national competition law and European competition law. Whereas rules include acts, statutes, regulations, directives, treaties, etc. For example, a company from country A wants to take over a company situated in country B. The question then is, which laws and rules are applicable when doing business on an international level?

There are several methods to enable companies to determine which laws and/or rules are applicable. One way is to look at the transaction amount of a take-over. This can determine whether European Law or national law is applicable. Another way is to look at the impact of the take-over with regard to the (European) competition. This can determine whether this take-over can be granted. Finally, does a take-over result in a dominant position of power with regard to the European Competition. If so, the take-over might not be granted.

With the project, we developed three types of agents, the law expert, personal law assistant and the law services broker. The *law expert* can determine whether a specific law is applicable, based on information and facts related to the location, the sort of agreement, etc. between companies. The *personal law assistant* assists end-users or other agents representing companies, to consult the system. Finally, the *law services broker* forms the one-stop shop to other agents, by mediating between the personal law assistant and the expert agents.

In the remainder of this section, we discuss the architecture of the system, message content ontology design and a simple scenario.

6.5.1 Architecture

The system is composed of different types of agents: the *law expert agent*, the *law services broker* and the *personal law assistant*. The multi-agent architecture is drawn in Figure 6.14.

6.5.1.1 Law Expert Agent

The *law expert agents* have the necessary knowledge about parts of European competition law. It means that they can reason about a part of a legal domain and exchange their finding with other agents. The *law expert agents* are able to agree on certain legal practices applicable to the question posed to them by the *personal law assistant*. In order to offer

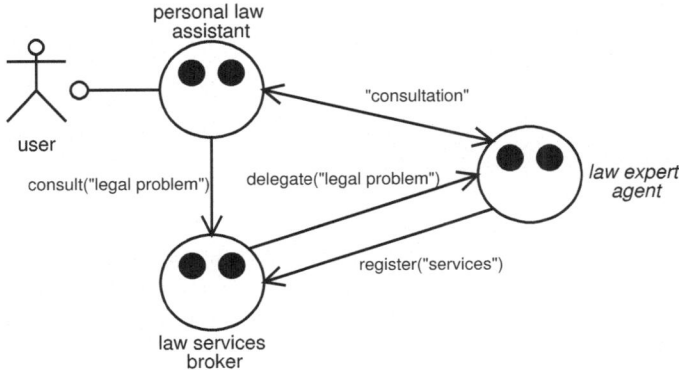

Figure 6.14
The Legal Advisor multi-agent architecture showing the agents involved: the *law expert agent*, the *law services broker* and the *personal law assistant*, and their interactions. The *law expert agent* is drawn as a prototype for the the *web expert*, the *article expert* and the *rules expert*. The "consultation" between the *law expert agent* and *personal law assistant* are based on a sequence of Tell (of type directive) and Answer (of type representative) sequence, based on the FIPA-Request protocol.

their services the agents register their competences at the *law services broker*. The design of a *law expert agent* is given in Table 6.6.

The first task of a *law expert agent*, i.e. register itself at the *law services broker*, is handled by the environment model. This is comparable to the platform life-cycle as discussed in Section 3.4.1 (p.63). The *law services broker* uses the registrations of the *law expert agents* in order to select the proper *law expert agent* that can solve the issues submitted by the *personal law assistant*. The second task is to provide answers to questions posed by the *personal law assistant*. The communication model is responsible for interaction with the *law services broker* and the *personal law assistant* on the basis of the Legaladvisor message content ontology. In the communication model, the agent uses the decode and encode functions in order to read and write messages. When a message is received, the agent first decodes this message from an ACL to the internal format of the agent, in this case Java instances. The communication model will dispatch the Java instances to the self model, which will instruct the planner. The planner model puts the task to provide consultation to the *personal law assistant* in the agent's agenda. Finally, the competence model starts to give consultation to the *personal law assistant*.

Three types of *law expert agents* are defined: the *web expert*, the *article expert* and the *rules expert*. The *web expert agent* is able to translate a question from the *personal law assistant* to a query for a search engine (e.g. Google). To make sure that the results are within the required domain, certain keywords, such as "law" are added to the search query. The technology used to wrap around search engines is based on the html analysis language: WebL (see Section 5.5.1.2). The article expert is able to match a question from

model	function	domain
communication	interact with *law services broker* interact with *personal law assistant*	Legaladvisor message content ontology
competence	provide legal advise	domain knowledge
self	instruct planner	*law expert agent*
planner	task selection, plan tasks	agent's agenda
environment	register at law services broker	the law services broker

Table 6.6
The five models of a generic *law expert agent* representing its capabilities split up in function and domain. The *web expert*, the *article expert* and the *rules expert* only differ from each other on the basis of the task *provide legal advise* and domain knowledge in the competence model.

the *personal law assistant* to an XML annotated set of laws. We used an "ad hoc" article annotation. A formalized schema for annotation is METAlex[31], which is used in markup of legal sources, such as the Rome Statute, Belgian Income Tax Law, Dutch Corporate Tax Law and Dutch Penal Code.

The rules expert consults a SWI-Prolog-driven knowledge base, which is able to reason with a set of production rules. If the reasoner has insufficient information about the legal situation, it sends a message back, asking for more specific information. To be able to query the Prolog KB from within the agent, the JPL[32] library is used.

After interviews with legal experts, it appeared that there are no knowledge bases available that cover European Law. The decision was made to use an available knowledge base, describing a set of law articles about the "opium laws" in the Netherlands, provided by the Department of Computer Science and Law of the University of Amsterdam[33].

6.5.1.2 Law Services Broker

The *law services broker* functions as a central hub in the system, it has a notion of existing *law expert agents* and is able to delegate questions to the *law expert agents* that are posed by the *personal law assistant*. Every *law expert agent* has to register at the *law services broker*. The "location" of the *law expert agents* is maintained by the environment model. The "services" of the *law expert agents* is maintained by the competence model.

On the basis of a matching strategy (such as pattern matching) and a question of a *personal law assistant*, the *law services broker* selects a *law expert agent*. The *law services broker* will delegate a consul to the selected *law expert agent*. The design of a *law services broker* is given in Table 6.7.

---

[31] See www.metalex.nl.

[32] See http://sourceforge.net/projects/jpl.

[33] See www.lri.jur.uva.nl.

model	function	domain
communication	interact with *personal law assistant* interact with *law expert agents*	Legaladvisor message content ontology
competence	register services of *law expert agents* match user question with service delegate consult	available service matching strategies type of questions
self	instruct planner	*law services broker*
planner	task selection, plan tasks	agent's agenda
environment	register *law expert agents*	available *law expert agents*

Table 6.7
The five models of the *law services broker* representing its capabilities split up in function and domain.

model	function	domain
communication	interact with *law services broker*, interact with *law expert agents* interact with user	Legaladvisor message content ontology user profiles
competence	consult *law services broker*, consult *law expert agent*, query users, present results	the *law services broker* domain knowledge
self	instruct planner	*personal law assistant*
planner	task selection, plan tasks	agent's agenda
environment	locate *law services brokers*	*law services brokers*, *law expert agent*

Table 6.8
The five models of the *personal law assistant*.

6.5.1.3   Personal Law Assistant

The *personal law assistant* is the agent with whom the end-user of the system interacts. The communication models maintains a user profile of the user and processes interaction with the user. Furthermore, this model interacts with the *law services broker* and *law expert agents* selected by the *law services broker* on the basis of the Legaladvisor message content ontology.

The competence model supports the user to consult the *law services broker* and *law expert agents*. Based on answers a user has given to queries, the *personal law assistant* can provide domain knowledge to *law services broker* and *law expert agents*. The answers of the *law expert agents* agents are presented as results to the user. This is operationalized by a web service which enables the user to provide its input. Furthermore, results of consults can be displayed. In Table 6.8, the design of the *personal law assistant* is given.

6.5.2   Message Content Ontology Design

By combining the ontology design of the Protégé tool with the Bean Generator, it was possible to create a Java object hierarchy which is used by the agents in the system. We will now look at the design of the *LegalAdvisorOntology*. A part of the ontology as designed in Protégé is given in Figure 6.15.

The LegalAdvisorOntology ontology contains a limited set of classes on the basis of the Minimal Ontology, in order to balance the expressive power of the ontology and the competences of the agents, which are in this case limited. Reason for this is that the agents have access to services with limited functionalities.

Conforming to the Minimal Ontology, we first defined subclasses of type *Action*. These subclasses are *Ask*, *AskYesNo*, *AskOption*, *Register*, *Consult*, *Delegate*, *Tell*, *TellYesNo* and *TellOption*. The action *Ask* is applied by the expert agents to inquire information. This action is specialized into *AskYesNo*, to inquire boolean questions and *AskOption*, to inquire for one or more options. *Register*, which is used to register agents at the broker. *Consult* is used by the UserAgent to consult the broker agent. *Delegate* is used by the BrokerAgent to delegate a legal problem to one or more expert agents. *Tell* is used to answer an *Ask* action. Similar to the *Ask* action. *Tell* is specialized into *TellYesNo* and *TellOption*.

Next we defined the subclasses of type *Concept*: *Option*, *LegalService* and *LegalProblem*. The concept *Option* defines the possible options used in the action *AskOption*. *LegalService* is a description of a service offered by an ExpertAgent. *LegalProblem* is a simplification of the problem owned by a UserAgent.

6.5.3 Simple Scenario

This section describes a simple example scenario to show how the agents within the system interact with each other, using the LegalAdvisorOntology. The scenario starts when the agent platform has been launched and the agents have been created. Each agents has to register its services at the *law services broker*. An example message sent from the webagent to the broker is:

> web expert to law services broker: (Register :legalservice (LegalService :type "keywordsearch"
> :description "Googlesearch"))

The message shows a description of the service that the agent can offer. As mentioned above, we did not use a full-fleshed ontology. Therefore, the service description is a very basic one.

The next step in the scenario is when a user enters information into a web form and submits this to the *personal law assistant*. Unknowing what the (semantic) content of the user's information is, it starts asking the *law services broker* for a suitable expert agent. The agent does this by forwarding the user's question to the broker:

> personal law assistant to law services broker: (Consult (LegalProblem :domain "competition law"
> :description (sequence "European" " competition" "law" "regulations"))"

The broker analyzes the content of the message, and tries to find an appropriate agent. This is done by applying a basic lookup mechanism in the broker's register. In this case, the broker decides to delegate the legal problem to the *web expert agent*. Therefore,

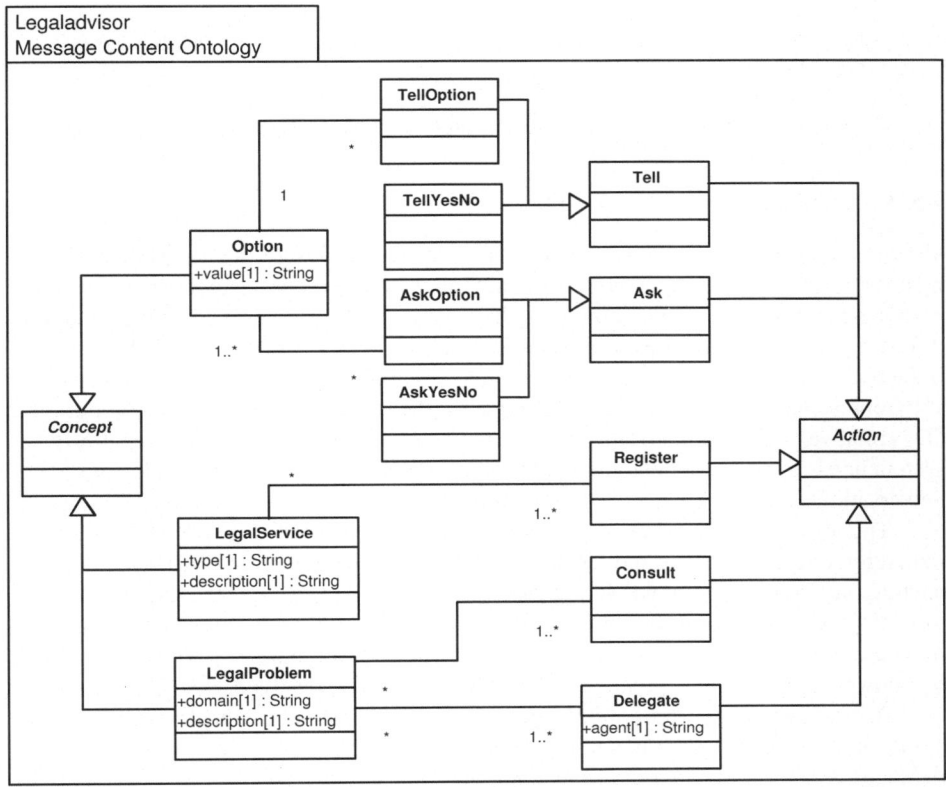

Figure 6.15
The Legaladvisor Message Content Ontology design for the Legal Advisor system, based on the Minimal Ontology.

the webagent is selected, since it can ask any question to Google. Whether the answer of Google is usable is to be decided by the end user.

This decision is then sent to the *web agent* by the message:

> law services broker to web expert: (Delegate (Consult (LegalProblem :domain "competition law"
> :description (sequence "European" "competition" "law" "regulations")) :agent "personal law assistant")

This message tells the *web expert* that it should find an answer to the specified LegalProblem and give the answer back to the agent "useragent". To find an answer to the LegalProblem, the *web expert* consults Google. The answer of Google, i.e. a list of URLs is translated into a sequence of the object Option and embedded into a TellOption action:

web expert to personal law assistant: (TellOption :options (sequence (Option value: "http://europa.eu.int")(Option value: "http://www.ellispub.com")(Option value: "http://www.etsi.org") . . .))

From there, the user agent presents the received answer to the end-user.

6.5.4   Evaluation

Although there have been a few concessions to the original design, we succeeded in building a stable and fully functional law assistance agent system. The system makes use of the relative simple message content ontology in order to show the generation and application of message content ontologies on a general level. The agents' functionality is limited, due to the unavailability of usable legal knowledge bases. We did not model an ontology that fully represents a legal domain. For example, in the musicshop example, the notion of a CD is relatively well-defined. However, the notion of a legal problem in the Legal Advisor System needs to be further elaborated. Furthermore, we only paid attention to the type of conversations, i.e. Tell-Answers combinations.

The legal services and legal problems are expressed as keywords. Real life conceptualization of legal services and legal problems need more elaborate constructs. For this, existing ontologies and knowledge bases could be included, such as the CIA world factbook that contains basic information related to countries, CYC containing common sense knowledge and various (in DAML represented) information sources[34]. The problem with this, however, is that conceptualization conflicts need to be resolved.

A drawback of the presented approach is that it does not consider complex constraints between concepts[35]. It is not (yet) possible to define what an allowed sequence of messages is. For example, a message containing the action class of type Ask, should be followed by a message containing an action class of type Tell. If we want to do so, we need to enhance the ontology mapping mechanism, in such a way that constraints can be stored in the ontology-mapping file.

6.6   Discussion

In this chapter, we addressed the problem of how agents can handle message-based communication. We have defined a framework for message content ontologies containing a Reference Model in order to provide semantics in message-based communication. The framework is built up out of a generic part and a specific part. The generic part is represented by an Agent Communication Meta Ontology that defines types of performatives and protocols based on (human) communication theory: speech acts and conversational interaction. The specific part is composed of a collection of domain dependent ontologies that describe the domain of the conversation, performatives, protocols and agent roles. We described and extended an existing categorization of speech acts for the definition of

---

[34] See www.cia.gov/cia/publications/factbook, www.opencyc.org and www.daml.org.
[35] Constraints on slots can be made, with facets as described in Table 6.5.

performatives. Furthermore, in order to show the variety of conversation protocols, we adjusted three existing protocols (i.e. Query, Request and Auction) and added two new ones (Negotiation and Supervision).

The Agent Communication Meta Ontology defines the subjects of agent communication: concepts, performatives, protocols and agent roles. We showed that a *message content ontology* is an instantiation of the Agent Communication Meta Ontology, which can be mapped onto a class diagram and specified in detail. From a theoretical point of view, it is appealing to define as much information as possible into a "full fledged" Reference Model. However, when designing an agent that is capable of handling this information, a lot of overhead emerges (due to the need for ontology operations and pre-negotiation activities). When making use of a full fledged Reference Model, the question is if all its concepts and relations are needed.

Based on our framework, we defined a "Minimal Ontology", which can be used in more pragmatic agent solutions. The ontology contains the classes Concept and Action, and the relation AllowedConcept. We explained that agents without an inference engine need a representation of an ontology in terms of their internal representation (such as Java beans) and means (such an ontology mapping file) to map instances of an ontology into their internal representation. On the basis of the presented tool, encoders and decoders can respectively be used for translating an agent's internal model to agent communication utterances and vice versa. However, in this approach, the ontology and ontology translation is hard coded. This means that if an ontology changes, the java code for the agent needs to be regenerated and the agent needs to be deployed again.

Both the construction of the Message Content Ontology Framework and the Minimal Ontology can be seen as a first step towards the standardization of ontologies in agent communication and conversation. A possible method to define message content ontologies starts with choosing an Agent Communication Meta Ontology as a Reference Model, such as defined in Section 6.3.1. Next, based on generic classes of the Agent Communication Meta Ontology, conversation specific concepts of a message content ontology need to be defined (see Section 6.3.4.1). Then, these concepts can be specified in more detail by defining their properties (or attributes) and relations (see Section 6.3.4.2). Finally, ontology operations (such as encoding and decoding, see Section 6.4.2) have to be defined and added into an agent model.

Future research on message content ontologies includes elaboration on means to represent both syntax and semantics of message content ontologies, handling issues related to accessibility, i.e. how to store ontologies and how to retrieve them, and from a methodological point of view, addressing problems related to redefinition of ontologies should be exploited.

For the case study, we designed a system with an information-driven character (cf. [Galbraith, 1973]) using notions of information processing actions (i.e. ask and tell). In the future, dedicated minimal ontologies suited for specific processes or specific domains can be defined. Other interesting domain are when agents with a knowledge-driven character communicate at the knowledge level. For this, content ontologies could be defined that can handle concepts like competences, knowledge, methods and protocols. A starting point can be UPML [Fensel et al., 1999b], see Section 5.2.

An alternative approach to ontology handling is having agents to manipulate existing ontologies and even to learn new ones. For example, agents could negotiate on the meaning of concepts and relations. Another alternative approach to ontology handling is that the agent sends serialized Java code[36] that represents (parts of) an ontology. The receiving agent can process this code into its own ontology model. Next to automatic generation of Java beans, semi-automatic generation of Java classes that define the behavior of agents can be considered. For example, *encoders* and *decoders* could take care of all aspects of conversation management. Tasks of conversation management are to keep track of state of conversations, follow interaction protocols and negotiate meaning. Probably the method of generating static code can be useful in well defined situations. However, when agents operate in dynamic environments and need to change their strategy and models at runtime, other techniques such as maintaining an explicit message content ontology and behavior patterns are to be considered.

---

[36]Within Java it is possible to translate (i.e. serialize) the structure and state of objects into a transportable format.

Chapter 7

Conclusions

In this book, we studied the use of human organizational principles for multi-agent architecture design. We explored the use of division of labor and coordination as principles for multi-agent design, which resulted in a framework for agent organizational design (Chapter 2). Next, we investigated how agents can make use of coordination mechanisms which resulted in an interoperability framework that identifies the problems that arise when having heterogeneous agents collaborate with each other. A selection of alternatives to solve interoperability problems, i.e. coordination strategies and ontology-based communication has been discussed (Chapter 3, 5 and 6). Finally, we presented a conceptual agent model that takes into account the capabilities of an agent(Chapter 4).

7.1 Application of Organizational Decomposition Principles and Coordination in Multi-Agent Systems

In order to answer the first research question *How can decomposition principles (i.e. division of labor) and coordination be applied in multi-agent systems?*, we assumed that despite the differences between intelligent agents and humans, mechanisms and patterns from the field of organizational design can be used as the basis for multi-agent architecture design.

In Chapter 2, we studied a number of coordination mechanisms ("Direct Supervision", "Standardization" and "Mutual Adjustment") and organizational structures ("Machine Bureaucracy", "Professional Bureaucracy" and "Adhocracy"). The result of this study is an organizational design framework, which consists of four perspectives: "task" that deals with tasks and task relations, "operation" which consists of objects, technical activities and jobs, "coordination" that is concerned with the control of technical activities through management activities and "organization" which deals with job allocation, positions and units. A collection of organizational design steps was presented containing three steps: process analysis, operations design and organizational design. To support the organizational design step, we extended "organigrams" with the notion of agents for representing a multi-agent system's organizational structure. Organigrams support the visualization of organizational structures by showing the agent staff, the grouping of the agents and the authority structure that connects the units and individual agents.

In order to choose an appropriate organizational structure, we used the following properties that distinguish between organizational structures: (1) environment (which can be stable, predictable or dynamic), (2) task nature (routine, skilled or innovative), (3) activity allocation (static, pigeonholing or innovative), (4) form of organization (steep, flat, none), (5) desired coordination mechanism (Direct Supervision, Standardization or Mutual Adjustment), (6) form of decision-making (centralized or decentralized) and (7) type of agents (controllable, cooperative or autonomous). For example, the Machine Bureaucracy can be applied when the environment is stable, the task nature routine, the activity location static, the decision-making centralized and the agents controllable.

A case study on distributed supply chain management shows the process from task decomposition via organizational design to three architectures of multi-agent system designs based on Mintzberg's organizational structures. Due to its repetitive nature, supply chain management can be seen as information-driven. Therefore, we applied Direct Supervision as a coordination mechanism, which is comparable to control strategies in conventional system design. If we see supply chain management as competence-driven, i.e. the process relies on the problem-solving skills that agents have, other organizational structures and coordination mechanisms can be applied. With the "pigeonholing" process, the competences of the agents can be categorized and mapped on a categorization of predetermined situations.

7.2   Coordination Mechanisms for Multi-Agent Systems

To answer the question *How can agents make use of coordination mechanisms?*, we investigated coordination mechanisms on a general level, using them as a metaphor to analyze control issues in multi-agent systems (see Chapter 2). In order to study the dynamics of the coordination mechanisms and means to implement them, we provided a framework for agent interoperation and elaborated on its levels in Chapters 3, 5 and 6.

The interoperability framework consists of four interoperability levels: "technical", "syntactic", "semantic" and "coordination". The first three levels correspond to traditional interoperability structures in agent communication, where the emphasis is on message transport, languages and ontologies. We added the coordination level in order to regulate communication patterns and the flow of information. To enable interoperability, we constructed a framework to abstract technique, representation, concepts and strategy. Issues handled on the "technical interoperability" (or transport) level are related to using shared message transport mechanisms and network protocols. Decisions related to envelope-encoding and message content languages are covered on the "syntactic interoperability" level. *Semantic interoperability* means that agents use shared ontologies in communication. A Reference Model for providing semantics to agent communication and a method to design message content ontologies was discussed in Chapter 6. Finally, decisions related to agents using shared procedures (e.g. "every agent has to register its services"), coordination strategies and the related notion of organizational roles (e.g. "Manager" and "Librarian") are covered by the "coordination interoperability" level. In Chapter 3, we discussed coordination mechanisms that can be applied on this level.

In order to assist agent engineers and Manager agents in reasoning about coordination, the following strategies have been represented in the form of coordination strategy methods: "Direct Supervision", "Standardization of Work" and "Mutual Adjustment". Agents that need coordination can agree to commit to one or more of these coordination strategies, supported by a coordination ontology that models the concepts and relationships describing the coordination domain. From experiments with the three coordination strategies we made the following observations: Direct Supervision shows a centralized model, i.e. all coordination knowledge (i.e. strategic and supervision) is concentrated in the Manager, who takes care of managing the relations between activities and Operators. In Standardization of Work, we can see a pattern of a decentralized model (Knowledge about coordination is distributed among the Operators), where the Manager only plays the role of a strategic planner. In Mutual Adjustment, there is no division of roles into Operators and Managers. As a result, the collaboration pattern shows a broadcast communication model where every agent tries to communicate with all available agents.

There are several considerations for choosing the appropriate strategy to use, such as the number of (available) agents and the nature of the task. When a task can easily be decomposed so that the system can be designed as a monolithic system, no coordination structure needs to be used. "Direct Supervision" is a good candidate when there is a limited set of agents, because the Operators do not need to be equipped with additional functions to reason about instructions as within Standardization of Work. In the latter strategy, the nature of the tasks is repetitive and can be solved in a distributed manner. In relation to the other two strategies the "Direct Supervision Manager" is the most expensive Manager, because it has strong couplings with all the Operators. Furthermore, it becomes more complex when the number of agents or tasks grows. When the number of agents is dynamic, "Standardization of Work" is to be considered. If the environment is dynamic, the nature of the tasks is heterogeneous and the number of agents is open then "Mutual Adjustment" should be applied. When Operators do not want to agree on having a Manager or the task description is not present, this strategy could be applied. These agents (or Operators) are the most expensive agents.

In Chapter 5, we addressed the problem of interoperation within the IBROW architecture, which provides support for the composition of applications from existing (web)services that reside on the Web. The intelligent agent metaphor enabled us to describe the services and their collaboration within the architecture as agents using roles and behaviors. Using the notion of separation of concerns, specialized agents are defined that operate within functional spaces. A lesson learned is that using separation of concerns instead of integration into one large monolithic system helped us to cluster heterogeneous services into one architecture. In order to enable the services (i.e. agents) to interact with each other, we applied common standards and available technology, such as FIPA compliant communication and procedures, agent toolkits and web technology. The agents collaborate using specialized ontologies and collaboration patterns on top of the interoperability framework. In addition, the Manager within the IBROW architecture uses the "pigeonholing" process to select Operators. The advantage of having agreed on standards, agent designers only have to deal with the coordination level of the interoperability framework. Within this level, they only have to specify ontologies and collaboration patterns.

In the "conference submissions" scenario we addressed the problem of having to classify over 600 submissions for ECAI2002 by hand in order to distribute them to reviewers. In our approach, we showed how to automate this process using a collection of configured "Problem-Solving Methods". This process is represented by an application configuration constructed by the broker, which is translated by the Manager into a "Multi-Agent Plan". The execution of this Multi-Agent Plan showed how Problem-Solving Methods from three libraries (i.e. data-transport, document analysis and classification) can interact with each other. Using graphical inspection tools via the agent console, we inspected parts of the dynamics (communication and internal behavior of agents) of the IBROW architecture.

The problem of how agents handle message-based communication was studied in Chapter 6. As a solution, we defined the "Message Content Ontology Framework" containing a theoretical "Reference Model" for an ontology-based communication, in which the meaning and intention of message contents is specified in "Message Content Ontologies" that provides semantics in message-based communication. The Message Content Ontology Framework consists of an "Agent Communication Meta Ontology" that defines types of performatives and protocols based on the Speech Acts Theory and Conversational Interaction Theory originated from (human) communication theory. The "Reference Model" is an instance of the "Agent Communication Meta Ontology" and consists of agent communication ontologies that describe the domain of the conversation, performatives, protocols and agent roles. Based on the framework, we defined a "Minimal Ontology", which can be used in pragmatic agent solutions. We argued that agents without an inference engine need a representation of an ontology in terms of their internal representation (such as Java beans) and means (such as an ontology mapping file) to map instances of an ontology into their internal representation. Based on the presented tool, encoders and decoders can be used for translating an agent's internal model to agent communication utterances and vice versa.

Both the construction of the Message Content Ontology Framework and the Minimal Ontology can be seen as a first step towards the standardization of ontologies in agent communication and conversation. A method to define message content ontologies starts with choosing an Agent Communication Meta Ontology as a Reference Model. Next, based on generic classes of the Agent Communication Meta Ontology, conversation specific concepts of a message content ontology need to be defined. Then, these concepts can be specified in more detail by defining their properties (or attributes) and relations. Finally, ontology operations (such as encoding and decoding) have to be defined and added into an agent model.

As a result of the studies carried out in Chapters 3, 5 and 6, we showed the levels of interoperation that are needed to support coordination mechanisms. Agents can make use of coordination mechanisms by coordination strategy methods and agreeing (statically or dynamically) on what role to play in a coordination strategy. We argued that organizational structures and coordination strategies are of interest to agent engineers because they can be used to allocate tasks to agents and control agents within multi-agent systems. If organizational structures and coordination PSMs are stored in libraries, agent engineers can model agent behaviors according to these coordination patterns. In addition, Managers can be equipped with knowledge to select a coordination strategy and to reason about it. Furthermore, a group of agents could negotiate about which coordination strategy to apply and how to execute it.

7.3 Agent Design Principles

The question *How can the capabilities and functionality of an individual intelligent agent be analyzed and designed?* is answered by the development of the Five Capabilities (5C) model (discussed in Chapter 4). The 5C model is a conceptual framework filled with a selection of generalized types of agent competences and provides design principles for individual agent design. The model defines five dimensions of agent intelligence: "communication model", "competence model", "self model", "planner model" and "environment model".

Each of the five models can play an important role in the development of an intelligent software agent. The analogy could also be applied to intelligent physical agents like robots. How each of the models will be filled in may vary depending on the particular kind of agent or the particular application. To illustrate variations of agents, we designed a number of agents with the 5C model. In Section 5.5.2.3, we showed the design for the Manager of the IBROW architecture. This agent is capable of interacting with other agents based on available message content ontologies. The competence model is able to construct Multi-Agent Plans, negotiate with Operators, execute Multi-Agent Plans, and negotiate with the Reconfigurator. The management of the agent's life cycles (cf. Section 3.4.2) is handled by the self model. The planner model is responsible for planning the actions required to follow the life cycles in the agent's agenda. Finally, the environment model is capable of searching for Operators and storing them in a repository of known Operators. Information related to relations with reconfigurator and user agents is also stored in the environment model. Furthermore, we showed how the 5C model can be implemented on top of existing agent technology, such as the JADE toolkit.

In order to show the overhead (due to pre-negotiation discussion) when applying the theoretical Message Content Ontology Framework, we analyzed the required functionality and knowledge, which resulted in an agent design that uses all five models (see Section 6.3). When putting ontology-based communication in operation, taking into account the current state of the art and the level of complexity of current multi-agent systems, we showed that only the communication and competence model are needed (see Section 6.4). Based on the "Bean Generator" tool, we showed that parts of the communication model can be generated automatically. This approach supports the idea that next to standardization of communication content, also standardization of communication handling is needed.

When analyzing the functionality of an intelligent agent, all five models can be used to identify functionality. Given the current state of the art, most technical agent designs only need a "communication model" for interaction with other agents and a "competence model" to offer their services. We argued this in Section 6.5, where the "Law Service Broker" is relatively simple and the "self model", "environment model" and "planner model" are seen as internal functional overhead. The cost to define and implement separate models for knowing the agent's goal, maintaining models of other agents and execution strategies can be larger than putting these functionalities into the communication and competence model. When there is no explicit reasoning on the agent's goal, the competence model maintains models of other agents, and the communication model handles execution strategies. In spite of these pragmatic simplifications the 5C model provides a powerful conceptual framework for reasoning about agent architectures.

7.4   Discussion and Future Research

To answer the research questions of this book, we (1) conducted a conceptual analysis of organizational concepts, organizational models and coordination mechanisms, (2) provided a framework for agent interoperation and (3) provided a conceptual framework for analyzing and designing the capabilities and functionality of an intelligent agent. Still several problems associated with the work presented remain.

Future research related to the agent organization framework may include elaborate research on specific organizational design theories and methods. In our work only a selection of organizational principles have been explored. A future agent organizational framework should assist designers in addressing more precisely an organization's overall task and environment. Furthermore, the framework could assist in the formalization of the overall behavior of a distributed intelligent system in terms of (human) organizational structure and behavior. More predictable and controllable behavior of agents could lead to reduction of the variability of systems. However, one of the prominent properties of agent intelligence is autonomy, i.e. independence. One of the challenges of individual agent design suited to operate within agent organizations is to find a balance between independence, predictability and controllability.

In order to inspect parts of the dynamics of a multi-agent system, such as the IBROW architecture, we used the "agent console". With the agent console, we can gain insights into the communication and internal behavior of agents. However, the expressive power of these graphical inspection tools is limited. Furthermore, when testing or debugging a multi-agent system, it is still difficult to start, restart, stop or suspend agents. Therefore, there is a need for more elaborate inspection and control tools in the form of intelligent debugging, where system inspection is on the knowledge level (e.g. "why did the state of the system change?") instead of inspecting at the symbol level (e.g. "what was the content of a message").

In our work on agent interoperation we concentrated on the semantic and coordination interoperability layers with the assumption that the technical and syntactical interoperability layer are standardized. In practice this assumption does not hold, because there is still many debate about "low level" standardization, such as transport protocols and communication languages. We first need to solve basic communication problems before we can focus on interesting aspects of communication, such as negotiation and bargaining, which can facilitate complex organizational models. One small step towards enabling complex organizational models is the application of message content ontologies that define the vocabulary of content of communication. Next step is having agents exchanging knowledge structures. For this, agents themselves should be able to add meaning to knowledge. A following step could be to support learning amongst agents, e.g. by feedback.

Most current research on agent models is technology-driven (i.e. on the symbol level) instead of capability-driven, because the models are based on a specific technology, infrastructure or a multi-agent environment. However, the fact that agents can be designed independently of each other and that agents posses a form of intelligence are promises of agent technology. At this moment, the available technology seems to restrict research on agent competences. For example, little is known about learning agent organizations. Both the research on agent models and multi-agent models should move from technology to capability (i.e. knowledge level).

From an agent organization point of view, the organizational structure "Adhocracy" using "Mutual Adjustment" as a coordination strategy is the most appealing. Given the current state of the art, the application of "Adhocracy" and "Mutual Adjustment" comes with many problems. For example, our model of "Mutual Adjustment" is based on a simple broadcast model, which does not guarantee success. In more complex situations, a more elaborate model for "Mutual Adjustment" needs to be designed. An extension to our model can be based on negotiation, where agents bargain or argue on coordination matters.

Adhocracy can typically be used in self-organizing applications, i.e. applications that can evolve in either time or space in response to dynamically changing requirements. In this type of application, there are typically several interacting software components (agents) that can act independently and in collaboration with each other, and with no central entity. If we would follow this definition as a metaphor, we would only have to specify a problem and a rough sketch of a problem-solving approach and the agents themselves would be able to elaborate on the problem-solving approach, allocate tasks, coordinate flows and solve the problem. However, before we can move from classical hierarchical decomposition and typical static control components to such an agent system, we need to give engineers and end-users a sense of control and means to guarantee that the system will achieve its goals.

When moving to real dynamic systems, agent engineers and end-users need to be convinced by the agent community that systems composed of self-organizing agents will lead to more robust, flexible, cheaper and more reliable systems. If we would follow this definition literally then there will be systems that can solve problems that are detected by the system itself, without any human intervention. In summary, the field of multi agent systems show promising roots to application that perform complex tasks but many technical and syntactical problems remain.

Summary

The general question addressed in this book *How can human organizational principles be used for multi-agent architectures?* is answered by an exploration of the possibilities to design multi-agent systems as artificial organizations. Three research lines are presented: *organizational modeling and coordination, interoperability* and *agent models*. Organizational modeling and coordination is concerned with how resources (i.e. people or agents) can be identified and related to each other. The (human) organizational principles we explored are: "division of labor" and "coordination". Division of labor consists of decomposing the work (or goal) into various distinct tasks. Coordination refers to managing relations between these tasks to achieve the work. The patterns of division of labor, responsibilities (i.e. people who do the work), clustering of responsibilities into units and coordination between units can be defined by "organizational structures". Organizations are complex entities formed to overcome various limitations of individual agencies, such as cognitive, physical, temporal and institutional limitations. The design of an organization should cover how one or more people are engaged in one or more tasks, where knowledge, capabilities and resources are distributed. Such a design can be seen as a set of networks and procedures that link agents, tasks, resources and skills.

Many human organizations can be viewed as information processing systems because many of their activities are concerned with transforming information from one form to another. In addition, organizational activity (like receiving orders, reporting and administrating) is frequently information-driven. Links between human organizations and computational systems are suggested by Fox, where distributed system are described by responsibilities of processes (i.e. agents), communication paths and a control regime that coordinates the whole. Furthermore, Malone and Crowston discusses the influence of coordination theory in resource allocation, management of unreliable actors, task assignment and information flow management.

Coordination is an essential activity in multi-agent systems, in that it permits agents to cooperate in order to achieve common goals. Based on division of labor, agents will perform a number of (specialized) tasks. When agents organized in a multi-agent system collaborate, they are capable of performing more complex actions than individual agents can. However, in order to achieve common and individual goals, agents need to interact in a coordinated manner. This means that an agent should be aware not only of the actions it can perform and the state it is in at any moment of the execution, but also of the actions other agents can perform and their states.

Chapter 2 presents a framework for multi-agent system design, which is based on human organizational notions and principles for distributed intelligent systems design. Organizational notions such as "task", "control", "job", "operation", "management", "coordination" and "organization" are framed into an organizational design framework. A collection of organizational design activities is presented that assists in a task-oriented decomposition of the overall task of a system into jobs and the reintegration of jobs using job allocation, coordination mechanisms and organizational structuring.

In order to allocate jobs to positions (i.e. agents), our approach makes use of an explicit separation of the performance of work and the control over it. "Operators" are responsible for performing the technical part of work, such as transforming input into output. "Managers" are responsible for the control over Operators. In order to coordinate Operators, we investigated a selection of coordination mechanisms described by Mintzberg: "Direct Supervision" where one individual takes all decisions for the work of others, "Mutual Adjustment" that achieves coordination by a process of informal communication between agents, and "Standardization of Work, Output and Skills".

Three organizational structures originating from Mintzberg are adjusted in order to coordinate agents and their work: "Machine Bureaucracy", "Professional Bureaucracy" and "Adhocracy". The Machine Bureaucracy is task-driven, seeing the organization as a single-purpose structure, which only uses one strategy to execute the overall task. The Professional Bureaucracy is competence-driven, where a part of the organization will first examine a case, match it to predetermined situations and then allocate specialized agents to it. In an Adhocracy, the organization is capable of reorganizing its own structure including dynamically changing the work flow, shifting responsibilities and adapting to changing environments. A case study on distributed supply chain management shows the process from task decomposition via organizational design to three multi-agent architectures based on the three organizational structures.

"Interoperability" is concerned with how to let agents communicate with each other, how to coordinate agent communication and how to add semantics to agent communication. Chapter 3 discusses "coordination mechanisms" in the form of "Problem Solving Methods", which can assist "Managers" and agent engineers in reasoning about coordination. Agents that need coordination can agree to commit to one or more coordination strategies. Underlying the Problem Solving Methods is a "coordination ontology" that models the concepts and relationships describing the coordination domain. The coordination strategies are based on the strategies described by Mintzberg.

From experiments with the three coordination strategies, we made the following observations: in Direct Supervision the coordination knowledge (i.e. strategic and supervision) is concentrated in the Manager, who takes care of managing the relations between activities and Operators. In Standardization of Work, we can see a pattern of a decentralized model (knowledge about coordination is distributed among the Operators), where the Manager only plays the role of a strategic planner. In Mutual Adjustment, there is no division of roles into Operators and Managers. As a result, the collaboration pattern shows a broadcast communication model where every agent tries to communicate with all available agents.

The "IBROW project" (IBROW stands for Intelligent BRokering On the Web) discussed in Chapter 5, has as goal to develop technologies for (semi-) automatic selection and configuration of new applications by reuse of existing services. Work on a multi-agent architecture capable of (semi)automatic reuse of Problem Solving Methods (PSMs) is discussed. Using the notion of separation of concerns, specialized agents are defined that operate within functional spaces. The agents within the architecture collaborate using specialized ontologies and collaboration patterns on top of an interoperability structure.

In a "conference submissions" scenario, we addressed the problem of having to classify over 600 submissions for the ECAI 2002 conference by hand in order to distribute them to reviewers. In our approach, we showed how to automate this process using a collection of configured PSMs. This process is represented by an application configuration constructed by a broker, which is translated by the Manager into a "Multi-Agent Plan" (MAP). The execution of this MAP showed how PSMs from three libraries (i.e. data-transport, document analysis and classification) can interact with each other. Using graphical inspection tools via the agent console, we inspected parts of the dynamics (communication and internal behavior of agents) of the IBROW architecture.

Chapter 6 focuses on the problem of how to add semantics to agent communication. Our approach is to look at "ontology-based communication", in which the meaning and intention of message contents is specified in "message content ontologies". In order to share semantics, agents commit to shared message content ontologies. We present a "Reference Model" for ontology-based communication based on "speech act" theory. A pragmatic approach is presented, taking into account the current state of the art in agent technology, which enables creation and use of message content ontologies to support ontology-based communication between agents. We describe a tool that assists agent engineers in designing message content ontologies and export them to Java source code. A case study on Legal Services illustrates conversations between agents based on a law message content ontology.

An "Agent Model" is concerned with guiding agent engineers in making conceptual, functional and technical design decisions when designing agents, taking into account typical agent intelligence competences, such as "autonomy", "interaction", "pro-activeness" and "reactiveness". In Chapter 4, we present the "Five Capabilities (5C) model" which is a conceptual framework based on a generalization of typical agent intelligence competences. The model defines five dimensions of agent intelligence: "communication model", "competence model", "self model", "planner model" and "environment model". Each of the five models plays an important role for the development of an intelligent software agent. How each of the models will be filled in may vary depending on the particular kind of agent or the particular application. It is possible that an agent design is based on the five models, but the technical model on a simplification.

The 5C model has been the design guide (for capabilities and functionality) for the development of a series of intelligent agent application prototypes (see Chapter 5 and 6) and commercial applications. The development of the applications showed that functional as well as technical constraints can be reflected in an intuitive manner along the five dimensions, using the notion of separation of concerns. Also several "non-agent" issues can be taken into account, such as functional constraints and technical/political constraints. Depending on the requirements of the application one can focus on each capability that needs attention, without losing oneself in the complexity of the entire design.

Chapter 7 concludes the book by answering the research questions and suggesting future work. The research questions are answered by (1) conducting a conceptual analysis of organizational concepts, organizational models and coordination mechanisms (2) providing a framework for agent interoperation and (3) providing a conceptual framework for analyzing and designing the capabilities and functionality of an intelligent agent. Future research includes extensions to the current agent organization framework, which should be of assistance in the organizational design decision process to bring coherence between the patterns of division of labor and patterns of coordination. Future research on the framework for agent interoperation may include study on agent negotiation in "Mutual Adjustment". Finally, the 5C model could be extended with a library of reusable model components.

Bibliography

[Austin, 1976] Austin, J. (1976). *How to Do Things with Words*. Oxford University Press.

[Bailin and Truszkowski, 2001] Bailin, S. and Truszkowski, W. (2001). Ontology Negotiation between Scientific Archives. In *Thirteenth International Conference on Scientific and Statistical Database Management*.

[Bellifemine et al., 2003] Bellifemine, F., G., C., Trucco, T., and Rimassa, G. (2003). *JADE Programmer's Guide*.

[Bellifemine et al., 2001] Bellifemine, F., Poggi, A., and Rimassa, G. (2001). Developing multi agent systems with a FIPA-compliant agent framework. *Software - Practice And Experience*, 31:103–128.

[Benjamins, 1993] Benjamins, V. (1993). *Problem Solving Methods For Diagnosis*. PhD thesis, University of Amsterdam.

[Benjamins and Fensel, 1998] Benjamins, V. and Fensel, D. (1998). Special issue on problem-solving methods. *International Journal of Human-Computer Studies (IJHCS)*, 49(4).

[Benjamins et al., 1998] Benjamins, V., Plaza, E., Motta, E., Fensel, D., Studer, R., Wielinga, B., Schreiber, A., and Zdrahal, Z. (1998). An Intelligent Brokering Service for Knowledge-Component Reuse on the World-WideWeb. In *Proceedings of the 11th Workshop on Knowledge Acquisition, Modeling and Management (KAW 98), Banff, Canada*.

[Berners-Lee et al., 2001] Berners-Lee, T., Hendler, J., and Lassila, O. (2001). The Semantic Web. *Scientific American*, 284(5):34–43.

[Bond and Gasser, 1988] Bond, A. and Gasser, L. (1988). *Readings in Distributed Artificial Intelligence*. Morgan Kaufmann publishers Inc.: San Mateo, CA, USA.

[Borst, 1997] Borst, W. N. (1997). *Construction of Engineering Ontologies*. PhD thesis, University of Twente, Enschede.

[Bradshaw, 1997] Bradshaw, J. (1997). *Software Agents*, pages 3–46. Menlo Park.

[Carley and Gasser, 1999] Carley, K. and Gasser, L. (1999). Computational Organizational Theory. *Multi-agent Systems*.

[Castelfranchi, 1995] Castelfranchi, C. (1995). Guarentees for autonomy in cognitive agents architecture. In *Intelligent Agents: Theories, Architectures, and Languages (LNAI Volume 890)*.

[Chavez and Maes, 1996] Chavez, A. and Maes, P. (1996). Kasbah: An agent marketplace for buying and selling goods. In *Proceedings of the First International Conference on the practical Application of Intelligent Agents and Multi-agent systems*.

[Corkill and Lander, 1998] Corkill, D. and Lander, S. (1998). Agent Organizations. *Object Magazine*, 8(4).

[Cranefield and Purvis, 1999] Cranefield, S. and Purvis, M. (1999). Uml as an ontology modelling language. In *Workshop on Intelligent Information Integration, 16th International Joint Conference on Artificial Intelligence (IJCAI-99)*.

[Davis and Smith, 1983] Davis, R. and Smith, R. (1983). Negotiation as a Metaphor for Distributed Problem Solving. *Artificial Intelligence*, 20(1):63–109.

[Dinkloh and Nimis, 2003] Dinkloh, M. and Nimis, J. (2003). A Tool for Integrated Design and Implementation of Conversations in Multiagent Systems. In *Workshop on Programming Multiagent Systems languages, frameworks, techniques and tools (ProMAS 2003) held at the 2nd International Conference on Autonomous Agents & Multiagent Systems*.

[Eriksson et al., 1995] Eriksson, H., Shahar, Y., Tu, S., Peurta, A., and Musen, M. (1995). Task Modeling with reusable problem-solving methods. *Artificial Intelligence*, 79:293–326.

[Esteva et al., 2001] Esteva, M., Rodríguez-Aguilar, J., Sierra, C., Garcia, P., and Arcos, J. L. (2001). On the Formal Specification of Electronic Institutions. In *Lecture Notes in Artificial Intelligence*, volume 1991, pages 126–147. Springer-Verlag.

[Etzioni and Weld, 1994] Etzioni, O. and Weld, D. (1994). A Softbot-Based Interface to the Internet. *Communications of the ACM*, 37(7):72–76.

[Fayol, 1949] Fayol, H. (1949). *General and industrial management*. New York: Pitman. First published in French in 1916.

[Fensel et al., 1999a] Fensel, D., Benjamins, V., Decker, S., Gaspari, M., Groenboom, R., Grosso, W., Musen, M., Motta, E., Plaza, E., Schreiber, A., Studer, R., and Wielinga, B. (1999a). The component model of UPML in a nutshell. In *Proceedings of the First Working IFIP Conference on Software Architecture (WICSA1), San Antonio, Texas*.

[Fensel et al., 1999b] Fensel, D., Benjamins, V., Motta, E., and Wielinga, B. (1999b). UPML: A framework for knowledge system reuse. In *Proceedings of IJCAI-99, Stockholm, Sweden.*

[Fensel and Motta, 2001] Fensel, D. and Motta, E. (2001). Structured Development of Problem Solving Methods. *IEEE Transactions on Knowledge and Data Engineering*, 13(6):931–932.

[Ferber, 1999] Ferber, J. (1999). *Multi-Agent Systems.* Addison-Wesley, Reading, MA.

[Fernández-López et al., 1999] Fernández-López, M., Gómez-Pérez, A., Sierra, J. P., and Sierra, A. P. (1999). Building a chemical ontology using Methontology and the Ontology Design Environment. *Intelligent Systems*, 14(1):37–45.

[FIPA, 2001] FIPA (2001). FIPA Ontology Service Specification. Technical Report XF000086, Foundation for Intelligent Physical Agents, http://www.fipa.org/specs/fipa00086/.

[FIPA, 2002a] FIPA (2002a). FIPA Abstract Architecture Specification. Technical Report SC00001L, Foundation for Intelligent Physical Agents, http://www.fipa.org/specs/fipa00001/.

[FIPA, 2002b] FIPA (2002b). FIPA ACL Message Structure Specification. Technical Report SC00061, Foundation for Intelligent Physical Agents, http://www.fipa.org/specs/fipa00061/.

[FIPA, 2002c] FIPA (2002c). FIPA Agent Management Specification. Technical Report SC00023, Foundation for Intelligent Physical Agents, http://www.fipa.org/specs/fipa00023/.

[FIPA, 2002d] FIPA (2002d). FIPA Communicative Act Library Specification. Technical Report SC00037J, Foundation for Intelligent Physical Agents, http://www.fipa.org/specs/fipa00037.

[FIPA, 2002e] FIPA (2002e). FIPA Contract Net Interaction Protocol Specification. Technical Report SC00029, Foundation for Intelligent Physical Agents, http://www.fipa.org/specs/fipa00029/.

[FIPA, 2002f] FIPA (2002f). FIPA Dutch Auction Interaction Protocol Specification. Technical Report XC00032, Foundation for Intelligent Physical Agents, http://www.fipa.org/specs/fipa00032/.

[FIPA, 2002g] FIPA (2002g). FIPA English Auction Interaction Protocol Specification. Technical Report XC00031, Foundation for Intelligent Physical Agents, http://www.fipa.org/specs/fipa00031/.

[FIPA, 2002h] FIPA (2002h). FIPA Request Interaction Protocol Specification. Technical Report SC00026H, Foundation for Intelligent Physical Agents, http://www.fipa.org/specs/fipa00026.

[FIPA, 2002i] FIPA (2002i). FIPA SL Content Language Specification. Technical Report SC00008, Foundation for Intelligent Physical Agents, http://www.fipa.org/specs/fipa00008/.

[Fox, 1981] Fox, M. (1981). An organizational view of distributed systems. *IEEE Transactions on system, man and cybernetics*, 11(1):70–80.

[Franklin and Graesser, 1996] Franklin, S. and Graesser, A. (1996). Is it an agent, or just a program? A taxonomy of Autonomous Agents. In *Proceedings of the Third International on Agent Theories, Architectures and Languages*.

[Frey et al., 2003] Frey, D., Nimis, J., Wörn, H., and Lockemann, P. (2003). Benchmarking and Robust Multi-agent-based Production Planning and Control. *The International Journal of Intelligent Real-Time Automation*. In Print.

[Galbraith, 1973] Galbraith, J. (1973). *Designing complex Organizations*. Addison-Wesley.

[Gaspari and Motta, 1994] Gaspari, M. and Motta, E. (1994). Symbol-level Requirements for Agent-level Programming. In Cohn, A., editor, *proc. of the 11th European Conference on Artificial Intelligence*.

[Geis, 1995] Geis, M. (1995). *Speech Acts and Conversational Interaction*. Cambridge University Press.

[Genesereth, 1997] Genesereth, M. (1997). An Agent-based Framework for Interoperability. *Software Agents, J.M. Bradshaw (Ed.)*, pages 317–345.

[Genesereth and Ketchpel, 1994] Genesereth, M. and Ketchpel, S. (1994). Software agents. *Communications of the ACM*, 37(7):48–53.

[Gomez-Perez, 1999] Gomez-Perez, A. (1999). Ontological engineering: A state of the art. *Expert Update*, 2(3):33–43.

[Gosselin, 1978] Gosselin, R. (1978). *A Study on the Interdependence of Medical Specialists in Quebec Teaching Hospitals*. PhD thesis, Faculty of Management, McGill University, Montreal.

[Gruber, 1993] Gruber, T. (1993). A Translation Approach to Portable Ontology Specifications. *Knowledge Acquisition*, 5(2):199–220.

[Gruber and Olsen, 1994] Gruber, T. and Olsen, G. (1994). An ontology for engineering mathematics. Technical Report KSL-94-18, Knowledge Systems Laboratory, Stanford University,.

[Gruninger and Fox, 1994] Gruninger, M. and Fox, M. (1994). The Role of Competency Questions in Enterprise Engineering. In *Workshop on Benchmarking - Theory and Practice*.

[Guarino, 1998] Guarino, N. (1998). Formal Ontology and Information Systems. In *1st International Conference on Formal Ontologies in Information Systems, FOIS'98, Trento*.

[Haddadi, 1995] Haddadi, A. (1995). *Communication and Cooperation in Agent Systems*. Berlin, Springer-Verlag.

[Haustein and Luedecke, 2000] Haustein, S. and Luedecke, S. (2000). Towards information agent interoperability. In *Cooperative Information Agents*, pages 208–219.

[Hendler, 2001] Hendler, J. (2001). Agents and the semantic web. *IEEE Intelligent Systems*, 16(2):30–37.

[Hewitt, 1991] Hewitt, C. (1991). Open systems semantics for distributed artificial intelligence. *Artificial intelligence*, 47(1):79–106.

[Huget, 2002] Huget, M. (2002). An Application of Agent UML to Supply Chain Management. In *Proceedings of Agent Oriented Information System (AOIS-02)*.

[Huhns and Stephens, 1999] Huhns, M. and Stephens, L. (1999). Multiagent systems and societies of agents. In Weiss, G., editor, *Multiagent Systems: A Modern Approach to Distributed Artificial Intelligence*, pages 79–120. The MIT Press, Cambridge, MA, USA.

[Jennings, 2000] Jennings, N. (2000). On agent-based software engineering. *Artificial Intelligence*, 177(2):277–296.

[Labrou et al., 1999] Labrou, Y., Finin, T., and Peng, Y. (1999). The current landscape of agent communication languages.

[Levinson, 1991] Levinson, S. (1991). *Pragmatics*. Cambridge University Press, Cambridge.

[Lomuscio et al., 2003] Lomuscio, A. R., Wooldridge, M., and Jennings, N. (2003). A classification scheme for negotiation in electronic commerce. *International Journal of Group Decision and Negotiation*, 12(1):31–56.

[Luck et al., 2003] Luck, M., McBurney, P., and Preist, C. (2003). *Agent Technology: Enabling Next Generation Computing: A Roadmap for Agent Based Computing*. AgentLink II.

[Maes, 1986] Maes, P. (1986). Introspection in knowledge representation. In *Proceedings of the 7th European Conference on Artificial Intelligence (ECAI)*.

[Maes, 1994] Maes, P. (1994). Agents that reduce work and information overload. *Communications of the ACM*, 37(7):31–40.

[Maes, 1998] Maes, P. (1998). Computational reflection. *The Knowledge Engineering Review*, 3(1):1–19.

[Malone, 1987] Malone, T. (1987). Modeling Coordination in Organizations and Markets. *Management Sciences*, 33(10)(1317-1332).

[Malone and Crowston, 1993] Malone, T. and Crowston, K. (1993). What is coordination theory and how can it help design cooperative work systems. *Readings in groupware and computer- supported cooperative work, assisting human-human collaboration.*

[Malone and Crowston, 1994] Malone, T. and Crowston, K. (1994). The interdisciplinary study of coordination. *ACM Computing Surveys*, 26(1):87–119.

[Mintzberg, 1993] Mintzberg, H. (1993). *Structures in fives: designing effective organizations.* Englewood Cliffs, N.J. Prentice Hall.

[Morgan, 1996] Morgan, G. (1996). *Images of organization.* Sage Publications.

[Motta, 1999] Motta, E. (1999). *Reusable Components for Knowledge Modelling: Principles and Case Studies in Parametric Design.* IOS Press, Amsterdam.

[Motta and Lu, 2000] Motta, E. and Lu, W. (2000). A library of Components for Classification Problem Solving. In *PKAW: The 2000 Pacific Knowledge Acquisition Workshop.*

[Neches et al., 1991] Neches, R., Fikes, R., Finin, T., T., G., Patil, R., Senatir, T., and Swarout, W. (1991). Enabling technology for knowledge sharing. *AI Magazine*, 12(3):36–56.

[Newell, 1982] Newell, A. (1982). The Knowledge Level. *Artificial Intelligence*, 18(1):87–127.

[Noy et al., 2000] Noy, N., Fergerson, R., and Musen, M. (2000). The knowledge model of Protege-2000: Combining interoperability and flexibility. In *2th International Conference on Knowledge Engineering and Knowledge Management (EKAW'2000), Juan-les-Pins, France.*

[Noy and McGuinness, 2001] Noy, N. and McGuinness, D. L. (2001). Ontology Development 101: A Guide to Creating Your First Ontology. 2001. Technical report, Stanford Medical Informatics.

[Nwana, 1996] Nwana, H. (1996). Software Agents: An Overview. *Knowledge Engineering Review*, 11(3):205–244.

[Odell et al., 2000] Odell, J., Van Dyke, H., and Bauer, B. (2000). Extending UML for agents. In Wagner, G., Lesperance Y., and Yu, E., editors, *Proc. Of the Agent-Oriented Information Systems Workshop at the 17th National Conference on Artificial Intelligence.*

[O'Hare and Jennings, 1996] O'Hare, G. and Jennings, N. (1996). *Foundations of Distributed Artificial Intelligence.* John Wiley & Sons.

[Omelayenko et al., 2000] Omelayenko, B., Crubézy, M., Fensel, D., Ding, Y., Motta, E., and Musen, M. (2000). Meta Data and UPML, UPML version 2.0. Technical report, Deliverable D5, IBROW project.

[Ossowski, 1999] Ossowski, S. (1999). *Co-ordination in Artificial Agent Societies.* Springer-Verlag New York.

[Pinto and Martins, 2000] Pinto, H. and Martins, J. (2000). Reusing Ontologies. In *AAAI 2000 Spring Symposium Series, Workshop on Bringing Knowledge to Business Processes.*

[Powers, 2003] Powers, S. (2003). *PracticalRDF*. O'Reilly.

[Rao and Georgeff, 1995] Rao, A. and Georgeff, M. (1995). BDI Agents: From Theory to Practice. In *Proceedings of the First International Conference on Multi-agent systems, (ICMAS-95)*, pages 312–319.

[Rodríguez-Aguilar et al., 1998] Rodríguez-Aguilar, J., Martin, F., Noriega, P., Garcia, P., and Sierra, C. (1998). Towards a test-bed for trading agents in electronic auction markets. *AI Communications*, 11(1):5–19.

[Schmidt et al., 2000] Schmidt, D., Stal, M., Rohnert, H., and Buschmann, F. (2000). *Pattern-Oriented Software Architecture: Patterns for Concurrent and Networked Objects.* Wiley and Sons.

[Schreiber et al., 1999] Schreiber, A., Akkermans, H., Anjewierden, A., de Hoog, R., Shadbolt, N., Van de Velde, W., and Wielinga, B. (1999). *Knowledge Engineering and Management: the CommonKADS Methodology.* The MIT Press.

[Searle, 1969] Searle, J. (1969). *Seech Acts.* Cambridge University Press.

[Shoham, 1993] Shoham, Y., . (1993). Agent oriented programming. *Artificial Intelligence*, 60(1):51–92.

[Singh, 1998] Singh, M. (1998), Agent Communication Languages: Rethinking the Principles. *IEEE Computer*, 31(12):40–47.

[Smith, 1776] Smith, A. (1776). *Wealth of Nations.*

[Sommerville, 1995] Sommerville, I. (1995). *Software Engineering.* Addison-Wesley.

[Studer et al., 1998] Studer, R., Benjamins, V., and Fensel, D. (1998). Knowledge engineering, principles and methods. *Data and Knowledge Engineering*, 25(1-2):161–197.

[Sycara et al., 2003] Sycara, K., Paolucci, M., van Velsen, M., and Giampapa, J. (2003). The RETSINA MAS Infrastructure. *Autonomous Agents and MAS*, 7(1).

[Taylor, 1947] Taylor, F. (1947). *Scientific management.* Harper & Row, New York. First published in 1911.

[Uschold and Grüninger, 1996] Uschold, M. and Grüninger, M. (1996). Ontologies: principles, methods, and applications. *Knowledge Engineering Review*, 11(2):93–155.

[Uschold et al., 1998] Uschold, M., King, M., Moralee, S., and Zorgios, Y. (1998). The Enterprise Ontology. *The Knowledge Engineering Review*.

[van Aart, 2004] van Aart, C. (2004). Organization Building Blocks for Design of Distributed Intelligent Systems. *International Journal of Human Computer Studies*. in press.

[van Aart and Jansweijer, 2003] van Aart, C. and Jansweijer, W. (2003). Interoperability. Technical report, Deliverable 10, IBROW project.

[van Aart et al., 2002a] van Aart, C., Pels, R., Giovanni, C., and Bergenti, F. (2002a). Creating and Using Ontologies in Agent Communication. *Workshop on Ontologies and Agent Systems at AAMAS 2002*.

[van Aart et al., 2000] van Aart, C., Van Marcke, K., and Eriksen, L. (2000). Agentbased Logistic Sevice Provision. In *Proc. the Fifth International Conference on the Practical Application of Intelligent Agents and Multi-Agent Technology (PAAM 2000), London*.

[van Aart et al., 2002b] van Aart, C., Van Marcke, K., Pels, R., and Smulders, J. (2002b). International Insurance Traffic with Software Agents. In F. van Harmelen, editor, *Proceedings of the 15th European Conference on Artificial Intelligence*. IOS Press, Amsterdam.

[van Heijst et al., 1997] van Heijst, G., Schreiber, A., and Wielinga, B. (1997). Using explicit ontologies for KBS development. *International Journal of Human-Computer Studies*, 46(2/3):183–292.

[Varga and Hajna, 2003] Varga, L. and Hajna, A. (2003). Engineering Web Service Invocations from Agent Systems. *Multi-Agent Systems and Applications III, Lecture Notes in Computer Science Vol. 2691*.

[Verharen, 1997] Verharen, E. (1997). *A Language-Action Perspective on the Design of Cooperative Information Agents*. PhD thesis, Katholieke Universiteit Brabant Tilburg.

[Weigand and Hasselbring, 2001] Weigand, H. and Hasselbring, W. (2001). An Extensible Business Communication Language. *International Journal of Cooperative Information System*, 10(4):423–411.

[Weiss, 1999] Weiss, G. (1999). *Multiagent Systems: A modern approach to distributed artificial intelligence*. MIT Press, London.

[Wielinga et al., 2003] Wielinga, B., Anjewierden, A., van Aart, C., and Jansweijer, W. (2003). Brokering in IBROW. Technical report, Deliverable 15, IBROW project.

[Wooldridge, 2002] Wooldridge, M. (2002). *An Introduction to Multi-Agent Systems*. John Wiley and Sons Ltd., Chichester, UK.

[Wooldridge and Jennings, 1995] Wooldridge, M. and Jennings, N. (1995). Intelligent agents: theory and practice. *The Knowledge Engineering Review*, 10(2):115–152.

[Wooldridge and Jennings, 1998] Wooldridge, M. and Jennings, N. (1998). Pitfalls of Agent-Oriented Development. In *Proceedings of the Second International COnference on Autonomous Agents*. ACM Press.

[Wooldridge et al., 2000] Wooldridge, M., Jennings, N., and Kinny, D. (2000). The Gaia methodology for agent-oriented analysis and design. *Internat. J. Autonomous Agents and Multi-Agent Systems 3*.

[Zambonelli et al., 2000] Zambonelli, F., Jennings, N., and Wooldridge, M. (2000). Organisational abstractions for the analysis and design of multi-agent systems. In *Proc. 1st int workshop on agent-oriented software engineering*.

Index

Whitestein Series in Software Agent Technologies

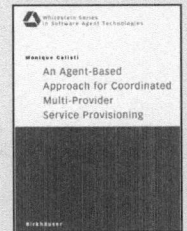

Edited by **Marius Walliser**, **Stefan Brantschen**,
Monique Calisti, and **Thomas Hempfling**

This series reports new developments in agent-based software technologies and agent-oriented software engineering methodologies,
with particular emphasis on applications in various scientific and
industrial areas. It includes research level monographs, polished
notes arising from research and industrial projects, outstanding PhD
theses, and proceedings of focused meetings and conferences. The
series aims at promoting advanced research as well as at facilitating
know-how transfer to industrial use.

Your Specialized Publisher in Mathematics

Birkhäuser

For orders originating from all over the world
except USA/Canada/Latin America:

Birkhäuser Verlag AG
c/o Springer GmbH & Co
Haberstrasse 7
D-69126 Heidelberg
Fax: +49 / 6221 / 345 4 229
e-mail: birkhauser@springer.de
http://www.birkhauser.ch

For orders originating in the
USA/Canada/Latin America:

Birkhäuser
333 Meadowland Parkway
USA-Secaucus
NJ 07094-2491
Fax: +1 201 348 4505
e-mail: orders@birkhauser.com

■ **Van Aart, Ch.**, Waalwijk, The Netherlands

Organizational Principles for Multi-Agent Architectures

2004. 216 pages. Softcover.
ISBN 3-7643-7213-3

■ **Neagu, N.**, Zürich, Switzerland

Constraint Satisfaction Techniques for Agent-Based Reasoning

2005. 184 pages. Softcover.
ISBN 3-7643-7217-6

An important aspect of multi-agent systems are
agent reasoning techniques for problem solving,
either at the level of a single agent or at the level of
distributed collaboration amongst multiple agents.
Constraint satisfaction problems are significant in
the domain of automated reasoning for artificial
intelligence. They can be applied to modeling and
solving of a wide range of combinatorial applications
such as planning, scheduling and resource sharing in
a variety of practical domains such as transportation,
production, supply-chains, network management
and human resource management. In this book we
study new techniques for solving constraint

satisfaction problems, with a special focus on
solution adaptation applied to agent reasoning.
Most work in constraint satisfaction has focused on
computing a solution to a given problem. In practice,
it often occurs that an existing solution needs to be
modified to satisfy additional criteria or
accommodate changes in the problem. For example,
a schedule or plan might need to be adjusted when
a resource is no longer available.
Based on constraint satisfaction problem structures
and their symmetries, we develop techniques for
adapting solutions in applications such as
replanning, rescheduling, reconfiguration, etc.,
which are important techniques for agent-based
reasoning. We show how these techniques can be
used for adapting solutions when the agent is
situated in dynamic and distributed environments.

This book is addressed to researchers in the artificial
intelligence domain who are interested in constraint
satisfaction techniques for agent reasoning.
Moreover, as these methods are important for many
applications such as planning, scheduling, diagnosis
and resource allocation, researchers and application
engineers in these domains may also benefit from
applying the techniques described in this book.

Whitestein Series in Software Agent Technologies

Your Specialized Publisher in Mathematics

Birkhäuser

■ **Vázquez-Salceda, J.**, Utrecht University, The Netherlands

The Role of Norms and Electronic Institutions in Multi-Agent Systems

2004. 292 pages. Softcover.
ISBN 3-7643-7057-2

This book presents a new framework for electronic organizations that defines a multi-level structure, from the most abstract level of the normative system to the final multi-agent implementation.
Our framework is specially suited for those complex, highly regulated domains that define restrictions at different levels of abstraction. In order to explore this problem, we study scenarios such as electronic health care and e-government.

The book discusses also the main issues surrounding the implementation of norms in agent-mediated institutions. The main observation is that norms are specified in regulations that are usually at a high level of abstraction. In order to be implemented, norms in regulations should be translated in operational representations (such as rules or procedures), to indicate how norms are to be implemented in the e-organization.

■ **Calisti, M.**, Zürich, Switzerland

An Agent-Based Approach for Coordinated Multi-Provider Service Provisioning

2002. 292 pages. Softcover.
ISBN 3-7643-6922-1

This book proposes a novel approach to improve multi-provider interactions based on the coordination of autonomous and self-motivated software entities acting on behalf of distinct operators. Coordination is achieved by means of distributed constraint satisfaction techniques integrated within economic mechanisms, which enable automated negotiations

to take place. This allows software agents to find efficient allocations of service demands spanning several networks without having to reveal strategic or confidential data. In addition, a novel way of addressing resource allocation and pricing in a compact framework is made possible by the use of powerful resource abstraction techniques

■ **Günter, M.**, Zürich, Switzerland

Customer-based IP Service Monitoring with Mobile Software Agents

2002. 168 pages. Softcover.
ISBN 3-7643-6917-5
Presenting mobile software agents for Internet service monitoring, this research monograph discusses newly standardized Internet technologies that allow service providers to offer secured Internet services with quality guarantees. Yet, today the customers of such services have no independent tool to verify (monitor) the service quality. This book shows why mobile software agents are best fit to fill the gap.

■ **Moreno, A.**, Tarragona, Spain / **Nealon, J.L.**, Oxford, U.K. (eds.)

Applications of Software Agent Technology in the Health Care Domain

2003. 212 pages. Softcover.
ISBN 3-7643-2662-X

This volume contains a collection of papers that provides a unique, novel and up-to-date overview of how software agents technology is being applied in very diverse problems in health care, ranging from community care to management of organ transplants. It also provides an introductory survey that highlights the main issues to be taken into account when deploying agents in the health care area.